MW01195951

March 2012

To

Sessica

Wishing you hours of enjoyment from the book.

[illegible]

Prannie Rhatigan's

Irish Seaweed Kitchen

The comprehensive guide
to healthy everyday cooking
with seaweeds

BOOKLINK

contents

contents

foreword

Even though there are said to be more than 50,000 edible plants in the sea, very few seaweeds are extensively used as food today, and most of these are used in Asia.

Seaweeds can be dried and used as a source of vitamins and minerals and many seaweeds contain valuable natural thickening or gelling agents that are very useful in a range of dishes. The earliest verified records of the clear use of seaweeds for this purpose came in 2008 from the early archaeological site of Monte Verde II in southern Chile where 9 seaweeds have been found at archaeological levels that confirm their use 14,500 years ago. Some of this material was near a worked cooking surface, and some had clear teeth marks. One of these, a kelp, is still sold today as dried 'quids' in Chilean markets.

China, Japan and Korea are the great centres of seaweed food utilization in the world. China has a particularly long history of seaweed utilisation, with very early mentions of seaweed in court poetry, specifically of seaweed gifts to the Emperor. Seventh – century Japanese court poetry expressed great appreciation of the fundamental beauty of seaweed as this extract demonstrates:

Upon the reefs
Grows the algae thickly;
On the rocky shoreline,
Grows the jeweled seaweed;
Soft as jeweled seaweed
Trembling, lay my girl;
Lush as thick green algae

Kakinomoto no Hitomaro
(662 – *c.*708)

There is also very early mention of seaweed use in a stanza describing an Irish monk's day:

Seal ag buain duilisg do charraig,
seal ag aclaidh,
seal ag tabhairt bhídh do bhoctaibh,
seal i gcaracair.

Anon. probably 12th century

A while gathering duileasc from the rock,
a while fishing,
a while giving food to the poor,
a while in a cell.

suggesting that duileasc (dillisk , dulse or creathnach) was valued both by the monks and by the wider population.

Séamas Mac An Iomaire's Cladaigh Chonamara (Stationery Office Dublin, 1938) mentions about 32 species of seaweed that were used in south – west Connemara at this time, indicating a much wider folk knowledge of seaweed in the west of Ireland than is generally appreciated.

Prannie Rhatigan has done a wonderful job in continuing this almost–lost tradition with this fascinating and taste-stimulating book of Irish seaweed cookery. I hope that some foreword – writer 14 centuries from now will speak of her book as a milestone in the revival of Irish marine algal cuisine.

MICHAEL D. GUIRY

PROFESSOR OF BOTANY,
NATIONAL UNIVERSITY OF IRELAND, GALWAY

introduction

As an island people, the Irish are no strangers to foods provided by the sea. In good times and in bad, there has always been seaweed, powerfully nutritious, sustaining, and available, linked to us through centuries of dependency, evolution, survival and migration. It has seeped into our folklore, our culture, and our songs. We have learned something of its medicinal power through centuries of experience: what we are about to learn through modern research in terms of health benefits will amaze us.

Edible seaweeds have always ranked highly in the culinary hierarchies of Japan, China and Korea where their health benefits have been extolled for centuries. What popularity they once enjoyed in the west has diminished over recent years, while their health giving properties have been mainly overlooked by western researchers. Because of its established status as a food in Asia, Asian countries show a considerable amount of scientific interest in the health benefits of seaweed consumption. The official Japanese Food Guide promotes seaweed as a source of nutrition, and various journals in Japan and China regularly publish articles on its health benefits. This said, there remains an enormous gap between the volume of published research on land vegetables and that which has been published to date on sea vegetables.

Fortunately, this is about to change. Influenced by contemporary Japanese cuisine, seaweed is beginning to take its place as mainstream urban fare, available both as trendy fast food in the form of sushi and wraps, and on the menus of many progressive restaurants.

This increase in consumption in the west is leading to more and more western research into the health benefits of seaweed as a food, which in turn suggests that seaweeds contain a wealth of substances that promote health and prevent disease. Already hailed as a nutritionally superior food, this bears testimony to the vast practical knowledge and belief in seaweed as a medicinal substance that has been accumulated over centuries by generations of people who recognised its health giving properties.

Like many before me, I grew up with the understanding that seaweeds were not just tasty, but healthy and nutritious too. My medical training however, dictates that I work from an evidence base and I can see that this evidence base is building. I look forward to the day when seaweeds will have mainstream preventative and therapeutic roles as proven and documented anti-viral, anti-cancer and anti-inflammatory substances. Other areas of medical concern in the developed world such as lowering blood pressure and lipids, and boosting the immune system are also among the specific areas of research demonstrating positive responses to the properties and actions of seaweeds.

Seaweeds have been described as 'the most nutritious form of vegetation on this planet' and my hope is that future nutritionists worldwide will soon be in a position to confidently recommend specific seaweed to the millions of people who could benefit so enormously from its health giving properties. Until then, we'll just have to rely on Grandmother's word that sleabhac is one of the best natural tonics around.

Prannie, Catherine, Johnny and Margaret Rhatigan going harvesting in winter in the late 1970s.

Which of course it is.

Ireland's long association with edible seaweeds, and with duileasc in particular, has certainly earned that plant the right to a position as a national culinary symbol; something akin to the pint of Guinness, the Aran sweater, the potato and the harp. Perhaps the growing trend towards a healthier lifestyle will reinstate crispy duileasc as a popular snack; a position it held among coastal dwellers here until well into the 20th century, when 'the men chewed it constantly and the women were never without it in their pockets...'

seaweed seasons

I grew up on the west coast of Ireland, where the rhythm of the tides and the lore of the sea still provide a timeless backdrop to everyday life for many of us. Against that backdrop, this book has written itself over many years.

As children, my father took us harvesting, where we learned about the glistening crop on the foreshore and how not to get cut off by the tides in early April. These trips to the sea revolved around the seasons, and followed a harvesting pattern.

Once the first frosts had sweetened the sleabhac – which was usually after Christmas – the cycle began. By St. Patrick's Day the egg wrack and black wrack had been put into large barrels to ferment with horse manure, and later on nettles and comfrey, to provide nutrient rich feeds for the organic vegetables and herb garden. The potatoes and peas had to be in by St. Patrick's Day or we were not on target in the garden. As the days lengthened, the first carraigín and Alaria were harvested for kitchen use and in April we raked the sand in special areas for cockles using a metal rake which 'clinked' against the shell. Soon after, the young sea spaghetti and kelps were harvested for use and the winter supply dried and stored.

Summer days brought the duileasc and the second flush of carraigín came ready for harvest. Other delicacies like sea lettuce, pepper duileasc, bladderwrack and channelled wrack each came ready in their own time, sometime between spring and the end of autumn. Looking back on all that, I realise that we as seaweed gatherers, were just a link in a long and basic chain of survival stretching back thousands of years. The stresses of modern living, coupled with an array of nutritionally poor foods make for a lifestyle as hazardous in some ways as that experienced by our early ancestors.

Luckily for them, they had seaweeds, mysterious nutritional powerhouses they chose from necessity, unaware of the massive health benefits. Luckily for us, seaweed remains a food option; a living treasure by the shore, more valuable by far than any golden coins that may lie buried beside it in the sand.

Wishing you many pleasant walks on the beach, many fruitful hours in your kitchen, and a lifetime of good health.

Prannie

Ralph Waldo Emerson's definition of a weed as a plant whose *virtues have not yet been discovered* is particularly true of seaweeds ...

ways to use seaweed

- **Ground or flaked**

  Add or sprinkle it onto food as you would a herb.
  Use as a condiment, as a salt and/or pepper replacement.

- **Whole, as a vegetable**

- **As a snack, dried or rehydrated**

  Duileasc was a favourite generations ago in Ireland, as nori/sleabhac is today in Japan.

- **As a recipe component**

  Follow any recipe in the book.

getting started

'Seaweeds, correctly called marine algae, are powerhouses of nutrients and they enhance the flavour and texture of food.'

- As a medical practitioner, I am frequently questioned on matters to do with acquiring better health. While physical activity and a positive attitude are essential elements to good health, my general advice mainly revolves around what you put on your plate: the food you eat is directly related to the state of your health and your attitude to life.
- If you already use seaweed in your diet, the recipes in this book will hopefully widen the horizons of possibility in terms of everyday cooking.
- If seaweeds are a new addition to your kitchen, the book aims to provide all the information you need for complete competency in cooking with seaweed.
- If you are somewhere in-between, you will find everything the everyday cook needs to add a spoon or two of good health and flavour to every meal they put on the table.
- To make the most of cooking with seaweed, a little planning will be helpful for people who have not previously used it in the kitchen.
- Start with easy to use seaweeds in simple recipes. Have a look at the seaweeds in the glossary/chart on page 14, and perhaps add the following to the contents of your kitchen press:
- A pack of Alaria, a pack or jar of seaweed stock, ground nori, sheet nori, some sea spaghetti and kelp. Irish seaweed suppliers produce some really flavoursome mixes, worth checking out in your local health food store or deli.

(see the list of suppliers on page 280)

storing seaweeds

Store seaweeds in a dry place away from direct light. If you need to store seaweeds in an unheated part of the house, double bag the seaweed in two plastic bags.

Seaweeds do keep indefinitely but ideally for about two years. Try to use up the seaweeds that you have from year to year. I find that the exception is the big kelps which seem to benefit from a flavour viewpoint if kept longer as they get more mature and become sweeter. One company in Japan still does this maturation and the process is called kuragakoi. This can take one to two years or sometimes even 10 years. Fresh seaweeds also keep well in the freezer.

... And finally a helpful hint on storing nori sheets from Duika Burges Watson, public health researcher *'I know the general advice is an airtight plastic bag out of the light for dried seaweeds, but if I'm using nori sheets for anything, I freeze the leftovers as they definitely keep better.'*

Glossary: a quick guide to the seaweeds in this book

	SEAWEED	HEALTH BENEFITS
Red Seaweeds	**Duileasc** *Palmaria palmata* dulse, dillisk, creathnach	Good source of minerals, vitamins and trace elements. Relatively low in sodium and high in potassium. Traditionally used as a substitute for chewing tobacco.
	Nori *Porphyra species* sleabhac, laver, sleabhcan, sloke	Rich in vitamins B, C, E and beta-carotene. Highest amount of protein compared to other seaweeds – up to 37% weight. Good balance of minerals and trace elements. Large amounts can be enjoyed without exceeding the recommended daily amounts of iodine as advised by World Health Organisation.
	Carraigín *Chondrus crispus (and Mastocarpus stellatus)* carrageen moss, irish moss	Used in cough mixtures around the world from Canada to New Zealand. Medicinally it has anti-viral and expectorant (phlegm loosening) properties for clearing chest infections and easing coughs. Acidic ingredients such as lemon are best added at the end of, not during, the cooking process. Nice balance of minerals, vitamins and trace elements and is particularly high in magnesium.
	Pepper Dulse *Osmundia pinnatifida*	Little nutritional research done.
Brown Seaweeds	**Sea Spaghetti** *Himanthalia elongata*	Good balance of minerals, vitamins and trace elements. Good source of calcium and magnesium.
	Sargassum *Sargassum muticum*	Very balanced range of minerals, vitamins and trace elements. Currently under research for its anti-viral properties. Has the lowest iodine of any of the brown seaweeds.
	Alaria *Alaria esculenta*	Alaria is almost identical to Japanese wakame biologically and nutritionally. High in calcium, B vitamins and many trace elements.Vitamin C content highest in late spring. Higher vitamin K values are found in early summer. High in vitamin B12 in late winter and early spring.
	Kelps *Laminaria digitata* oarweed *Laminaria hyperborea,* forest kelp kombu	Both contain a wide range of minerals, vitamins and trace elements. Contain high levels of iodine so consume small to moderate quantities to stay within the WHO recommended levels. The carbohydrate content differers; the blades of hyperborea can have up to 25% mannitol in spring while digitata has only about 5%.
	Sugar Kelp *Saccharina latissima*	A very sweet and delicious seaweed it has a wide range of minerals, vitamins and trace elements. As with Laminaria digitata and Laminaria hyperborea it contains high levels of iodine so take care with preparation in order to stay within World Health Organisation recommended levels.
	Bladder wrack *Fucus vesiculosus*	Best harvested in summer for a high Vitamin A content and in autumn for a high vitamin C content. Balanced range of vitamins, minerals and trace elements.
	Egg Wrack *Ascophyllum nodosum*	A wide range of minerals, vitamins and trace elements.
	Channelled Wrack *Pelvetia canaliculata*	Many trace elements and is high in selenium and vitamin C.
Green Seaweeds	**Sea Lettuce** *Ulva lactuca* or *Ulva rigida*	High levels of iron, Vitamin B12, calcium, manganese and magnesium. Vitamin C content highest when harvested in early summer. High in protein.
	Sea Grass *Ulva intestinalis*	Calcium levels are high in addition to having a broad range of trace elements and vitamins.
	Green Sea Velvet *Codium fragile*	Good source of iron and trace elements.

Further on in the book you will find more details on each seaweed including a nutritional values chart.

CULINARY USES

CULINARY USES
Spicy flavour. Delicious as a snack uncooked or on its own simply dried. Rich, salty nut-like taste and unique mouth feel. Soaked briefly in water and added to salads. Tasty addition to breads and scones. As a surprise ingredient in brown bread ice cream.
Mild, slightly nutty taste. Thin, papery black or dark green sheets for making sushi. Toasted and crumbled over salads. As an ingredient in stews, soups and casseroles, even in pesto. Can also be added to desserts for extra depth of flavour and texture. Pairs wonderfully with chocolate and ginger.
Traditionally used to set blancmange and jellies. Natural setting agent for any liquid, sweet or savoury. Can be used to thicken soups and casseroles. Improves the texture of home made ice cream. Eaten as a salad in Japan.
Adds a wonderfully peppery note to sauces for fish. Great as part of a condiment.
Adds a beefy flavour when used in soups, stews and casseroles. Nutty-like flavour when used in salads and with pasta. Use in a dish with 'regular' spaghetti to add variety, colour, flavour and texture.
Delicious in salads.
Excellent for miso soup and makes delicious calcium rich vegetable soups and stews. Imparts a chicken-like flavour when cooked with rice.Can be used uncooked in salads if pre-soaked or marinated in lemon juice. Alaria has a more delicate taste but needs a longer cooking time (40 minutes) than the cultivated Japanese wakame (15 minutes). Soak prior to cooking and use the soaking water.
Can be added to beans during cooking to enhance flavour and reduce cooking time. Used to make a traditional soup stock, Dashi in Japan. A tasty savoury party snack when marinated and oven crisped. Used as a condiment for meats, cheeses, vegetables and fish.
Can be soaked and made into crisps. Uses are similar to kelp but with a sweeter taste. Can be used in biscuits, cakes, tarts and cookies.
The tips can be marinated, lightly steamed and eaten in salads. Use as a base to steam and flavour fish and eat some of the tips with the fish. Delicious as part of a condiment mix. Makes a great stock.
Traditionally used to feed animals – reported benefits: increased milk quality from cows, increased yolk content in eggs and increased wool production in sheep. Needs further research.
Very tasty addition to foods.
A bright, colourful addition to salads. Delicious in omelettes. Can be added to breads such as focaccia. Cook with fish or in meaty casseroles. Unexpected vibrant taste when compared to the mildness of land lettuce.
Warning: Ulva likes nutrient rich waters (often associated with raw sewage) and CAN grow in polluted areas. If not properly washed there is some risk of E. coli infection.
Contains high levels of agaropectin gel, useful for setting liquids.

These are based on available research and were current at the time of going to press.

preparing seaweeds

Soaking and chopping seaweeds is self explanatory, but if you wish to flake or grind seaweeds for use, even though they are dry, they will need to have all traces of moisture expelled before you can crumble them easily.

To grind or flake seaweeds there are
4 options:

This information is repeated on the bookmark to guide you through seaweed preparation.

First ...

Remove dry seaweed of choice from storage bag.

1
speedy oven method

Place on a tray or oven proof plate and put in a hot oven. Watch it closely. It needs to be checked every minute or so. Remove from the oven and check to see if it can be crumbled. Place back in the oven if not crisp enough to crumble. Nori crisps faster than Alaria. Duileasc takes longer. Kelps and sea spaghetti usually take the longest of all. Seaweed can burn easily and this method is only recommended if you are short on time and is economical if the oven is already on.

2

slow oven method or dehydrator

Place in a cool oven overnight – ideally not hotter than 105°, F 40°C to retain vital nutrients. This is an easy and safe way of crisping seaweed when you have planned ahead and can crush and store seaweed in sealed bags for later use.

3

pan method

Place on a dry heavy pan and set over low heat until crisp, turning often with a small pincers and pressing the seaweed into the pan. Test with your fingers by tearing or crushing to see if it is becoming crisp. Depending on the humidity of the seaweed to start with, this can take 30 minutes or more. It is a gentle way of removing the moisture and there is no danger of burning or over heating the seaweed.

4

grill method

The grill can be used to crisp seaweeds. Place a layer of greaseproof paper over the seaweed to prevent browning or burning and keep on the bottom slot, well away from the heat at the top. This can be useful if the seaweed has been rinsed of salt and is damp or wet. It can take 10 minutes turning often.

And finally …

When all moisture is expelled using a method outlined above, and the seaweed is crisp it can be crushed in a pestle and mortar, with a rolling pin, between the fingers or whizzed in a coffee grinder depending on whether you need a ground or flaked result. Store excess in a sealed container.

As seaweed has a surprisingly varied culinary following, I invited not only celebrity chefs, but friends, colleagues and family who are good cooks to select a favourite recipe which we then worked on together, experimenting with particular seaweeds and flavours. Some of the recipes include seaweed as a key ingredient while others received a seaweed makeover, many with spectacular results. The relative ease with which these food fusions were effected is encouraging for people who want to introduce seaweed into their own kitchens; in fact many of the testers who had not previously cooked with it, found it a versatile ingredient which incorporated easily into several food combinations.

As cooking is not an exact science, minor variations in measurements won't make a great difference to the end result. It is important, however, not to mix the imperial and metric measurements given with each recipe. Medium eggs 55 – 60g work best when eggs are required in a recipe. Oven times are included while preparation times are not; preparing food is a task each cook times differently, and trying a new recipe invariably takes longer to assemble than something you have been cooking for years. As some of the seaweeds require marinating or soaking, it is a good idea to read a new recipe through once before getting started.

There are many recognisable old favourites among the recipes, so initially you will probably find something familiar – with a spoon or two of dried seaweed included. The seaweed presence varies from recipe to recipe, and can of course be altered to suit your taste. Whether you are already a fan of the scrumptious smoky bacon flavour of dried smoked duileasc, just beginning to get a taste for the mild chicken flavour of Alaria in cooked dishes, or an outright sleabhac connoisseur, there is something here for you.

- All recipes in this book have been created by Prannie and Johnny except where otherwise stated.
- A full list of all recipes using a specific seaweed can be found in the index (page 282) under the name of that seaweed.
- If you fancy a nibble of fresh seaweed please, please NEVER pull seaweed from the rocks. Use a scissors or sharp knife and give the seaweed a little haircut. In this way you will do no harm.
- If on thyroid medication consult with your practitioner before consuming seaweed

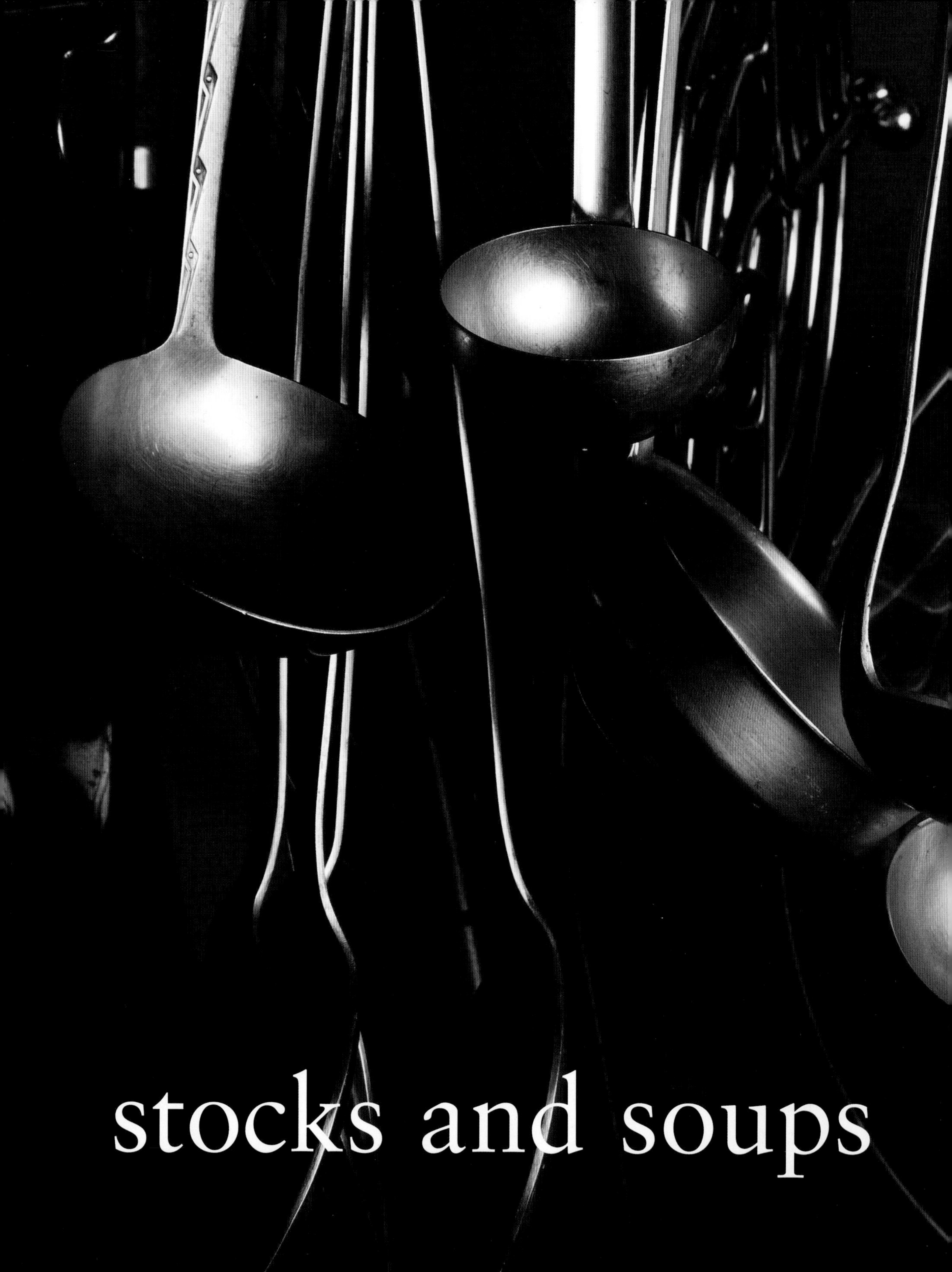

stocks and soups

My approach to making a tasty stock is to use a range of Irish seaweeds resulting in great flavour and a balanced nutritional base. My rule of thumb is to use a small amount of a variety of seaweeds on a daily basis, and this is also true when making stocks.

Irish seaweed harvesters (see page 280) supply the basics for stock making so you can choose an already ground version or a pack containing large pieces to simmer and then chop back into the finished product.

basic sea and land vegetable stock

This is a stock made in Ireland with Irish seaweeds – but the seaweeds (or variations of them) are available worldwide.

Here is our tried and tested stock pot favourite that seems to be forever on the go. The stock can be cooled and refrigerated or frozen and may be used for any recipe requiring vegetable stock in this book.

If you wish to choose just one seaweed for stock I recommend either Alaria or sea spaghetti, both of which can be chopped and put back in with the finished soup.

Alaria gives a mild chicken flavour and is an essential part of miso soup. Sea spaghetti gives a beefy flavour and makes a soup hearty. For a stock with the maximum punch of layered flavours try a mix of sea and land vegetables.

Seaweed used: Alaria, sea spaghetti, kelp, bladderwrack, nori, mixed seaweeds

3 litres (5 pints) of water
***Alaria**, 30cm (1 foot) length or about 15g (1/2 oz) of dried weight, rinsed under the cold tap*
***sea spaghetti**, about 15 – 20g (3/4 oz) of dried weight, rinsed under the cold tap*
***kelp**, 2.5cm (1 inch piece), rinsed under the cold tap*
***bladderwrack** if available, about 10 – 15g (1/2 oz) of dried weight, rinsed under a cold tap*
*1 tablespoon **nori** (optional)*
*a sprinkle of other **mixed seaweeds** of choice (optional)*
1 medium onion including skin for colour, sliced roughly
1 small carrot, sliced roughly
1 closed fistful dried porcini mushrooms
half a stick of celery
1 – 2 cloves of garlic

Herbs
sprig of thyme, sprig of parsley including stalks, a few coriander stalks
1 teaspoon bonito (dried fish) flakes (optional)

1 Place all the ingredients in a large pot, cover, and bring slowly to the boil. Simmer gently for 1 hour.

2 Remove the Alaria, sea spaghetti and bladderwrack and reserve. These can be chopped and returned to the finished soup. Remove kelp if it hasn't disintegrated and reuse when cooking beans or freeze until you have sufficient quantities to make a kelp condiment. (See page 254.)

3 Strain into a large bowl or jug.

4 Any easily retrieved porcini can be reserved and chopped into the soup.

5 The remaining ingredients in the colander – disintegrated kelp, carrot, onion, garlic, herbs and bonito flakes – can be chopped and used to add fibre to dog food, or composted.

QUICK VERSION

On occasions when you are short on time just simmer the seaweeds in water for about 30 minutes to soften them and stir in some Marigold stock, about 4 teaspoons per litre, at the end of the cooking.

I have no hesitation in recommending the organic Swiss vegetable bouillon powder from this company as it is free from all additives and a very useful alternative to making your own.

There are very few brand names mentioned in this book but this just has to be included as an essential kitchen ingredient for busy people.

herb and vegetable broth
with duileasc and cheese,
from Gerry Galvin

Gerry Galvin, who ran the famous Drimcong House restaurant in the west of Ireland for many years, is a great seaweed fan and uses it in the basic staples such as bread and soup.

'A simple recipe using duileasc which is unfussy and healthy.'

Seaweed used: Duileasc
Serves 3 – 4 in small portions

400ml (13½ fl oz) vegetable stock
150ml (5fl oz) dry white wine
1 tablespoon balsamic vinegar
55g (2oz) grated hard cheese
55g (2oz) chopped ***duileasc***
55g (2oz) finely chopped mixed fresh herbs such as mint, parsley, fennel, marjoram

1 Bring stock, wine and vinegar to the boil and simmer for 3 minutes.

2 Serve in soup bowls with little dishes of cheese, duileasc and herbs available separately for diners to flavour each portion of broth to their own liking.

From a study of the effects of heat on anti – tumour activity carried out by Jane Teas, PhD, cancer researcher: 'In a seaweed extract prepared at room temperature, there was cancer cell inhibition of 38%; if made after boiling the seaweed, this increased to 76%, but when microwaved, it decreased to less than 30%.'

vietnamese soup

Rick Epping who has travelled widely in Asia, calls this a Faux Pho because it is his interpretation of a Pho or Vietnamese working man's staple soup. It was traditionally eaten for breakfast in North Vietnam but these days can be eaten at any time. There are many variations in the meats but always the same greens and types of basil and noodles.

Seaweed used: Nori and Alaria
Serves 6 – 8

Broth

2 litres (3½ pints) stock. Use chicken stock from page 41 or land and sea vegetable stock (see page 22) or use water and 2 chicken stock cubes or water and about 3 tablespoons Marigold stock.

6 – 12 inch (15–30cm) piece **Alaria** ***– snipped into 1 – 2.5cm (½ or 1 inch) pieces***
1 teaspoon nam pla or fish sauce of choice
600g (1lb 6oz) beef very thinly sliced
To make the beef easier to slice thinly, either half freeze until just stiff, about 1½ hours or use frozen meat and let it half thaw

1 – 2 toes ginger, sliced thinly
1 red chilli, sliced thinly
2 large mushrooms, sliced thinly
1 bunch spring onions (green onions), cut coarsely
125g (4½ oz) of thin rice noodles
2 bunches mung or mixed bean sprouts
2 teaspoons **nori flakes**

Dressing

1 lime, halved
1 bunch mixed basil: Thai, lemon and sweet
1 bunch coriander, chopped coarsely
Tamari or soy sauce (optional)
¼ red chilli extra for dressing soup (optional)

1 Bring the stock to a rolling boil. Add the Alaria and simmer, covered, for 30 – 40 minutes until the midrib has softened.

2 Add the nam pla and the meat to the rolling broth.

3 Add the ginger, chilli and mushrooms and boil for 5 minutes until the meat is cooked.

4 Add the spring onions and simmer for 5 minutes.

5 Add the noodles, mung or mixed bean sprouts, and 2 teaspoons of nori flakes and remove from the heat for 3 minutes. Ladle into big bowls.

To dress the soup
Squeeze some lime juice directly into each bowl, add the basils and coriander, and extra chilli if using. Add a dash of soy or more sprouts to taste.

COOK'S TIP

Ask your butcher for very thinly sliced raw beef cut into 2.5cm (1 inch) strips x 3.5cm (1½ inch).

VEGETARIANS

use land and sea vegetable stock and add 450g (1lb) cooked aduki beans to the broth when adding the noodles. Use 200g (7oz) of dried beans to get 450g (1lb) cooked beans or use 2 x 400g (14oz) cans of cooked beans.

Rick Epping is a folk musician and harmonica craftsman.

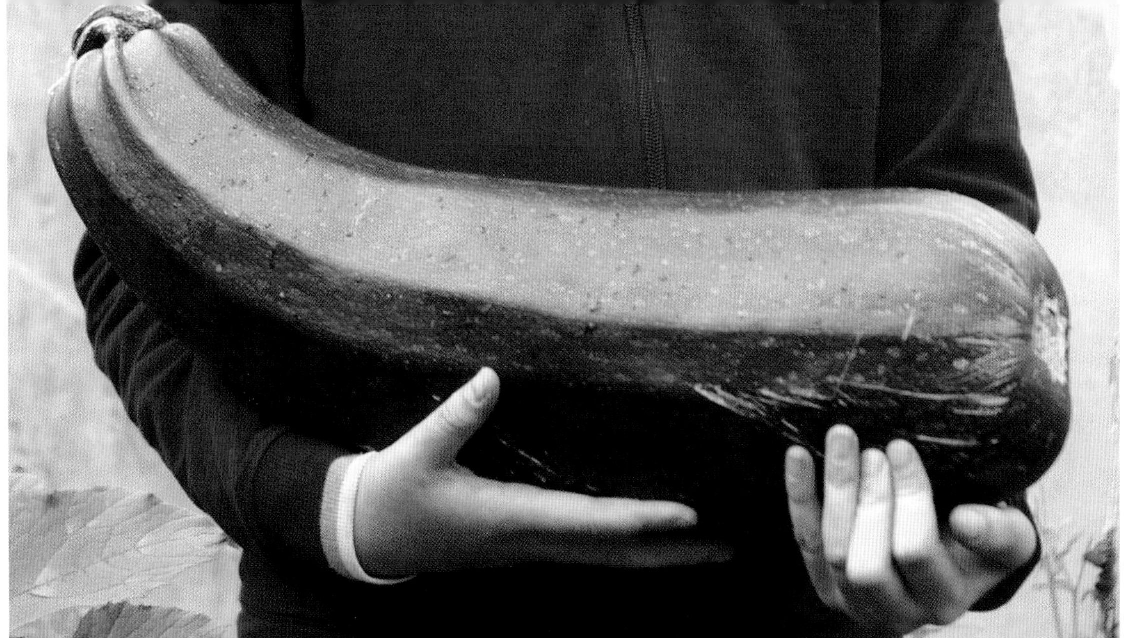

curried courgette and sweet potato soup

Gerry Harrington once spotted a monster courgette in our garden and turned it into this great soup. Add 55 – 115g (2 – 4oz) of washed red lentils at the same time as the vegetables and transform the soup into a meal in itself.

Seaweed used: Alaria
Serves 4 – 6

dash of olive oil
small knob of butter
3 shallot onions, or 1 large onion, chopped roughly
1 teaspoon turmeric
1$^1/_2$ teaspoons mild madras curry powder or paste
1 large courgette, cubed
1 large sweet potato, cubed
10 – 15cm (4 – 6 inches) ***Alaria****, snipped into small pieces and soaked for 10 minutes or longer in warm water*
1.5 litres (2$^3/_4$ pints) vegetable stock
coriander or parsley to garnish

COOK'S TIP

For this recipe 1.5 litres stock can be made from 2 tablespoons Marigold stock.

1. Heat the oil and butter in a large pot over moderate heat and sweat the onions until soft. Add the turmeric and curry powder and sauté for 2 minutes.
2. Add the courgette and sweet potato. Drain the Alaria, reserve the soaking water and add to the pot later when adding stock. Add the drained Alaria, stir well and sauté for 1 minute, cover and sweat on low heat for 10 minutes
3. Add the stock and reserved soaking water, bring to a simmer and cook until the vegetables are soft which will take no more than 10 – 15 minutes as these vegetables cook quickly.
4. Blend until creamy and season as desired.
5. Garnish with coriander or parsley and serve with crusty bread.

Test Kitchen Comment: 'Fabulous, very simple, delicious and quick to make.'

Recipe from Gerry Harrington, traditional fiddle player and chef.

pumpkin and Alaria soup

A soup that combines the warmth and colour of late summer harvest with the fruits of the shoreline, harvested in the spring.

This is a great recipe to introduce seaweeds to the uninitiated. The seaweed is visible and has a mild chicken – like flavour. For anyone nervous about trying seaweed, serve a bowl before you add the chopped Alaria back into the main pot, and encourage them to add a small amount. Important to the end result is the kind of pumpkin or squash you use. It is vital to get a truly flavoursome pumpkin or squash, such as Hokkaido, also called Uchi Kuri.

Seaweed used: Alaria
Serves 6 – 8

***Alaria** 1 x 15cm (6 inch) piece, (up to 4 x 15cm (6 inch) pieces can be used, according to taste)*
2 litres (3¼ pints) cold water
1 – 2 tablespoons olive oil
3 onions, chopped
3 cloves of garlic, chopped
1 pumpkin, about 1 – 1.2kg (2lb) weight, chopped
1 medium – large sweet potato, chopped
1 – 2 small dried chillies,
1 heaped tablespoon of Marigold stock

Garnish
1 tablespoon parsley, chopped finely
25g (1oz) walnuts, chopped roughly

Jack O Lantern type pumpkins make great spooky faced candle holders but lack any flavour for soup making

1 Rinse the Alaria briefly under a cold tap and place in a medium saucepan with the water. Cover, bring to the boil and simmer briskly for 35 – 45 minutes until the midstem of the Alaria has started to soften.

2 Meanwhile put the olive oil into a large saucepan and add the onion, garlic, pumpkin and sweet potato. Crumble in the chilli, cover and allow to sweat gently over very low heat for 30 minutes. Turn occasionally with a wooden spoon.

3 Add the Alaria with its cooking water and the stock powder to the pot of vegetables, cover and bring to the boil. Simmer briskly for about 10 minutes until the vegetables are soft and the midstem of the Alaria is very soft.

4 Remove the Alaria to a chopping board and cut into bite size pieces.

5 Blend the soup until smooth, add back the chopped Alaria and stir.

6 To serve, ladle into bowls, sprinkle with parsley and garnish with a few chopped walnuts.

Every child should know how to grow a pumpkin and turn it into food. There is lots of fun and magic involved. Pumpkins are easy to grow, so why not encourage a child you know to grow and harvest his or her own with a view to preparing pumpkin soup with you in the autumn? It's an interesting project, an important lifestyle lesson, and you will be amazed at how fast both child and pumpkin can grow over the summer.

nettle soup

The medicinal properties of the nettle combine with calcium rich Alaria and delicious fresh herbs to make a soup that tastes of the countryside.

Wear gloves and handle the nettle plants with care – they sting. Pick only the fresh young leaves at the top of the nettle. Never use a nettle that is in flower. Remove stalks and wash leaves.

Seaweed used: Alaria
Serves 4 – 5

15 – 30cm (6 – 12 inch) piece ***Alaria****, soaked for 30 minutes in just enough lukewarm water to cover it, chopped finely*
150 – 200g (5 – 7oz) young nettle leaves
2 tablespoons olive oil or 55g (2oz) butter
1 small or medium onion, chopped
250g (9oz) cooked parsnips, peeled and diced
900ml (1½ pints) milk or rice milk
1 teaspoon each of chopped fresh marjoram, sage and lemon thyme or half the amount if using dried
1 dessertspoon fresh chopped lovage or half the amount if using dried
2 teaspoons vegetable stock powder such as Marigold
½ – 1 teaspoon sea salt
2 tablespoons cream (optional)
2 tablespoons parsley, chopped

Gaby Wieland is the author of *Neantog Cookbook – Gaby's Favourite Recipes*.

1. Heat the oil in a medium saucepan, add the onion and cook gently over moderate heat until transparent. Add the nettles, Alaria and soaking water and cook gently for about 10 minutes.
2. Add the parsnips, milk, herbs, vegetable stock powder and sea salt and simmer for another 10 minutes or until the parsnips are tender. Blend until smooth.
3. Ladle into bowls; add a dash of cream if using and some parsley.

GROWING WILD...

- The humble stinging nettle grows wild in Ireland, and is often vastly undervalued for its health giving properties.
- Nettles are an ideal spring tonic rich in Vitamins B and C and beta – carotenes as well as iron, chlorophyll and copper.

COOK'S TIP

If nettles are unavailable, use fresh spinach and grate a little nutmeg in towards the end of cooking.

miso

Japanese researcher Yamamoto reported in his study of 39,713 Japanese nurses, that consuming six bowls or more of miso soup per week had a statistically significant reduction in breast cancer incidence.

The miso broth contains phytoestrogens from both fermented soy beans and seaweed. The isoflavones contained in miso soup may also play a role in reducing the risk of breast cancer.

Based on data from US breast cancer studies, the recommended daily intake of seaweed is 75 mg/kg body weight. This is approximately 5g of dried seaweed per day for an average European woman. These studies suggest that seaweeds have a protective effect in eostrogen metabolism and may provide a dietary chemoprevention in breast cancer.

All good reasons to snip some Alaria into a pot of your favourite soup or experiment using miso with Alaria.

To make miso soup

Traditionally miso soup is made by boiling Laminaria for about 15 minutes, removing the Laminaria, then adding other vegetables, a little tofu and some wakame which is our Alaria.

Seaweed used: Alaria
Serves 1

handful of finely chopped selection of seasonal vegetables
300ml (1/2 pint) of stock/water
1 tablespoon of chopped, cooked ***Alaria***
a jar or packet of white or yellow miso as these are more mild and delicate than the dark versions

Try Domini Kemp's soup on the next page for another quick way to enjoy miso.

1. Cook the vegetables in the water or vegetable/chicken stock for a few minutes until just tender. Add the Alaria and stir to heat through. Remove from the boil.
2. Dissolve a tablespoon of miso in a few tablespoons of the hot stock. Stir into the vegetables and stock pot. Add more to taste if needed. Don't re–boil.

Alternative method

1. Simmer about 1/2 tablespoon of dried snipped Alaria for 30 minutes.
2. Add chopped vegetables and simmer until tender.
3. Remove from heat. Stir in miso and taste. Garnish with herbs.

hot noodle soup

from Domini Kemp

Domini Kemp, with her sister Peaches, opened Itsa Bagel, now a highly successful food company, in Dublin in 1999.

Currently with The Irish Times Magazine as a food writer, she co–wrote New Irish Cooking and more recently published her own book *Real Food, Real Fast*.

'This is an incredibly simple store cupboard hot–pot of miso broth, sea vegetables, onions, garlic and any other vegetables you have handy such as bok choi, spinach or broccoli. I always have frozen peas on hand as they are nutritious, especially when fresh vegetables are not as fresh as they could be.'

Seaweed used: Mixed sea vegetables
Serves 2 large portions

1 teaspoon olive oil
1 large onion, peeled and sliced
5 cloves garlic, peeled and sliced
1 knob ginger peeled and chopped
1 handful **mixed sea vegetables**
1.5 litres (2½ pints) water
150g (5 oz) noodles, soba, rice, or somen
150g (5 oz) frozen peas or other green vegetables
1 sachet miso soup
1 teaspoon sesame oil (optional)
1 – 2 teaspoons soy sauce
1 teaspoon Chinese hot sauce (optional)
1 tablespoon sweet chilli sauce (optional)

1. Heat the olive oil in a large saucepan over moderate heat, add the onion, and cook until soft.
2. Stir with a wooden spoon and then add garlic, ginger, sea vegetables and water. Bring to the boil and add noodles, following the cooking instructions on the packet.
3. Add the peas and cook for 1 minute. Add remaining ingredients when the noodles are just cooked.
4. Ladle into large bowls and serve at once.

COOK'S TIP

The sweet chilli sauce and Chinese hot sauce are optional flavours and not essential to the soup. Feel free to experiment with different Asian condiments. A poached egg on top makes it into a filling meal.

roasted red pepper and red lentil soup

Participants on my seaweed courses over the years often appreciated wrapping their hands around a steaming mug of this hearty soup after a bracing walk on the shore.

With its rich red colour, this blend of peppers, seaweed stock, lentils, garlic and tomatoes is as substantial as it is appetising.

Seaweed used: Kelp, mixed seaweed
Serves 4

1 x 5 – 7.5cm (2 – 3 inch) piece of ***kelp,*** *snipped and soaked in warm water for 10 minutes*
5g or 1 very small fistful dried porcini mushrooms
1 – 2 tablespoon olive oil or 25g (1oz) butter
1 onion, chopped roughly
6 garlic cloves, chopped roughly
2 medium carrots, chopped roughly
400g tin (14 oz) plum tomatoes or equivalent in fresh or frozen
1 litre (1¾ pints) land and sea vegetable stock, (see page 22) or
1 litre (1¾ pints) water, 1 tablespoon marigold stock and 1 tablespoon ***mixed seaweeds***
2 large red peppers, roasted, see next column
½ – 1 teaspoon brown sugar
150g (5oz) red lentils, well washed and soaked in cold water for 5 minutes
1 teaspoon marjoram

Garnish
parsley, chives and walnuts, chopped

1 Soak the porcini in cold water for 3 minutes and then rinse under the cold tap to remove forest grit. Snip in half with scissors and set aside.

2 Heat some olive oil in a large saucepan and sweat the onion and garlic for 5 minutes with the lid on. Add in the diced carrot and allow to sweat for another 10 minutes.

3 Add the tomatoes, stock or water with stock and seaweeds, porcini, red peppers, kelp with soaking water, brown sugar and lentils. Stir well.

4 Simmer gently for 10 to 20 minutes until the lentils are cooked. Add the marjoram and blend until smooth.

5 Ladle into wide bowls and garnish with parsley, chives and walnuts.

To roast red peppers

Preheat oven 180°C/350°F/Gas 4

1 Cut peppers in half lengthways and remove seeds. Place on baking tray and place in oven for about 20 minutes until skins become charred.

2 Remove from the oven and allow to cool before removing charred skins and chopping roughly.

cooking with kelp

A stroll on any of Ireland's Atlantic facing beaches after the May storms will almost certainly bring you face to face with the might of the waves in the form of the May weed; long, brown seaweeds torn from their rock beds and hurled onto the shore...

This is kelp, the cash crop from the sea which was used as fertiliser, or burned, and the ashes sold for iodine production all along the coast until late into the 20th century.

Half way across the world, the same plant is also gathered in Japan but valued in a very different way. Essential to Japanese cooking, dashi is a traditional stock made from a strip of mature kombu or kelp, cold water, fish (bonito) flakes and little else. It takes 15 minutes or so of a simmer under the boil for the flavours to develop after which the kombu is removed and saved to tenderise beans or be transformed into a condiment to top rice.

Japanese chefs living in Ireland and using Irish seaweeds find it difficult to get the same flavour using this traditional method. In order to get the same flavoursome dashi stock they need to soak the kombu overnight and then boil for 1 hour or longer. They think that this could be due to the "hard" (limescale content of the) water in Ireland; even Japanese kombu behaves differently in parts of Ireland than in Japan.

Dashi kombu* is said to be at its best when it has matured for two years. This is often confusing because what is meant is that it is harvested when it is about two years old, specifically during the harvesting season which runs from the 10th July until about the 10th September. After or before this period the kombu is not considered to be of good enough quality. One year old kombu is called water kombu and does not contain the rich components needed for good flavour. Traditionally the two year old harvested kombu is air dried in four to six hours which encourages the white umami rich mannite to develop on the fronds. It is then dispatched without further maturation.

The amino acid glutamate, naturally occurring in kombu, makes it one of the highly rated 'Umami Foods'. In 1908 Kikunae Ikeda, a Japanese chemist, first isolated glutamates from kombu and named the taste sensation *umami*. Umami can be translated roughly as 'delicious' and has the effect of enhancing the flavour of foods; similar umami glutamates are

also found in mushrooms, tomatoes and Parmesan cheese. It wasn't until 2001 that scientists in California demonstrated that humans have a specific receptor for 'umami' flavours and that umami was accepted as the fifth taste sensation after salty, sour, bitter and sweet.

When using kelp to make stock in Ireland I have to use a mix of sea and land vegetables including porcini mushrooms to get a flavour similar to that produced by Japanese chefs who use kelp only. Our Irish kelp is different to Japanese kelp and is not handled or dried for the specific purposes of making stock.

A longer simmering period to release flavour is not an ideal solution either as even though some iodine will be released into the air the iodine remaining in the stockpot could well exceed what the body requires and contain more, in fact, than the WHO (World Health Organisation) recommends as a daily allowance. Many French chefs never allow kombu to boil as they claim it impairs the flavour by making the stock bitter.

It is best to stay below 1000 micrograms (μg) per day for iodine, as more can be harmful, especially for people who are sensitive to iodine and don't have a way to eliminate excess from the body. Having said that, Laminaria makes a great tasting snack and is very safe and delicious in other recipes as long as it is prepared properly.

Store it in paper bags, soak it in fresh cold water for 30 minutes or blanch in boiling water for 10–20 seconds, discard the water, and cook as required in moderate amounts. This allows the iodine to come down to acceptable levels where it can be safely enjoyed. Small amounts can of course be safely eaten without any soaking.

** Dashi: a light seaweed stock, usually with dried bonito (fish) added*

sea food chowder

from Ian Mannix BIM seafood advisor

A tried and tested chowder recipe is something that will never let you down, and can be served as a lunch or a supper. You can use many types of white fish for this dish such as pollack, haddock, hake and whiting. As well as white fish you can also add smoked fish.

'I always use smoked coley or haddock in mine as it adds a great flavour. The crisped duileasc with its aroma of bacon substitutes for the bacon sometimes used in chowder recipes. Use to taste as the blend of flavours in this soup is already rich and delicious.'

Seaweed used: Duileasc, mixed seaweeds
Serves 6

10 medium sized potatoes, washed, peeled and cut into 6 chunks per potato
750ml (1¼ pints) milk
2 medium carrots, chopped into thin rings
400g (14 oz) mix of white fish and undyed smoked fish, cut into 2.5cm (1 inch) chunks
1 onion, diced
2 cloves garlic, crushed
a knob of butter
2 teaspoons **mixed seaweeds**, *chopped finely*
1 teaspoon sea salt or a mix of salt and **duileasc**
2 scant teaspoons vegetable stock powder
200g (7oz) cooked prawns, (thawed and well drained if using frozen)
2 tablespoons **duileasc** *or* **smoked duileasc**, *dried and chopped finely*
100ml (3½ fl oz) single cream
handful chopped parsley
100g (3½ oz) smoked salmon, chopped (optional)
toasted **duileasc** *or* **duileasc crisps**

(see recipe for 'dulse' crisps on page 253)

1. Boil ⅓ of the potatoes in a saucepan for about 15 – 20 minutes or until tender. Drain and set aside. These will be used to make the soup thick.
2. Put the milk into the saucepan, set over moderate heat and bring to just under the boil. Add the rest of the potatoes and simmer for 10 minutes. Add the carrots and the white fish and simmer for about 3 minutes.
3. Meanwhile heat a pan over moderate heat and fry the onion and garlic in butter until soft, not coloured. Set aside.
4. Add about 6 tablespoons of the heated milk to the cooked potatoes. Add the seaweeds, sea salt or duileasc and salt mix, and vegetable stock and blend with a hand held blender to a smooth, creamy consistency. Add to the saucepan and stir gently for a minute to thicken the soup.
5. Add the prawns, duileasc and cooked onions to the saucepan. Allow the flavours to infuse over a low heat for 15 minutes.
6. Remove from the heat, add the cream parsley and the smoked salmon if using. Stir gently, return to low heat and cook for 1 minute. Ladle into bowls.
7. To serve, sprinkle with toasted chopped duileasc or some duileasc crisps. Chowder improves with sitting over very low heat, without stirring, for up to an hour before adding the salmon, cream and parsley to serve.

fish stock or fumet de poisson

Eithna's was a celebrated fish restaurant right on the harbour in picturesque Mullaghmore, Co. Sligo, for many years. This is Eithna O'Sullivan's fish stock which is the basis for many of her renowned recipes...

Fish stock is used as an essential ingredient for many fish and shellfish dishes. It is usually made from the bones and heads of prime white fish, for example turbot, sole, john dory, monkfish, lemon sole or brill. Unlike other stocks it does not require long cooking, and is better left to simmer rather than boil. The time is also important as if left too long to cook it becomes bitter and gluey. To get the full flavour from the vegetables, cook them first for about 20 minutes and then add the fish and seaweed.

Seaweed used: Kelp, duileasc, mixed sea vegetables

1 onion peeled and sliced roughly
1 carrot peeled and chopped roughly
white part of 2 leeks sliced
1 stalk of celery sliced
bouquet garni, parsley, bay leaf, thyme, fennel
10 crushed black peppercorns
2 litres (3½ pints) cold water
450ml (¾pint) white wine
2 teaspoons wine vinegar
1.5kg (3½lb) of uncooked white fish, bones and heads cleaned and rinsed
55g (2oz) of ***dried mixed sea vegetables****, or 20cm (8 inch) piece of* ***dried kelp****, (soaked for 30 minutes in cold water and water discarded)*
2 x 15cm (6 inch) pieces ***fresh or dried duileasc****, chopped*

1 Place all the vegetables, bouquet garni and peppercorns in a large saucepan and cover with 1 litre (2 pints) of cold water.

2 Bring to the boil and boil for ten minutes, add the white wine and vinegar and simmer for ten minutes.

3 Add the second litre of cold water, the fish bones and seaweed to the stockpot.

4 Bring to just below boiling and simmer for 20 minutes, no longer. Strain.

The stock can be used as a base for many fish sauces or for fish soups and chowders. It can be reduced further to make it more concentrated and frozen in smaller quantities.

Recipe from Eithna O'Sullivan
www.goodfoodtocook.com

chicken stock

All the goodness of traditional chicken stock, with the nutrients and flavour of Alaria, provides a rich stock base in any recipe.

Seaweed used: Alaria

organic chicken carcass; a chicken that has been already roasted for a meal, all meat removed
dash of brandy
water, enough to cover chicken which is about 2 to 2.5 litres (about 4 pints)
1 carrot, halved
1 onion, quartered
1 stick of celery, roughly chopped
2 cloves of garlic, whole
a few whole red peppercorns
7.5cm (3 inch) piece of Alaria, or ground seaweed stock
fresh herbs of choice: 1 sprig of rosemary, 2 sprigs of parsley, including stalks, 1 bay leaf, 1 sprig of lemon balm if available or use the equivalent in dry herbs if fresh herbs not available

1 Place the carcass with all the extra parts including stray bones, pieces of skin and jelly into a pot. Allow to sit over low heat for 15 minutes or so until the fats melt.

2 Add a dash of brandy or leftover wine. Put on the lid and turn up the heat to moderate. Allow the carcass to cook a little for 1 – 2 minutes. Using a barbecue tongs turn the carcass over. Put the lid back and cook the other side.

3 Do this a few times until the alcohol evaporates and parts of the carcass are lightly browned on both sides. The smells coming from the kitchen at this stage are wonderful.

4 Add the water, carrot, onion, celery, garlic, peppercorns, seaweed and herbs, bring to under a boil and simmer gently for 1 hour, then strain. Discard the contents of the sieve.

5 Cool the stock and refrigerate. Skim off any fat when cold. Freeze the stock in 1 litre ($1^3/_4$ pints) or smaller containers for later use.

COOK'S TIP

A great stock for risotto, especially the mushroom risotto on page 75.

starters and light lunches

smoked mackerel pâté

One of the great flavours of the Irish Atlantic seaboard, the taste and smell of mackerel evokes long summer evenings spent fishing, then home to a late supper of pan–fried mackerel, brown bread and homemade butter. If we were lucky, there was a mug of buttermilk there too; we churned at least twice a week in the summer in an old wooden churn that leaked a bit and was hard on the arms.

Mackerel pâté, in many variations, evolved from the volume of mackerel available to us and the fact that my father once got a present of a fish smoker for Father's Day.

Here is my mother's most popular version...

Seaweed used:
Mixed seaweeds or duileasc
Serves 4

1 egg, hard boiled
55g (2oz) cream cheese
1 teaspoon horseradish
1 unwaxed lemon, juice and zest
1 teaspoon mixed seaweed
1 large fillet smoked mackerel 175g (6oz), or 3 small fillets

For a smooth pâté use the food processor, and for a coarser one, use a fork.

1. Mash the hard boiled egg and cream cheese together, then add the horseradish, lemon and seaweed.
2. Remove the skin and bones from mackerel fillet and flake into the mixture. Stir to combine.
3. Refrigerate to allow the flavours mingle. Remove at least 30 minutes before serving to bring to room temperature.
4. Serve with fingers of toast or small crackers.

shellfish canapés

Both the crab pâté and prawn butter are versatile, delicious and freeze well. The seaweeds add that extra layer of taste that makes both pâtés favourites at drinks parties, or with aperitifs. Impressive as a starter served in single portion dishes with a selection of crudités or oven dried seaweed crisps made from sea spaghetti or duileasc.

Both of these recipes come from neighbours Pam and Dan Nelson who run a great kitchen party.

CRAB PÂTÉ

Seaweed used: Nori or bladderwrack
Serves 8 – 10 as finger food

340g (12oz) cream cheese, full fat
3 tablespoons mayonnaise
1/8 teaspoon curry powder
*1 – 2 teaspoons **nori or bladderwrack,** ground*
1 tablespoon onion, grated
1/2 – 1 tablespoon lemon juice, to taste
1/4 – 1/2 tablespoon Worcestershire sauce
175g (6oz) fresh or frozen crabmeat, defrosted

1. Mash the cheese in a large bowl. Add the mayonnaise, curry powder, seaweed, onion, lemon juice and Worcestershire sauce. Mix well.
2. Stir in the crabmeat. Season if necessary and chill for one hour to allow the flavours to blend, or until serving.
3. The pâté can be placed in a mould that has been lightly oiled with sunflower oil, and refrigerated for 4 hours. Unmould onto a flat surface, then chill again before serving.
4. Serve on a bed of lettuce or sea lettuce. Goes well with thin rye crackers, Melba toast or crudités.

PRAWN BUTTER

Seaweed used: Alaria
Serves 8 – 10 as finger food

225g (8oz) cream cheese, mashed
115g (4oz) butter softened
125g (4 1/2 oz) sweet prawns, finely minced
3 spring onions (green onions) chopped finely
*1 teaspoon **Alaria,** ground finely*
1/2 teaspoon curry powder
2 teaspoons sugar
1 teaspoon lemon juice

1. Place all the ingredients in a food processor and process everything together.
2. Use as a dip for small crackers and duileasc crisps, or as a spread for crispbread.

COOK'S TIP

Don't use tinned crab unless it is of the highest quality, and don't use light cream cheese.

tomato tart with two cheeses

This is a colourful and nutritious meal contributed by Catherine, our editor. If you have a bountiful crop of tomatoes, this tart is one way of making the most of them. The tomatoes, prepared in the oven with olive oil and Alaria can be used hot or cold as a succulent starter, or as a side dish with any meat or fish.

Seaweed used: Alaria
Serves 4

TOMATO DRESSING

3 large ripe tomatoes, halved
2 tablespoons olive oil
2 rounded teaspoons of ***ground Alaria***

TART

200g (7oz) ready made puff pastry
200g (7oz) ricotta cheese
100g (31/2oz) Parmesan shavings
2 large eggs
1 dessertspoon milk
4 black olives, stoned and chopped roughly
2 rounded teaspoons ***ground Alaria***

Preheat oven to 180°C/350°F/Gas 4 and grease a 28cm (10 1/2") diameter round tart tin.

1. Place the tomatoes on a baking tray, brush with olive oil and sprinkle over the Alaria. Bake until slightly dried out and soft, about 50 minutes. Set aside.
2. Roll the pastry to a thickness of 3mm (1/8 inch) and line the tin leaving a generous lip of pastry over the edge of the tin to counteract shrinkage. Bake blind for 5 minutes.
3. Place all the ingredients except the olives into a food processer and process on medium for about 30 seconds or until just mixed. Too much blending will shred the Parmesan, and you won't get the delicious melted Parmesan pieces when served hot.
4. Spread the mixture over the pastry base and then press the tomatoes into the filling in the design of your choice. Sprinkle the olives over the top, but not on the tomatoes and bake for 25 – 30 minutes or until the filling is set and the pastry golden. Serve with a mixed leaf salad.

COOK'S TIP

To cook pastry evenly at the bottom, place a baking tray in the oven to preheat with the oven.
Place the tin with the uncooked pastry on the hot tray and cook as normal in the centre of the oven.

Catherine Rhatigan

sea spaghetti and cheese straws

This recipe really maximises the delicate flavour of sea spaghetti and my advice is to make more than you need; children love them and never once have I had leftovers. Use bladderwrack if available instead of nori for an additional subtle nutty flavour. Prepare and cook as for nori.

Seaweed used:
Sea spaghetti and nori or bladderwrack
Serves 6

20g (/4 oz) dried sea spaghetti
2 tablespoons or juice of 1 lemon

PASTRY

75g (2½ oz) butter
75g (2½ oz) plain flour
75g (2½ oz) mature cheddar, grated
¾ teaspoon dry mustard
½ teaspoon nori flakes or ground bladderwrack
(for bladderwrack preparation see bookmark.)

TO PREPARE THE SEA SPAGHETTI

1. Soak sea spaghetti in cold water for 30 minutes to rehydrate, drain and place in bowl. Add lemon juice and stir to coat.
2. Allow to marinate for 30 – 60 minutes.
3. Place in a steamer and steam until soft and similar to al dente spaghetti. Depending on the thickness of the seaweed this takes between 5 – 12 minutes.
4. Remove from the steamer. Pat dry with kitchen paper.

TO PREPARE THE PASTRY

Place the butter, flour, cheese, mustard and nori flakes in a food processor and pulse until the ingredients form a ball. Wrap the dough in cling film and refrigerate for 1 – 2 hours.

WHEN READY TO BAKE STRAWS

1. Grease two baking trays.
2. Press and roll out the dough as thinly as possible to a rectangle measuring about 15 x 30cm (6" x 12").
3. Lay one strand of sea spaghetti out on the edge of the dough and press it gently into the dough. Roll the pressed sea spaghetti over just once, to barely encase (*see photograph above).*
4. Cut into 7.5cm (3 inch) pieces and place on baking tray. Repeat process with strands of sea spaghetti until all the dough is used.
5. Chill in the freezer or fridge for 20 – 30 minutes. Preheat the oven to 190°C/375°F/Gas 5.
6. Bake for 10 minutes in the centre of the oven until golden brown.
7. Remove and leave on baking tray for 2 minutes to settle.
8. Carefully transfer to wire rack. Eat warm or cold.

COOK'S TIP

The straws are perfect for entertaining as they can be prepared in advance and stored uncooked, either in the fridge for 24 hours, or in the freezer until needed, before popping them into the oven for ten minutes or slightly longer if straight from the freezer.

three omelettes

Omelettes always look better and taste lighter if they rise a little. To get this effect, beat in plenty of air, and finish the cooking under a moderately hot grill. Ingredients other than milk and eggs should be light, finely chopped and in small quantities. Good free range hen or duck eggs from the market make all the difference. Serve with crusty bread and salad.

OMELETTE WITH SEA LETTUCE

Seaweed used: Sea lettuce or nori
Serves 3

2 eggs, beaten with a twist of salt
1 tablespoon milk
1 tablespoon crème fraîche (optional)
1 handful ***fresh sea lettuce****, washed, soaked for*
10 minutes, drained and chopped finely, or
1 tablespoon dried ***sea lettuce*** *or* ***nori***
1 handful spinach leaves, chopped finely
25g (1oz) cheese, grated
olive oil for cooking

Preheat grill to 180°C/350°F/Gas 4.

1. Add the milk to the eggs and crème fraîche and whisk thoroughly. Add the sea lettuce, spinach and cheese to the eggs and whisk again.
2. Heat the oil in the pan over moderate heat until hot, and add the egg mixture. Cook for about 1 minute or until the bottom of the omelette starts to firm. You can check this by removing the pan from the heat and shaking it slightly; the top should still be fluid, and the base firmer. Lift an edge and have a quick look if unsure.
3. Place the pan in the oven or under the grill for about 2 – 3 minutes, or until the omelette starts to rise and turn golden. If using an oven with a grill, check the pan handle is heatproof. Serve immediately.

OMELETTE WITH ALARIA

Seaweed used: Marinated Alaria
Serves 3

2 eggs, beaten with a twist of salt
1 tablespoon milk
1 tablespoon olive oil
1 shallot, chopped finely
3 medium mushrooms, sliced
1 clove garlic, crushed
1 tablespoon marinated ***Alaria***
(see recipe page 98)

1. Add the milk to the eggs and whisk thoroughly.
2. Cook the shallot and mushrooms in olive oil over moderate heat for 2 minutes.
3. Add the garlic and cook for 10 seconds.
4. Add the Alaria to the egg mixture and pour over the shallots, mushrooms and garlic.
5. Cook for 1 – 2 minutes and finish cooking under the grill as in omelette one.

COOK'S TIP

A really flat omelette can be made into a sandwich by spreading pesto, crisped seaweed, mayonnaise or fresh herbs in the centre.

Sligo market duck eggs

OMELETTE WITH DUILEASC

Seaweed used: Duileasc
Serves 3

2 eggs, beaten with a twist of salt
1 tablespoon milk
olive oil, for frying
1 large or 2 small shallots, chopped finely
8g ($^1/_4$ oz) duileasc, flakes or small pieces
$^1/_2$ red pepper, diced
2 cloves garlic
1 very small dried chilli, crumbled, or $^1/_2$ – $^1/_4$ teaspoon chilli flakes
25g (1oz) cheese
1 tablespoon duileasc crisps

(optional – see recipe on page 253)

1 Add the milk to the eggs and whisk.

2 Cook the shallot, duileasc and red pepper over moderate heat for 2 minutes in a small amount of olive oil. Add the garlic and stir for 10 seconds.

3 Add the chilli to the eggs, whisk well, and pour over the vegetables in the pan.

4 Cook for 1 minute or until the bottom of the omelette has cooked.

5 Sprinkle cheese on top and finish cooking as before. Top with duileasc crisps.

memories of sleabhac

Among my father's oldest friends were the Waters brothers originally from Innishmurray Island, just off the coast of North Sligo. Paddy and John Andrew moved away from the area, but Mick and my father were lifelong friends. Sleabhac... sloke... nori... sleabhcán... slough... call it what you will, was an intrinsic part of the island lifestyle, the islanders believing that everyone needed two 'good feeds' of sleabhac early in the New Year to purify the body. With its high protein content, balanced range of minerals, vitamins and trace elements, it was actually a perfect boost to the system and a great way to help the body fight off infection during the winter months.

My father's belief in this new year nutritional boost resulted in our heading to the beach over the days of Christmas, basins at the ready, to harvest sleabhac. It was always great fun, and even as kids, there was a tremendous satisfaction in the careful harvesting, watching the purple – black glistening prize slowly fill the basins. Before the winter evening closed in we piled back into the car, chugged and bumped up the track to the main road, and into the village, where we drew to a halt outside the door of my father's favourite public house; bearers of great treasure. In we trooped and very soon, my father was benignly dispensing little portions in bags to old men in big overcoats who normally huddled over a pint, but became animated at the thought of fresh sleabhac.

memories of sleabhac

On Innishmurray, sleabhac was harvested right after the first heavy frost of the season which was usually in early January. Traditionally it was simmered for up to 4 hours, then seasoned with a little salt and pepper and mixed with very finely diced onion. It was eaten on its own or with potato or bread.

One of the difficult things about preparing sleabhac is getting all the sand rinsed out. My mother washed it at least ten times before putting it into a big pot on the Aga. Once cooked, the first sleabhac of the season was shared among neighbours and friends who appreciated it.

In the seventies we were among the very few who harvested from the shore: folk memory still associated the practice with extreme poverty, and I remember some folk reacting with exaggerated aversion at the thought of eating seaweed. We, on the other hand, thanks to my parents, learned to respect sleabhac for what it is.

My neighbour **John Keegan** remembers coming home from school to a sleabhac dinner twice a week during the season. His mother Mary Ellen plucked the finer variety which grew on the rocks, had very little sand in it, but was riskier to harvest. The older people were aware of the risks, and usually worked in pairs and groups. They used their fingers to 'fluff' the sleabhac up against the rock so they could get a grip on it.

John has eaten sleabhac all his life, plucking it as his mother did, from the more exposed rocks where most people agree, the slough is sweeter, needs little rinsing and less cooking time. After a very quick rinse under running water he squeezes it dry and without adding extra water, steams it in a saucepan with a tight fitting lid, using a small serrated knife to chop it against the sides of the pot every ten minutes or so to break it up as it steams. A 'cut as you stir' method. After 30 to 40 minutes, depending on the sleabhac, he serves it from the pot, nothing added. I found it pure and sweet with a hint of saltiness.

In Donegal this method of fluffing up the plant so it could be more easily plucked was called 'rolling', because otherwise it would be too 'giortach' or short, to pluck. **Grainne Rua,** from Glencolmcille recounts that the shorter, sweeter, better quality sleabhac grows on the exposed rocks and is more difficult to harvest, but worth it. You have to roll it onto the handle of a spoon and 'roll like mad' until you have a roll about 1½ inches thick and 5 – 6 inches long – 'a rollog'.

Jimmy Nellie, who rolls the sleabhac for her claims it has aphrodisiac qualities for males if harvested at the right phase of the moon, but no one knows for sure which phase that is exactly...

Beezie McGowan from Ardtrasna in Sligo also favours the short, rock–exposed sleabhac over the longer, more easily accessible variety that we always plucked. A sleabhac connoisseur, who has dined on it all her life, she passes for a sprightly seventy–year–old, although approaching ninety. She cooked up a pot of the longer sleabhac variety for me once, not her usual choice, and commented on the length of time it took to both wash and cook, compared to the shorter plant she favours. At the end of

memories of sleabhac

all that, she was totally unimpressed by the flavour, despite the knob of garlic butter she melted in the centre of the sleabhac before eating it.

For my part, I grew up with the longer sleabhac, and was more than happy to take the rest of the contents of the pot home with me, once Beezie had ladled it into jars. Beezie's mother, Annie, often cooked sleabhac with a piece of back bacon added to the pot for flavour, while Beezie sometimes fries it, washed and squeezed, in a pan over moderate heat with melted garlic butter.

A few miles down the coastline in Mayo **Annette O'Leary** claims that sleabhcán is never ever washed. Instead, people go to the exposed rocks where the sleabhcan is always plucked sand free. Nor do they roll it like they do in Donegal; instead they wait for a very dry breezy day when the seaweed dries on the rocks and can be peeled off in one sheet.

Annette learned her craft from her mother **Annie Caine,** and grandmother **Mary Weir,** who made great use of old flour bags, which they first bleached and used as pillow cases, and which, when their stay in the linen press had expired, were bleached again in the sun and transformed into very handy bags for harvesting seaweeds. The sleabhcan was plucked and dried on the shore in the space of one well chosen, dry and breezy day in early Spring. The bags were packed with the dried, or semi dried seaweed, making it much lighter to carry home.

Traditionally the sleabhcan was boiled, while another variety of nori known locally as 'tripidi' is better eaten raw or roasted. "Triopallach" means a cluster or bunch and refers to the seaweed that is clustered between the dualacins or small black shelled mussels.

For both Annette and I, the modern kitchen has contributed to how sleabhcan can be treated and stored. We both find that freezing it shortens the cooking time to between 1 hour and $1^1/_2$ hours, as opposed to the traditional 4 hours.

She also roasts her sleabhcan straight from the shore by placing it unwashed, on parchment on a baking tray at gas mark 3 for 15 minutes. She turns it over, lifts off the parchment and gives it another 15 minutes or so until it can be crumbled. When cool she stores it in an airtight container and enjoys it sprinkled over an egg in a cup or on raw tomatoes or lightly steamed carrots.

Another great way to store and prepare it is to freeze it in a block straight from the shore. When needed, thinly slice it with a sharp knife, lay it out on parchment and roast it using the method described.

laver bread cakes

Herbalist and author, Judith Hoade baked this traditional Welsh bread for 'A Taste of Wales', which was part of a television series entitled 'Regional Cooking' in Britain in the seventies. The original version uses fried bacon and bacon fat, and is also included here. Judith has replaced the bacon with onion and I have replaced it with duileasc. Combining both options makes very appetising cakes. Laver bread served this way with eggs makes a tasty breakfast with a difference. The traditional recipe is: Mix cooked laver in coarse or fine oatmeal. Fry diced bacon in some fat and remove from the pan. Shape the oatmeal and laver mixture into little cakes and fry in the bacon fat, to give them flavour.

This recipe is a mix of Judith's and mine, using a combination of onion and duileasc to replace bacon, making it suitable for vegetarians.

Seaweed used: Laver and duileasc
Serves 4 as a starter

115g (4oz) ***laver/nori/sleabhac seaweed, cooked until soft, drained and chopped***
25g (1oz) fine oatmeal or fine millet flakes
butter, a knob plus extra for frying
olive oil for frying
1 onion, diced
5 – 10g (1/4 oz) ***duileasc,*** *snipped into 2.5cm (1 inch) pieces*

COOK'S TIP

Fried duileasc gives off a wonderful bacony smell when cooking and tastes like bacon too.

1. Mix the oatmeal or millet with the laver and set aside to soak for 5 minutes.
2. Fry the onion in butter and set aside.
3. Place the snipped duileasc on the pan and toast/cook until crisped.
4. Form the laver/oatmeal mixture into small cakes about 5cm (2 inches) in diameter and 1.5cm (3/4 inch) thick.
5. Heat some oil and more butter in the pan over moderate heat and cook the laver cakes until golden on each side. This takes about 2 minutes (each side).
6. Drain on kitchen paper.
7. Serve topped with crisped duileasc and some onion on the side. Sweet chilli sauce works well as an accompaniment.

Yumiko Matsui picking nori

nori tsukudani

This is the Tokyo style of stewing nori, and is a very old method of cooking the seaweed. The recipe comes from the mother of our Japanese photographer.

Seaweed used: Nori
Serves 2 – 3

about 150g (5 oz) freshly plucked nori,
rinsed under cold running water
1 tablespoon mirin or 1 teaspoon sugar
a pinch of salt
2 tablespoons soy sauce or tamari
1 teaspoon of dashi powder
250ml (8½ fl oz) water

Place all the ingredients together in a medium sized pot, bring to a simmer over moderate heat and cook for about 30 minutes until the mixture develops a rich, dense, sweet, yet savoury taste.

Approximately 9000 million sheets of nori are consumed in Japan every year.

HOW TO SERVE

1 teaspoon of Tsukudani can be added to leftover boiled rice. Pour green tea onto the rice to warm it and top with this stewed seaweed. Add a little wasabi paste to taste. Great as a quick snack or when hunger sets in at midnight after a few beers.
It can also be used to top vegetables or sushi and is very often used as the centre of rice balls or spread on bread. Delicious whatever way you use it.

Yumiko Matsui

COOK'S TIP

4 sheets of dried nori rehydrated in 1 cup of water for 10 minutes can be used instead of fresh nori. Use nori and soaking water along with the rest of the ingredients and method as above. Fresh nori gives a better result.

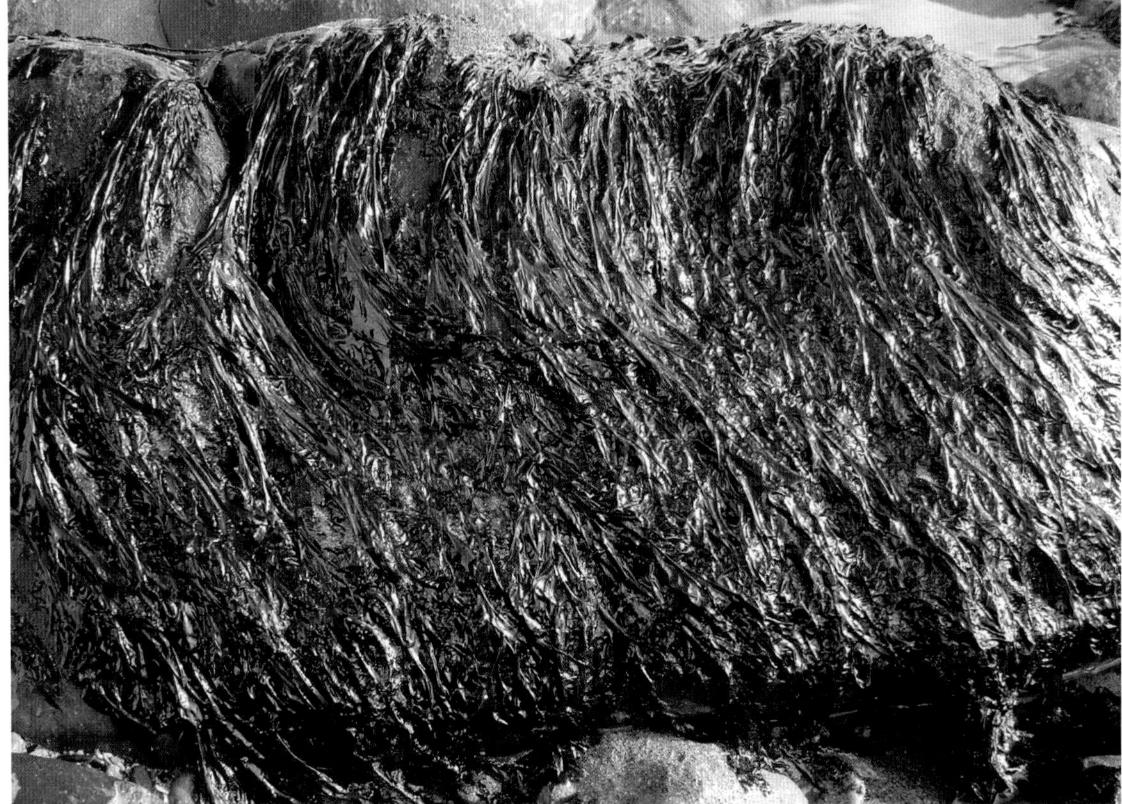

sleabhac pâté

Sleabhac has its own distinctive flavour, to which lemon juice and olive oil only have been added. More of either can be added to taste. If you are using fresh sleabhac, be sure to wash it thoroughly to remove all grains of sand. This is more difficult than you might think. When you think it is free of sand, wash it one more time.

Seaweed used: Sleabhac
Serves 4

a handful of fresh* sleabhac*, about 150g (5oz) or 4 sheets* nori *rehydrated in just enough cold water to make a stiff paste.

Follow recipe from step 3 opposite
olive oil to taste
lemon juice to taste
pinch of salt

1 Wash sleabhac well, then cook until soft by simmering for 3 – 4 hours, or see 'memories of sleabhac' on page 53 for a faster cooking method.

2 Drain well in a sieve, save the water for stock, and chop finely.

3 Add a few drops of very good quality olive oil and a squeeze of lemon.

4 Add a pinch of salt if not washed in seawater. Taste and adjust seasoning.

5 Spread on toast, crackers, Rye Vita or Melba toast.

nori pancakes with st tola cheese
and mixed salad leaves

An imaginative dish which can be prepared in advance and finished in the oven while a starter is being served. The amount of seaweed used is determined by the chef, which gives plenty of space for individual tastes.

First prepare the roasted red peppers and the tomato sauce as they each need to cook for nearly an hour. While they are cooking prepare the pancakes.

Seaweed used: Sleabhac
Serves 4

NORI

About 100g (3½oz) of freshly harvested nori, washed and steamed for 30 minutes or 3 sheets of dried nori soaked briefly in water and roughly torn

TOMATO SAUCE

2 tins tomatoes, standard size
4 cloves garlic, chopped finely
2 small onions, chopped roughly
1 teaspoon sugar or honey
salt and pepper to season

To prepare the tomato sauce

1. Place all the ingredients in a small saucepan and bring to the boil. Simmer very gently, uncovered for 40 – 60 mins.
2. The sauce is ready when it has reduced by about half and the onions are tender. Taste and season again, if necessary.
3. Add a couple of tablespoons of the prepared nori to the tomato sauce and blend with a hand or electric blender. Taste and add a little more nori if required.
4. Repeat this process until you have a blend and taste that suits you. Reserve remaining nori for another recipe, for example, pâté or pesto.

ROASTED RED PEPPERS, ONIONS AND GARLIC

3 red peppers, halved, seeds removed and sliced thinly lengthways
4 cloves garlic sliced roughly
2 large onions sliced roughly
3 sprigs rosemary
4 sprigs thyme
4 tablespoons olive oil
salt and pepper to season

To prepare the roasted red peppers, onions and garlic

Preheat the oven to 180°C/350°F/Gas 4

1. Place the peppers, garlic, onion, rosemary and thyme sprigs in an ovenproof dish. Add the olive oil and seasoning and toss gently to coat the vegetables in oil.
2. Place in the oven for 40 – 50 minutes or until the skins of the peppers are just turning black.

PANCAKES

200ml (7fl oz) milk mixed with 75ml (3fl oz) water
2 large eggs
pinch of salt
115g (4oz) plain flour
butter to cook pancakes
125g (4¼ oz) St Tola cheese or any mature goats' cheese

To prepare the pancakes

1 Place the milk, water and eggs into a blender and blend for 30 seconds. Add the salt to the flour and blend for a minute until it becomes a smooth batter. Pour the batter into a jug.

2 Heat a little butter in the frying pan over high heat, until hot. Turn the heat down and add a couple of tablespoons of batter to the pan. By swirling it around you should be able to get a thin coating of the batter around the whole frying pan. You may need to add more at this stage.

3 After about one minute use a spatula to turn the pancake. Give the second side another minute or two. Remove to a plate.

4 Continue the process until you have cooked eight pancakes.

Putting it all together

Preheat the oven to 220°C/425°F/Gas 7.

1 Take one pancake and put about two generous tablespoons of the tomato and nori sauce on it spreading evenly. Add a sprinkling of roasted red peppers and onions on top.

2 Crumble some goats' cheese onto this and roll the pancake.

3 Repeat for each pancake, and place in one or two buttered ovenproof dishes.

Cover the dishes with foil or parchment to prevent the pancakes from drying out as they heat up.
Cook for 30 minutes or until dish is thoroughly hot.

SALAD LEAVES AND BALSAMIC VINAIGRETTE

Any generous mix of salad leaves, organic if possible. Try to include some rocket
50ml (2fl oz) balsamic vinegar
150ml (¼ pint) olive oil
1 teaspoon honey
salt and pepper to taste
sprinkle of mixed seaweeds
This quantity will be more than you need, but the dressing will keep for your next salad or you can make half

To prepare the salad with balsamic vinaigrette

Combine all the ingredients in a screw – topped jar and shake vigorously. Add to the salad leaves just before serving.

COOK'S TIP

Any leftover sauce and vegetables make a great topping for pizza.

Recipe from Maire Nunan, teacher.
Maire put this dish together when our Japanese photographer Yumiko arrived in her kitchen with a bag of freshly harvested sleabhac.

seaweed crêpes with prawns

For something quick, easy and different, try this seafood crêpe, created in Malaysia.

Seaweed used: Nori
Serves 2 – 3 (makes 3 crêpes)
Recipe doubles easily to make 6 crêpes

3 teaspoons light soy sauce
2 teaspoons sesame oil
1 clove garlic, crushed
6 medium sized prawns, shelled and cubed, weight – about 55g (2oz)
3 eggs
3 teaspoons white flour, spelt works well
*4 **nori sheets,** toasted and chopped finely or pulsed in coffee grinder*
80ml (3fl oz) water
25g (1oz) butter for cooking prawns
25g (1oz) butter or 3 teaspoons oil for cooking crêpes

1. Combine 1 teaspoon of light soy sauce, 1 teaspoon sesame oil and garlic in a small bowl to make a marinade.
2. Add prawns to marinate for about 10 minutes while preparing the rest of the ingredients.
3. Combine the eggs with the remainder of the light soy sauce and sesame oil, flour, seaweed and water and beat well or pulse in a liquidizer.
4. Remove the prawns from the marinade and fry lightly over moderate heat in butter until just barely cooked and still crunchy. Remove from the pan and keep warm.
5. Add more butter or oil to the pan and add about 80ml or 1/3 of the beaten egg mixture to the pan to make a crêpe. When the bottom of the crêpe has set after about one minute, put a tablespoon – which is about 1/3 of the seasoned prawns on top of crêpes and roll it up like a sushi roll.
6. Cook over moderate heat for about 1½ minutes, turn and cook for a further 1½ minutes until the centre of the crêpe is fully cooked. Or you can finish cooking in a hot oven 220°C/425°F/Gas 7 if the oven is already on. Remove and keep warm.

Serve hot, garnished with green salad and a chilli dip.

COOK'S TIP

If using frozen cooked prawns leave whole, thaw, marinate but don't fry. They will heat through when the crêpe is cooking.

When asked to contribute a recipe, enterprising seaweed fans Barry and Maggie O'Dowd went straight to the source and called up friends in Asia. Between them all they came up with this recipe.
A case of too many cooks getting it just right!

mother of the sea

Although we associate sleabhac / nori with Japan there is a fascinating link to a botanist called Kathleen Drew Baker who lived in Manchester in the 1920s. Prior to her marriage, she had been studying the life cycle of nori but once married, was no longer allowed to work in the University, this being the rule at that time.

Kathleen's husband who also worked at the university, set up tanks at their home and at their holiday cottage in North Wales so she could continue her research. Her son recalls (in conversation with Duika Burges Watson) that when eating boiled eggs for breakfast, both he and the neighbours' children used peel off the very fine membranes and keep them for his mother which she used as substrate in her seaweed research.

Her work led to the discovery of what is called the "conchocelis phase" or what was the missing link in the life history of nori. Prior to this nori was called 'gambler's grass' in Japan because the life cycle was unknown and as there was no guarantee of a profitable crop, it was a most unpredictable seaweed to rely on for an income. Kathleen published her work in 1949 and the Japanese immediately put it to good use, resulting in a renewed and flourishing nori industry. In 1957, she died tragically after a short illness aged 56.

She is rightly credited with saving the nori industry in Japan, and in 1963 Japanese fishermen, no longer at risk from nori crop failure, put up a statue to 'the mother of the sea'.

Unveiled on 14th April, there is a remembrance ceremony in her honour every year in the middle of the cherry blossom season. The statue overlooks the Ariake Sea, and offerings are regularly brought to thank the Shinto gods for assisting her discovery.

dressed crab with cucumber and Alaria salad

from Chapter One

This recipe is from Chapter One, the acclaimed Dublin restaurant which was awarded Food and Wine Magazine Best Dublin Restaurant Award 2008.

Owner Ross Lewis says: 'This recipe is Garrett Byrne's, our head chef here. He came across seaweed as an ingredient while travelling in Asia and Australia.'

Seaweed used: Alaria
Serves 4

½ cucumber
*115g (4oz) pack dried **Alaria,** soaked in warm water*
for 15 minutes, rinsed and patted dry. Leaves removed from midstem and set aside
Save midrib for stock
250g (9oz) white crab meat, cooked
100g (3½ oz) brown crabmeat, cooked, optional
If not using, add more white meat to make up a total weight of 350g (12½ oz)
2 limes

CRAB DRESSING
3¾ tablespoons rice wine vinegar
3½ tablespoons dashi or stock
120ml (3½ fl oz) mirin
2 tablespoons soy sauce

SALAD DRESSING
120ml (3¾ fl oz) rice wine vinegar
75ml (2½ fl oz) soy sauce
15g (½ oz) sugar

1 Peel the cucumber, cut lengthways and scrape out the seeds. Slice as thinly as possible, put in a bowl, salt lightly and leave for 2 hours. Rinse under cold water and set aside.

To prepare the crab dressing

Put all the ingredients into a small saucepan, bring to the boil for 1 minute and then allow to cool completely.

To prepare the salad dressing

As above, put all the ingredients into a small saucepan, bring to the boil for 1 minute and then allow to cool completely.

To serve

1 Place the white/brown crab meat on a cold plate and spoon over the cold crab dressing.

2 Toss the Alaria leaves and the cucumber in the prepared cold salad dressing and arrange beside the dressed crab.

3 Place half a lime on each plate.

scallop dangaku on pickled cucumbers with nori jus

from Seamus O'Connell

Seamus O'Connell, described as one of Ireland's most original culinary talents, has a long association with the Ivory Tower restaurant.

'This dish is a play on the flavours of sushi while the scallop, gently roasted with a miso glaze and sesame crust, comes from the traditional miso coated tofu dengaku which is sold on the streets of Tokyo.

Miso dengaku can be made with any of the different colours and types of miso for the sweet scallop, though the lightest yellow or white miso is preferred.

Once kept sealed in the fridge, it doesn't deteriorate for 2 – 3 weeks, so the amount I give is double what is needed, it is versatile stuff and I'm sure you will find your own uses for it.'

In Japan, food is rarely served as hot as we like it in the west, the Japanese realise that the tongue is much more sensitive to subtle flavours around blood temperature. So here the sauce and vegetables are served at room temperature and the scallop just warm in the middle.

Seaweed used: Nori
Serves 4

1 cucumber
25g (1oz) sea salt

MISO CUSTARD
100g (3½oz) miso shiro paste – (soya bean miso – yellow or white)
70g (2½oz) sugar
1 egg yolk
1 teaspoon shoyu (soy sauce)
1 teaspoon sake, or sweet sherry

CUCUMBER DRESSING
3 – 4 umeboshi plums or paste
20g (¾oz) sugar
80ml (3fl oz) rice wine vinegar

NORI JUS
*1 sheet **nori seaweed,** roasted and roughly crumbled*
75ml (2½fl oz) fish or prawn stock or dashi (kombu and dried bonito stock)
1 teaspoon wasabi paste ((Japanese horseradish)
1 teaspoon shoyu (soy sauce)

SCALLOPS
40ml (1½fl oz) sesame oil
500g (1lb 2oz) scallops: 4x100g (3½oz) each or 8 x 70g (2½oz) each
4 pinches sesame seeds

GARNISH
3 scallions, minced
4 pinches pickled ginger

1 Cut the cucumber into thirds. Leave the peel on and push lengthways through a mandolin with fine teeth to give spaghetti – like results. Alternatively cut the cucumbers into thin strips and then cut again to have matchstick thick strings. Toss with the salt and leave the colander to drain for 5 – 10 minutes.

2 Next make the miso 'custard': combine miso, sugar, egg yolk, shoyu (soy sauce) and sake in a small bowl and whisk over a pan of boiling water until it loosens and then thickens slightly. This takes about 5 – 10 minutes. Set aside.

3 Now make the dressing for the cucumbers – stone the umeboshi plums, then put them into the smallest blender you have. Add the sugar and rice wine vinegar and blend until smooth.

4 Wash the salt off the cucumbers and drain. Toss with dressing in a bowl and set aside. Heat the grill or the oven grill to high setting.

5 Make the nori jus. Soak the nori sheet broken up in the fish stock with wasabi paste for about 5 minutes. Add shoyu and blend until smooth. Set aside.

6 In the frying pan heat the sesame oil on high heat – when it smokes add the scallops and sear for 2 minutes. Turn off the heat, cover the top of each scallop with a teaspoon of the miso custard, spreading evenly.

7 Coat each with a pinch of sesame seeds and place under the grill 15cm (6 inches) from the element.

8 Grill the scallops for 3 – 4 minutes or until the miso and sesame seem to colour and crisp up. Remove from grill.

TO SERVE

On small white flat plates, place a mound of cucumbers in the centre, place a scallop or two on top (depending how large they are); dribble the nori jus in dramatic black blobs around the scallop on the plate, garnish with finely minced scallion and pickled ginger.

www.seamusoconnell.com

seaweed hummus

This is a very different way of making hummus. You have to start two days in advance, as the chickpeas are actually sprouted before cooking, making them very digestible. Those inclined towards flatulence after eating beans will find this recipe helpful.

Seaweed used: Alaria
Serves 8

250g/½ packet of organic chickpeas
3 or 4x13cm (5 inch) pieces of Alaria
3 cloves garlic, crushed
4 tablespoons dark or light tahini
4 – 5 tablespoons olive oil, extra virgin, cold pressed
juice of 1 or 2 lemons
1 – 2 tablespoons tamari

Optional extras:
a pinch of paprika
a few drops of toasted sesame oil

Recipe from Jessica Reid, artist

To prepare the chickpeas

1 Rinse well and soak overnight in plenty of cold water.

2 Rinse well again, drain and leave to sprout for two days until germination begins and the tails have sprouted.

3 Rinse with cold water 2 – 3 times a day.

HUMMUS

1 Place the chickpeas and Alaria in a pot with enough water to cover and boil for 1 hour until soft. If necessary keep topping up the water. The seaweed will disintegrate.

2 Finish the cooking by boiling the pot almost dry. Leave a little of the cooking water to get the right consistency when blending.

3 Transfer the chickpeas and seaweed to a food processer and process until smooth.

4 Add garlic, tahini, olive oil, lemon juice and tamari and process briefly.

5 Add paprika and sesame oil, if using, process again and check seasoning.

6 Serve as a dip with carrot and celery sticks or on bread with salad.

a quick hummus

It takes seconds to make hummus using a tin or two of cooked white beans such as chickpeas, cannellini beans or butter beans, rinsed and drained.

Seaweed used: Mixed seaweeds
Serves 4

2 x 400g (14oz) tins cannellini beans, or 450g (1lb) cooked and drained
2 – 3 crushed garlic cloves
2 tablespoons tahini
4 tablespoons olive oil
juice of a lemon
*1 heaped tablespoon ground **Alaria** or mixed seaweeds*
25g (1oz) chopped coriander leaves
½ teaspoon ground coriander seeds
2 tablespoons parsley
1 teaspoon vegetable stock powder
¾ – 1 teaspoon Dijon mustard
3g (1 large pinch) of mixed seaweed

COARSE HUMMUS

Put the ingredients into a food processor and pulse just to break up.
Refrigerate.

SMOOTH HUMMUS

Process all the ingredients in a food processor until smooth.
Refrigerate.

WHEN COOKING BEANS

- 200g (7oz) dried (uncooked) beans is the equivalent of 2x400g (14oz) cans of undrained cooked beans.
- 100g (3½oz) dried (uncooked) beans equals 1x400g (14oz) can of undrained cooked beans.
- A 400g can contains 225g (8oz) cooked beans when drained.
- When cooking beans remember to place a piece of **kelp** in the water to shorten the cooking time.

filo pie
with sea spaghetti, mushrooms and apples

Chef Mike Harris surpasses himself with this original blend of apple, apricot, nuts, mushrooms, mustard seeds and sea spaghetti encased in delicate and mouth – watering filo pastry. Substantial, not difficult to prepare, and very impressive.

Seaweed used: Sea spaghetti
Serves 6

25g (1oz) sea spaghetti
60ml (2¼ fl oz) olive oil
15g (½oz) black mustard seeds
1 large onion, chopped
100g (3½oz) oyster or other mushrooms chopped roughly
50g (1¾oz) mixed nuts, chopped
50g (1¾oz) unsulphured apricots soaked for ten minutes, drained and chopped roughly
50g (1¾oz) pine nuts
30ml (1¼fl oz) tamari
10 sheets filo pastry – defrosted if frozen
melted butter
1 apple, cored and roughly chopped

COOK'S TIP

Walnuts and hazelnuts worked well in test kitchen, as did 30g (1¼oz) of dried oyster mushrooms, rehydrated.

TO PREPARE THE SEA SPAGHETTI

1. Soak in cold water for 10 – 15 minutes, drain and chop roughly.
2. Preheat the oven to 200°C/400°F/Gas 6
3. Grease an ovenproof dish, ideally rectangular to fit filo pastry, or fold the pastry to fit.
4. Heat the olive oil in a pan over moderate heat, add mustard seeds and cover. Allow the mustard seeds to pop, then add the onions and mushrooms and fry briefly. Add the seaweed, nuts, apricots, pine nuts and tamari to the pan and mix well. Remove from the heat and allow to cool.
5. Lay two sheets of pastry on the bottom of the dish, brushing each one with butter.
6. Add the apple to the cooled pie mixture and spoon half the mixture on top of the pastry, spreading out evenly. Lay two more sheets of pastry on top of the mixture. Spoon the remaining mixture on top and spread evenly. Cover with the remaining six sheets of filo pastry, being sure to brush each sheet with butter. Cut into portions prior to cooking. If you try to cut it after cooking, the filo pastry will shatter.
7. Cook in the centre of oven for 30 – 40 minutes until the pastry is golden brown. Serve immediately.

potato stir-fry with sea veg and seafood

Once the potatoes have been cooked, the remainder of this delicious meal is quickly prepared in one pot. The ultimate no fuss option.

Seaweed used: mixed sea vegetables
Serves 2

5 medium potatoes, peeled and chopped into bite sized cubes
12 – 15g (1/2 oz) ***mixed sea vegetables***
50ml (1 3/4 fl oz) olive oil
1 onion, sliced
1 garlic clove, crushed
1/2 each green, red and yellow pepper, sliced
1 red chilli, chopped seeds removed (optional)
2 portions smoked salmon, thinly sliced, or 2 portions of cooked seafood of your choice

1. Place potatoes in a steamer. Steam for about 5 – 10 minutes until almost cooked but still firm when pierced with a fork. Set aside.
2. Place the sea vegetables on a dry pan or wok over moderate heat and toast until crispy.
3. Remove from the pan.
4. Add the olive oil to the wok/pan. Add the onions, garlic, peppers and chillies and toss to cook evenly for about 2 – 3 minutes.
5. Add the potatoes and heat thoroughly to finish cooking.
6. Add in crisped sea vegetables and seafood of choice, toss ingredients together and serve warm.

COOK'S TIP

This also works well without the seafood for a vegetarian option. Sliced cooked day old potatoes also work well.

Recipe from Manus McGonigle, Quality Sea Veg, Donegal, a seaweed harvester who enjoys the mix of seafood and seaweed readily available to him on the north west coast.

tortilla

One evening we found a handsome young Spaniard in our garden, which is about two minutes from Streedagh Beach, Sligo where three of the Spanish Armada Ships were wrecked in 1588. An artist, he had arrived from Spain to make a documentary about the event. His mother, Gloria cooked this dish for us, fusing basic ingredients from both countries.

Tested in Germany where it is also a well known potato dish, the addition of duileasc so delighted people who had never before tasted seaweed that they wouldn't cook the dish again without it!

Seaweed used: Duileasc
Serves 4

60ml (2fl oz) olive oil
6 medium size potatoes, sliced
1 medium onion, sliced
1 medium red onion, sliced
6 eggs, beaten
40g (1½oz) ***duileasc****, rehydrated for 10 minutes and chopped*

COOK'S TIP

Slice the potatoes medium to thin so they need less time to cook. Though it may be tempting to use cooked potatoes the traditional recipe calls for uncooked.

1. Heat the oil in a frying pan over moderate heat, and add the sliced potatoes. Fry, but do not brown.
2. When the potatoes are almost cooked, add the onions and fry until soft.
3. Remove from the pan and cool.
4. Place the potatoes and onions in a mixing bowl and mix in the eggs and the duileasc.
5. Lightly grease a 27cm (10½") pan and fry the egg mixture over moderate heat until the eggs are set.
6. Turn the contents of the pan over onto a plate and slide back into frying pan, uncooked side down, and cook until lightly browned.
7. Cut in wedges and serve with bread.

Xavi Munoz, artist.

seaweed and porcini mushroom risotto

Although it may seem odd to feature a recipe from landlocked Switzerland in a seaweed cookery book, the harvesting component of the dish is strikingly similar. We harvest on the shore, and the Swiss, equally passionately, harvest in the upland forests for mushrooms of all kinds.

Seaweed used: Sea spaghetti and Alaria
Serves: 2 – 3

*20g (3/4 oz) **dried sea spaghetti,** snipped into 5mm (1/2 inch) pieces*
25g (1oz) dried porcini
450ml (14fl oz) lukewarm water
25g (1oz) butter
1 small onion, finely chopped
250g (9oz) risotto rice, preferably Carnaroli
200ml (7fl oz) white wine
350ml (12fl oz) chicken stock, hot
1 small garlic clove, crushed
pinch of nutmeg
100g (3 1/2 oz) Parmesan cheese, grated
*2 dessertspoons **Alaria,** ground finely*
few sprigs of parsley
Vegetarians can use a vegetable and / or seaweed bouillon instead of chicken stock.

Andrea Oestreich, a forensic toxicologist, is a native of Graubünden, Switzerland and remembers mushroom harvesting as a child on early autumn mornings with his parents in the alpine woods, some 6000 feet above sea level.

This risotto has been Andrea's party piece for many years and he was very reluctant to have it invaded by alien sea plants... However, even he had to agree that it brought the dish to a new level.

To prepare the sea spaghetti and porcini

1. Rinse the sea spaghetti briefly under a cold tap to remove any sand and then soak for 1 hour in the measured lukewarm water. Soak the porcini in cold water for 3 minutes and rinse well under cold tap to remove forest grit. Add to bowl of soaking sea spaghetti for 1 hour.

To prepare the risotto

1. Melt the butter in a saucepan over moderate heat, add the finely chopped onion and cook until translucent. Add all the rice and stir well to coat with the butter and onion mixture.
2. Add the wine and stir over moderate heat to evaporate it.
3. Add the mushrooms, sea spaghetti and the soak water to the chicken stock and keep hot.
4. Using a soup ladle, add the hot chicken stock to the rice mix, 1 ladleful at a time, stirring constantly. The secret here is to never stop stirring! When nearly all of the stock has been absorbed, add the garlic.
5. The mushrooms and sea spaghetti will sink to the bottom of the stock pot or jug. Be sure to include these ingredients as the stock is ladled into the rice. The risotto is ready to eat approximately 20 minutes after the first ladleful has been added to the rice.
6. Add a pinch of nutmeg. Just before serving, add the Parmesan cheese and Alaria and mix gently. Serve immediately with a sprig of parsely.

I'M IN THE
GARDEN

7

salads and vegetables

popeye's gratin

While visiting friends in Canada, we were pleasantly surprised by the widespread availability of kale, swede, pumpkin, spinach and cabbage in shops and mainstream restaurants. It was delightful to see the elevation these sometimes neglected vegetables received.

This recipe from Canadians Shirley–Anne and Bob Thomson, features the classic combination of spinach and cheese, and is given an extra flavour lift by the addition of duileasc.

Seaweed used: Duileasc
Serves 4 – 5

560g (1¼ lb) spinach, cooked, drained and chopped
1 egg, beaten
325ml (11fl oz) crème fraîche or yogurt with a dash of cream
1 can French onion soup mix
20g (¾ oz) duileasc, cut into 2.5cm (1 inch) pieces
55g (2oz) bread crumbs
115g (4oz) grated cheddar cheese

Preheat the oven to 180°C/350°F/Gas 4

1 Combine the egg and spinach in a bowl and stir in the crème fraîche and soup mix. Pour into a casserole dish.

2 Mix the duileasc with the bread crumbs and cheddar cheese and spread evenly over the spinach mix.

3 Place in the centre shelf of the oven and bake for about 40 minutes, or until the breadcrumbs are golden and the cheese bubbling.

COOK'S TIP

1.2kg (2½ lb) fresh spinach yields about 560g (1¼ lb) of cooked spinach.

While meat contains Vitamin B12, few land plants provide a good source of this essential vitamin. 100g of fresh sea lettuce Ulva lactuca can provide up to 35% of the RDA, (recommended daily allowance for adults).
It is particularly valued by the natives of Chile, where it is known as 'luche'.

beetroot and sea lettuce salad

This colourful recipe comes from the award winning kitchen of the Tobergal Lane Café in Sligo, and was created by owner and Eurotoque chef Brid Torrades. Containing just two basic main ingredients, it is easy to make and brings an understated sophistication to your table whatever the occasion. The beetroot can be used either raw or parboiled.

Seaweed used: Sea lettuce
Serves 3 – 4

2 medium sized fresh beetroot
3/4 level tablespoon Dijon mustard
4 tablespoons olive oil
2 tablespoons wine vinegar
1 generous handful of fresh sea lettuce, rinsed and shredded

1 Wash the raw beetroot, peel lightly and grate coarsely. If you prefer you can wash and parboil the unpeeled beetroot for 10 minutes, then peel lightly and grate coarsely.

2 Make the vinaigrette by combining the mustard, olive oil and wine vinegar in a salad bowl and stirring well.

3 Toss the beetroot and the sea lettuce in the dressing to coat, and serve.

COOK'S TIP

Use a sharp serrated knife to shred the sea lettuce.

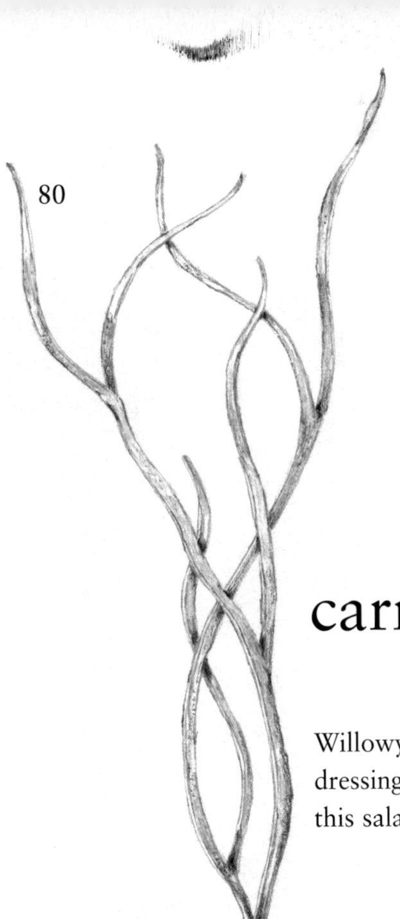

carrot and sea spaghetti salad

Willowy sea spaghetti and delicate carrot strips combine with a sweet garlicky dressing to create a salad as delightful to look at as it is to eat. Easy to prepare, this salad never fails to delight even first time seaweed tasters.

Seaweed used: sea spaghetti
Serves 4 – 6

*15g (½oz) **sea spaghetti,** dried or a handful of **fresh sea spaghetti***
2 tablespoons lemon juice
1 tablespoon wine vinegar
4 – 5 carrots, washed well, not peeled, and sliced into long, fine lengths with a potato peeler

DRESSING
3 tablespoons good quality olive oil
1½ tablespoons lemon juice
1 teaspoon coarse whole grain mustard and honey
*1 tablespoon **mixed seaweed***
2 cloves garlic, crushed
A pinch of cayenne pepper
A pinch of grey sea salt

To prepare the sea spaghetti

1. Rinse the dried sea spaghetti and soak in warm water for 1 hour or briefly steam until al dente. If using fresh sea spaghetti, rinse well and steam for 10 minutes until al dente.
2. Rinse the seaweed again and then marinate in lemon juice and wine vinegar for a few hours or overnight.
3. Some can be left full length to decorate – chop the remainder into 2.5 – 5cm (1 – 2 inch) pieces.

To prepare the salad

1. Combine the dressing ingredients in a small jug or bowl.
2. Pour the dressing over the carrots and sea spaghetti and allow to marinate for at least an hour.

Diane Roemer, artist and teacher

duileasc champ

Many years ago when Chef Shaun Paul Brady phoned up the owners of Carraig Fhada Seaweeds to ask for a few recipes, Betty and Frank were away and their son took the call.

He was in a bit of a rush but his basic instructions were perfect: 'Just throw in duileasc with spuds and you can't go wrong.'

The resulting recipe has been a firm favourite ever since.

Seaweed used: Duileasc
Serves 4

675g (1½lb) baby potatoes, scrubbed and lightly peeled
salt, 1 teaspoon
45ml (1½fl oz) double cream
4 tablespoons white wine
juice of ¼ lemon
*2 tablespoons **duileasc**, chopped finely*

1. In a large saucepan, cook the potatoes in well–salted boiling water for 15 – 20 minutes, or until tender.
2. Drain well and return to the pan with double cream, white wine and lemon juice.
3. Gently crush each potato against the side of the pan with the back of a fork.
4. Add the duileasc and season to taste. For a quick and easy seaweed mash, add 1½ tablespoons of crushed duileasc to regular mashed potatoes; a great accompaniment to any fish dish.

champ with mixed seaweeds

from Domini Kemp

Seaweed used: Mixed sea vegetables
Serves 4 – 6

300ml (½ pint) milk
1 large bunch spring onions, chopped
*1 handful dried **mixed sea vegetables***
6 – 8 potatoes, medium sized, peeled and cooked in boiling water until tender
1 bunch parsley, flat or curly, chopped finely
75g (2½ oz) butter
salt and pepper to season

1. In a medium sized saucepan, heat the milk then add the spring onions and sea vegetables. Bring the milk almost to the boil, remove from the heat and leave to infuse.
2. Drain and mash the potatoes and add the milk mixture gradually. Mix well.
3. Add the parsley and butter. Season and mix well, adjusting seasoning if necessary.
4. Serve immediately.

Delicious served with pan–fried salmon with hoisin and ginger glaze (see recipe on page 148).

potatoes with mustard seeds and duileasc

Potatoes and duileasc both hold time honoured places of importance in the Irish diet and the combination possibilities of these two ingredients are practically endless. Here is another delicious variation.

Seaweed used: Duileasc
Serves 6

1kg (2lb 3½ oz) potatoes, preferably waxy
pinch of sea salt
6 tablespoons olive oil
bunch of scallions, chopped finely
2 tablespoons mustard seeds
½ teaspoon turmeric
small bunch of flat leafed parsley, rinsed and chopped
25g (1oz)* duileasc, *rinsed under cold running water and chopped roughly

COOK'S TIP

Potatoes can be steamed.

Rebecca Hussey, organic gardener

1. If the potatoes are new, scrub them clean leaving the skin on, otherwise peel and chop them to a uniform size of about 2.5cm (1 inch) cubes. Place them in a pan with enough water to cover, and bring to the boil. Add a pinch of sea salt and simmer very gently for 15 – 20 minutes until the potatoes are cooked through but still firm and holding their shape. Drain in a colander and set aside.
2. Wash the saucepan and dry thoroughly, pour in the olive oil, heat over a moderate heat and add the finely chopped scallions and the mustard seeds.
3. Stir gently until the contents of the saucepan begin to sizzle, then remove from the heat and add the turmeric.
4. Return to a low heat and add the potatoes to the spices, tossing gently until they are coated with the mixture. Add the duileasc and parsley, and serve warm.

baked hoisin onions wrapped in kelp

A meltingly delicious and unusual accompaniment. This is a great side dish with lamb chops and will enhance any vegetarian meal.

Onion fairs are still popular in parts of Europe, including Brittany and Wales, and take place in late Autumn. In addition to the most intricate of hand–woven onion and garlic bunches, the array of tarts, pies, chutneys, jams and preserves on sale at the stalls is enormous, and generally homemade. For onion lovers, the fair in November in Berne, Switzerland, with all its sights, sounds and smells, is well worth a visit.

Seaweed used: Kelp
Serves 4

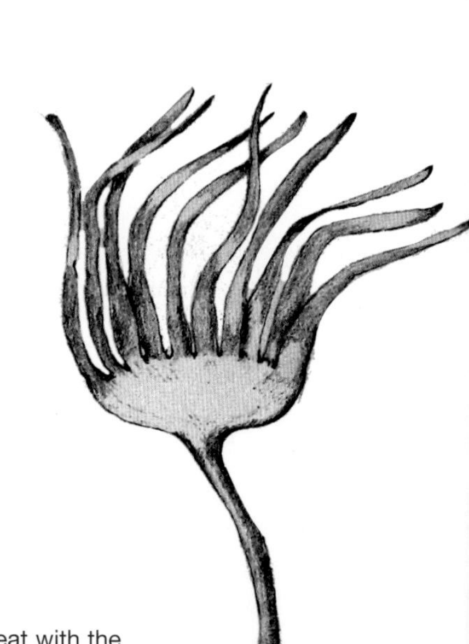

***4 strips of kelp:** 17.5 – 20cm by 5cm wide (2 x 9 – 10 inches), soaked for 40 minutes in warm water*
4 tablespoons hoisin sauce
1 heaped teaspoon dark brown sugar
4 large onions, peeled and cut into quarters with the base kept intact
4 cocktail sticks to secure kelp
2 tablespoons water

Preheat the oven to 190°C/375°F/Gas 5.
Use a lidded casserole dish that will snugly hold the 4 onions.

1 Mix the hoisin sauce with the sugar and set aside.

2 Wrap a strip of kelp around an onion. Secure with a cocktail stick. Repeat with the remaining 3 onions. Put the water and onions into the casserole dish.

3 Spoon the hoisin evenly over the onions, pushing the sauce down through the onion cuts.

4 Bake for 1 hour or until the onions are meltingly soft. Baste with the sauce when cooked and allow to sit for 10 minutes before serving.

Laminaria digitata (kombu, kelp) contains more fibre than an equivalent portion of prunes or apples.

kale and duileasc

This is a finger–licking dish which leaves guests or family competing for the last bit in the pot.

Seaweed used: Duileasc
Serves 4 as a side dish

1 large bunch kale
55g (2oz) duileasc, dried
olive oil or flax oil, to drizzle
Parmesan cheese (optional)
pine nuts (optional)

1. Wash the kale and remove tough stalks.
2. Place in a steamer and steam for about 20 minutes, until tender.
3. Meanwhile, place the duileasc on a dry pan over low to moderate heat until it crisps up and all excess moisture has been expelled. Remove from heat and crumble into small pieces with fingers or pestle and mortar.
4. To serve, chop the kale roughly with a serrated knife. Place a serving of kale on each plate and top with crisped duileasc. Drizzle with flax or olive oil, a shaving of Parmesan and a sprinkle of pine nuts, if using.

Minerals such as iron are present in seaweeds at higher levels than in many well known sources, such as meat. Nutritional analysis reveals that an 8g serving of duileasc has four times more iron than a 100g serving of raw sirloin steak.

baked goats' cheese

with duileasc and garden lettuces

from Alice Waters

'We have had this dish on the menu in the Chez Panisse Café every day since we opened and vary the accompaniments according to what's available, adding slices of ripe pear and watercress in the fall, or rocket leaves and hazelnut oil in summer. Delicious as a first course, it can also be served after a meal, as a combination salad–and–cheese course. Investigate fresh local goats' cheeses in your area, or use French chèvre. The goats' cheese can marinate from overnight to up to a week.'

Alice Waters

'She's hailed by the French as one of the greatest cooks, she invented Californian cuisine and she turned the gastronomic world on to organic food.'

Jay Rayner, Observer Food Monthly

Seaweed used: Duileasc
Serves 4

225g (8oz) fresh goats' cheese, a log about 5 x 13cm (2 x 5 inches)
250ml (8½fl oz) extra–virgin olive oil
3 – 4 sprigs fresh thyme, chopped
1 small sprig rosemary, chopped
½ sourdough baguette, 75g (2½oz), preferably a day old
*2½ tablespoons **duileasc,** finely ground*
1 tablespoon red wine vinegar
1 teaspoon sherry vinegar
salt and pepper
60ml (2fl oz) extra–virgin olive oil, walnut oil, or a combination
Freshly ground pepper
250g (9oz) garden lettuces, washed and dried
*1 handful **mixed dried seaweeds**, rehydrated in a little cold water for 10 minutes and well drained (optional)*

1. Carefully slice the goats' cheese into 8 discs about 1cm (1/2 inch) thick. Pour olive oil over the discs and sprinkle with the chopped herbs. Cover and store in a cool place for several hours or up to a week.
2. Preheat the oven to 150°C/300°F/Gas 2. Cut the baguette in half lengthwise and place in the oven for 20 minutes or so, until dry and lightly coloured. Grate into fine crumbs on a box grater or in a food processor. The breadcrumbs can be made in advance and stored until needed. Stir in the flaked duileasc and set aside.
3. Preheat the oven to 200°C/400°F/Gas 6. Remove the cheese discs from the marinade and roll them in the bread and duileasc crumbs, coating thoroughly. Place the cheeses on a small baking sheet and bake for about 6 minutes. Remove from the oven and allow to cool a little to firm up.
4. Measure the vinegars into a small bowl and add a big pinch of salt. Whisk in the oil and a little freshly ground pepper. Taste for seasoning and adjust. Lightly toss the lettuces and mixed seaweeds if using, in the vinaigrette and arrange on salad plates. Using a metal spatula, carefully place 2 discs of the baked cheese on each plate, and serve.

FOUNDATION

Created by Alice Waters in 1997, the Chez Panisse Foundation supports public school programmes that use food to educate, nurture and empower youth.

Our local Primary school's organic garden is loosely modelled on one of the Foundation's flagship programmes The Edible Schoolyard, which is used as an outdoor classroom in Berkeley, California.

bean pâté

This pâté was very enthusiastically received at a Community Food Project* cooking session. Normally made with a glut of fresh beans it can be made in winter using rehydrated dried beans or tinned beans.

Ingrid Foley, a Community Food Project gardener, created this recipe and says: 'I first tried this broad bean pâté when I was inundated with beans; not always everyone's favourite. The texture of the bean makes it ideal for a pâté, particularly when the beans are more mature. The beauty of the recipe is that you don't have to peel the beans, so preparation is really easy and quick. The recipe is merely a guide. Adjust it as you will with various herbs or some onion. The mixed seaweeds enhance it beautifully. My kids, who wouldn't touch a broad bean in its whole form, love it!'

Seaweed used: Dried mixed seaweeds
Serves 10 – 12

500g (1lb 2oz) fresh broad beans shelled or cooked butter beans when beans are out of season
3 – 4 cloves garlic
2 fresh tomatoes, chopped or 2 sundried tomatoes
2 tablespoons basil/parsley
1 tablespoon coriander, chopped roughly (optional)
*2 teaspoons **mixed seaweeds,** ground or flaked*
juice of ½ lemon
125ml (4fl oz) olive oil

1. In a large saucepan, cover the broad beans with water, bring to the boil, and cook for about 10 – 12 minutes until tender. Drain well.
2. Place in a food processor along with the garlic, tomatoes, herbs and seaweed and process on medium until roughly mixed.
3. Add the lemon juice and process again, then add oil gradually and process to a smooth consistency. More oil may be needed if a runnier texture is desired. Adjust seasoning to taste.
4. Serve it on brown bread, toast, crackers or as pasta sauce.

***The Community Food Project facilitates members of the community in growing, harvesting and cooking food together as a healthy way of life. Funded by the Irish Health Service Executive and run under the guidance of a trained organic gardener, several gardens exist in the north west of Ireland and the programme is steadily expanding.**

apple, celery and carrot salad

This salad has lots of texture, colour and crunch, comes with a creamy dressing, and is a pleasant alternative to a leafy salad.

Seaweed used: Alaria or nori
Serves 4

DRESSING

*1 tablespoon **nori flakes** or **ground Alaria** (see bookmark)*
300g (10oz) Greek yogurt or half crème fraîche and half Greek yogurt. If using the crème fraîche/yoghurt mix, omit the olive oil
1 tablespoon runny honey
1 tablespoon olive oil
sea salt to taste

COOK'S TIP

If you prepare this in advance, store in a cool place and mix well before bringing to the table. Don't chop the celery and apples too finely, or you lose the crunch.

SALAD

3 sticks celery, washed and chopped into bite size pieces
6 small organic carrots, scrubbed and cut into rounds
6 small eating apples, washed
$^1/_2$ tablespoon lemon juice
25g (1oz) pine nuts or walnuts or a mix of both

1. In a large salad bowl, whisk together the dressing ingredients, adjusting the flavouring to taste. Add the celery and carrots to the bowl.
2. Chop the apples and add to the salad bowl with the lemon juice to stop them discolouring. Toss well to coat.
3. Add the nuts, toss, and serve.

Great with omelette or baked fish.

sargassum salad for boat owners!

When Jane Teas came to stay with me after the International Seaweed (Phycology) Conference held in Ireland in June 2008, I was delighted to hear that she had a use for sargassum. This invasive seaweed had been making an appearance on Irish shores, and over the last few summers I had more than once encountered exasperated boat owners grappling with its long fronds to keep them clear of their propellers and doing a lot of cursing into the bargain. I am delighted to tell them that they can harvest it from a clean area, bring it home and eat it – in moderation of course. Within 10 minutes they will have a tasty salad on the table to complement dinner.

Seaweed used: Sargassum seaweed – fresh or dried Serves 4

About 15g (1/2 oz) of ***dried sargassum***
olive oil, enough to coat the seaweed.
Dried sargassum will absorb about 10 times its weight in water, so you only need to rehydrate small amounts for use.

THE DRESSING

1 tablespoon umeboshi plum vinegar
1/8 teaspoon fresh dill
1 clove garlic, minced
few twists of freshly ground red pepper

SALAD OF CHOICE

lettuce leaves, washed and torn into pieces
cucumber, sliced
radish, sliced
avocado, sliced with a squeeze of lemon
onion, sliced finely

1. Soak the sargassum for about 10 minutes in fresh water if using dried. Try to add just enough water so that the sargassum is rehydrated and there is little water left over. Drain, pat dry with kitchen towel, slice into 2.5 – 5mm (1/2 – 1 inch) pieces and put into a large salad bowl.
2. Add enough olive oil to the bowl to coat the chopped fresh or rehydrated seaweed. Toss well. It is important to toss the olive oil and seaweed so that the dressing ingredients will mix well on the surface of the plant.
3. Mix the dressing and add to the seaweed. Toss the salad ingredients with the dressed seaweed to mix well.

COOK'S TIP

1 tablespoon umeboshi vinegar can be substituted by mixing 1/4 teaspoon umeboshi paste with 2 teaspoons hot water and 1 teaspoon lemon juice

Sargassum has a very balanced range of nutrients in addition to having anti-viral properties. I found it heartening to hear from Jane that her experimental work on small numbers of HIV patients over the last 5 years is very positive and has led to increases in patient CD4 helper cells.

spinach, sesame and ginger prawn salad

This exotic salad was created one evening when I was experimenting with the pickled ginger used for sushi.

It can be prepared with or without the prawns and makes a great starter served in individual dishes.

Seaweed Used: Nori
Serves 3 – 4

SALAD
85g (3 oz) small sweet prawns, cooked
2 large handfuls baby spinach, washed, torn and hard stalks removed
1 avocado, sliced and tossed in lemon juice
half a mango, sliced
1 tablespoon pickled pink sushi ginger, drained

DRESSING
1 teaspoon toasted sesame oil
2 tablespoons olive oil
1 1/2 teaspoons lemon juice
1 teaspoon runny honey

TOPPING
Toasted sesame seeds
Toasted pieces of torn nori for sprinkling

1. Measure the dressing ingredients into a large salad bowl and mix well to combine. Add all the salad ingredients to the bowl and toss to dress lightly.
2. Divide the salad into individual serving bowls, making sure that a little of each ingredient goes into each serving.
3. Sprinkle seeds and nori on each portion and serve.

pumpkin and ginger with mixed seaweeds

This is a favourite of my husband Johnnys' and blends the taste and colour of autumn into a versatile side dish that goes with just about everything. Use the very small Hokkaido / Uchi Kuri orange squash (below) when in season – these should be available in your local farmers' market. Don't use the Jack O Lantern type (opposite) as they don't have as much flavour.

Seaweed used: Mixed seaweeds or Alaria
Serves 4

1 small or 1/2 a medium orange pumpkin (squash)
2 – 3 tablespoons olive oil and a small knob of butter
2 cloves garlic
1.5cm (3/4 inch) – small toe of ginger
75ml (2 1/2 fl oz) water
2 tablespoons ***mixed seaweeds,*** *chopped, or 1 tablespoon ground* ***Alaria***

Variation
sweet potato can be used instead of pumpkin or squash for a change

1 Cut the pumpkin into half, then quarters and remove the pith and seeds. No need to remove the skin if organic. Just remove any damaged parts. Cut into 2.5cm (1 inch) pieces. Heat the olive oil and butter in a wide pan over moderate heat.

2 Crush the garlic and ginger through a garlic press and add to the pan, then add the pumpkin. Increase the heat and toss ingredients in the pan to coat with oil and butter, and cook for 1 minute.

3 Reduce the heat. Add water and sprinkle on the seaweeds. Cover with a tight fitting lid and leave on the stove to cook over moderate heat for 6 minutes or until just cooked. Alternatively, if the oven is on, the covered pan can be placed in the oven to cook for about 6 minutes at 190°C/375°F/Gas 5.

4 Pierce a piece of pumpkin with a fork. If the flesh pierces easily, the pumpkin is cooked. Remove from the oven or stove and mix gently.

5 Serve as a side dish with just about everything in the autumn.

COOK'S TIP

Try not to peel much of the skin; just use a potato peeler to skim off any of the very hard parts at either end.

Memories of Alaria

The Irish historically referred to Alaria as 'fern weed' or 'sea fern'. Apparently St. Ciaran had a meal every evening of barley bread and spring water with two roots of sea fern, believed to refer to the edible seaweed dabberlocks (Alaria esculenta).

Wakame is very similar to Alaria and is highly prized in Japan, where it is used for making nutritious and health giving miso soup.

Alaria salad

We visited Larch Hanson at his home in Maine one midsummer on a full moon when the tides were perfect, and helped him harvest Alaria. It was a memorable experience.

After a deliciously healthy dinner which he whipped up in minutes, he entertained us to a poetry reading of his own material. In one of his poems he uses the analogy of choosing the perfect wave to land exactly at the Alaria beds to describe finding the right marriage partner: the idea being to neither fall short nor end up on the rocks.

Thrice married he has landed on the rocks a few times but is ever the romantic and poet.

A trained chef, this is how Larch makes a salad using his favourite seaweed, Alaria.

'I use Alaria because I like the flavour, and it's high in calcium. I cut it finely with a scissors before reconstituting it in water. One could reconstitute it first, then chop it finely with a scissors or a knife. It's a matter of personal preference. I don`t want to throw out the soak water because the water contains a lot of nutrients, so I more or less sprinkle the seaweed with water, and keep turning it over. Think of it as making a pancake batter, and you want enough water to wet the flour, but not so much that it's runny. I also squeeze lemon juice into the soak water, because lemon will help release minerals from the seaweed.

'While the Alaria is reconstituting, I make a marinade. I grate ginger and squeeze the juice out of the pulp. Sometimes I will cut ginger in small chunks and extract the juice from my juicer. Either way works. I squeeze orange juice for a fragrant sweetener. One could also use raw unpasteurised honey and stir that into the marinade. I use toasted sesame oil. I add a dash of tamari. One could also add a dash of brown rice vinegar. So there you have it: Alaria, lemon, ginger juice, orange juice and / or raw honey, toasted sesame oil, a dash of tamari and / or brown rice vinegar. Mix it all together to suit your taste. The longer it soaks, the more tender it becomes.

'I can imagine using this seaweed salad with chopped apples, and I can also imagine adding it to a dark green salad that includes romaine or baby greens, cucumber and parsley. Grated carrots would be another good addition. When I cook carrots with Alaria, I sometimes add one clove of garlic. It always is delicious.'

Larch Hanson, Seaweed harvester from Maine Seaweed Company

puy lentils and Alaria with goats' cheese salad

The combination of oils and spices in the salad dressing here perfectly complements the robust flavour of goats' cheese, while the Alaria gives the puy lentils a real flavour lift. Take time to really savour the first mouthful.

Seaweed used: Alaria
Serves 4

225g (8oz) puy lentils
1 red onion, chopped finely
olive oil, for frying
1 bay leaf
½ tablespoon thyme, destalked and finely chopped
15cm (6 inch) piece ***Alaria*** *(about 5g) snipped into 0.5 – 1cm (¼ – ½ inch) pieces*
875ml (1 pint 10fl oz) stock

DRESSING
1 garlic clove, crushed
1 level teaspoon mustard powder
2 tablespoons lemon juice
2 tablespoons walnut oil
3 tablespoons olive oil

85g (3oz) walnuts
1 tablespoon ***mixed sea vegetables,*** *chopped*
1 large handful rocket leaves
115g (4oz) firm white goats' cheese, crumbled

COOK'S TIP

For an extra vegetable boost add more lightly dressed salad leaves and mop up the salad dressing with some crusty bread.

1 Rinse the lentils under cold running water, place in saucepan, cover with cold water and bring to the boil. Simmer for 5 minutes. Drain and rinse well, to remove indigestible starches. Set aside.

2 In a large heavy based saucepan sauté the onion in olive oil over moderate heat until softened.

3 Add the par–cooked lentils, bay leaf, thyme and Alaria and stir briefly.

4 Pour in the stock, cover and simmer for 40 minutes until cooked. Drain any remaining liquid and keep warm.

To prepare dressing and assemble the salad

1 In a large bowl combine the garlic, mustard, lemon juice and oils. Toss the hot lentils in the dressing.

2 Add half of the walnuts, half of the sea vegetables and the rocket, and toss well.

3 Sprinkle cheese over the top and toss again. Scatter the remaining mixed sea vegetables and walnuts over the salad. Serve warm.

Puy lentils are ideal for salads because of their unique peppery flavour and the fact they hold their shape during cooking. They are identified by the area of cultivation where they are grown in the Le Puy region of France.

cannellini bean salad with marinated Alaria

A delightful concoction comprising beans, fruit, chilli, fresh herbs and Alaria. Guaranteed to surprise and delight.

Seaweed used: Alaria, kelp for cooking beans
Serves 4

25g (1oz) raisins
juice of 2 lemons
100ml (3½fl oz) olive oil
½ onion chopped finely
2 garlic cloves, chopped finely
½ red chilli, seeds removed, sliced finely
¼ teaspoon black onion seeds
450g (1lb) cooked cannellini beans or 2 tins
2 bananas
½ a mango, fresh, cubed or chopped roughly
marinated Alaria (see recipe opposite)
large fistful coriander leaves, chopped
coriander leaves to decorate

To prepare the salad

1. Soak the raisins in lemon juice to allow them to plump up.
2. Heat the oil in a large frying pan and sauté onion until transparent. Add the garlic, chilli and onion seeds and sauté for 2 – 3 minutes. Set aside to cool.
3. Rinse the cannellini beans under cold running water, drain well and place in a large bowl.
4. Add the lemon juice and raisins stirring to coat the beans. Toss in the cooled onion and chilli. Slice the bananas and toss in immediately to prevent blackening. Add the mango, marinated Alaria and coriander. Mix gently and decorate with the coriander leaves.

MARINATED ALARIA

Alaria needs to be simmered for around 40 minutes because the midrib is quite tough. Marinated Alaria can be used to stir through other salads, or as a side dish with grains.

2 x 15cm (6 inch) pieces of fresh Alaria cut into 1–2.5cm (½ – 1 inch) pieces or same length (about 3g) of dried Alaria, snipped as above
1 tablespoon tamari or soy sauce
3 garlic cloves, crushed
2 teaspoons honey
1 tablespoon olive oil
1 teaspoon grated ginger
A dash of toasted sesame oil

1. Soak the Alaria in just enough tepid water to cover it for 20 minutes.
2. In a small saucepan, combine the rest of the ingredients except the sesame oil and boil for 1 minute over moderate heat.
3. Add the Alaria and a little of the soak water to the saucepan and bring back to the boil, uncovered. Simmer for 40 minutes or until the mid rib is very tender.
4. Add some more of the soak water if needed and continue to boil until the mid rib is very soft.
5. Remove from the heat, add a dash of toasted sesame oil and taste for sweetness, adding more honey if needed.

Cooking dried beans

As a general guide use just less than half the cooked quantities if using dried beans.

For this recipe use 200g (7oz) of dried cannellini beans. Rinse well under a cold tap and soak in plenty of water overnight with a piece of kelp to help soften the beans. Change the water and bring to the boil. Boil for 5 minutes then rinse and drain. This helps to remove the indigestible starches.

Cover the beans with cold water again and add back in the piece of kelp. Bring to the boil and simmer until cooked, about one hour. Drain and rinse with cold water. Discard the kelp as it will have disintegrated. See extra note on beans page 69.

basic seaweed smoothie

to get you started

Smoothies taste great, are easy to make, and give you a great green boost in one glass. Start small, and increase the green and seaweed content as you progress.

There are endless possibilities and with a little experimentation you can custom–make your own. Victoria Boutenko originally came up with the idea: check out her website at **www.rawfamily.com** for more ideas and information.

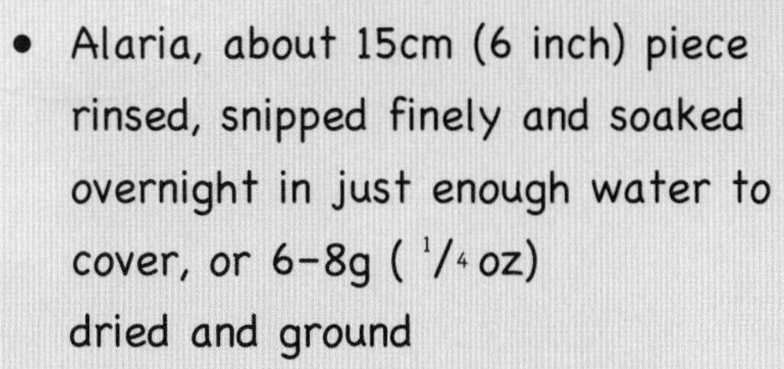

- Alaria, about 15cm (6 inch) piece rinsed, snipped finely and soaked overnight in just enough water to cover, or 6–8g (1/4 oz) dried and ground
- 1 banana chilled or else peeled, chopped and frozen overnight, or 2 chilled pears
- 1/4 pineapple, including core, chopped
- 300 ml (1/2 pint) cold water.
- 6 large green leaves, well washed
- a little local honey or agave to sweeten if needed

GOOD NEWS ABOUT SEAWEED

Research has shown that seaweeds have an apoptotic effect on cancer cells. This means that they cause cancer cells to die while otherwise protecting normal healthy cells.

• Put everything, including the soak water into a blender and blend until smooth.

• It is important to vary the ingredients in the recipe, choosing small amounts from a wide variety.

• Have a look at my version overleaf for a list of favourite ingredients.

get the most from your smoothie...

'The important thing about seaweeds is that they are just not land plants... they have so much more to offer with specific components such as alginates, fucoidans, laminarins, fucoxanthines, phyto–defensive compounds, and specific lipids... all of which just don't occur in land plants and each of which to date has shown strong anti cancer properties.
So to reduce seaweeds to land plant minerals, vitamins, proteins and carbohydrates is to overlook their richness and potential value...
they aren't just some land plant that is weird and grows in the water.'

Jane Teas PhD, cancer researcher

my addictive green smoothie

This is our breakfast. Power–packed full of seaweed, fruit and vegetables, this smoothie keeps us energised and hunger at bay until lunchtime and beyond. We start virtually every day with this, since it was introduced to me in its original form by friend and raw food collaborator, Gaby. By the end of the first week of experimentation I had created my own signature seaweed smoothie about which I enthuse endlessly.

Already popular with many food–conscious celebrities, smoothies taste great and this seaweed version packs a major nutrient punch from land and sea sources.

Prepare the smoothie every second day if pressed for time and store, covered in the fridge for up to 24 hours. Remember to soak the seaweed the night before. If you have forgotten then soak it for at least 10 minutes in the morning.

If you do not enjoy icy cold drinks, then use fresh ripe bananas or other fruit.

It can take you 20 minutes or longer to drink / eat the smoothie and you will need a spoon if it is thick. Put it into a container with a lid if you are on the move. Don't rush it!

If you want to do just one thing for your health, not to mention your taste buds and your skin, enjoy this smoothie on a daily basis. When you reach your next birthday, acknowledge gracefully, then start counting backwards. You will not be disbelieved.

Seaweed used: Alaria

Yield 1½ – 2 litres using a Vitaprep blender with a 2 litre jug. Adjust the quantities to suit your blender jug.

*6 – 8g (¼oz) dried **Alaria,** rinsed and soaked in a cup of cold water overnight.*

***Juice:** 250ml (8½fl oz) blueberry juice or juice from 2 – 3 ruby grapefruit, or apple juice*

***Seasonal greens:** 4 handfuls, choose from spinach, chard, 1 – 2 dandelion leaves, beet greens, young nettle tops in spring, broccoli, 1 – 2 leaves of kale, lettuce, rocket, collard greens*

***Herbs:** a sprig of mint,lemon balm, coriander or fennel. Hedgerow herbs when in season.*

***Fruit:** ¼ pineapple (ripe), core included or a handful of frozen berries or half an apple and 2 – 3 frozen or fresh bananas, or 3 – 4 pears.*

***Spices/seeds:** 1 inch of ginger. Ground hemp and flax seeds.*

***Optional extras:** a shake of cocoa nibs, bee pollen to sweeten: a dash of local honey or agave*

1 Pour the soaking water from the Alaria into a blender. Chop the Alaria roughly and add to the blender with the juice and pineapple. Blend on high before adding the rest of the ingredients.

2 Gradually add all the greens and fruit leaving the chopped bananas until the end. Add more water or juice if you like. Taste while it is still in the blender so you can adjust the flavour.

3 If the smoothie is too bitter add a little more banana or a small amount of local honey or agave.

Two things to remember

Use produce in season and always vary the ingredients.

COOK'S TIP

To freeze bananas pack them into a plastic container that will hold three bananas and slice into 1cm (½ inch) pieces. Freeze until required.
Frozen bananas make the smoothie thick.

the BBC challenge

When a BBC Northern Ireland crew came to film our garden some years ago for a *Secret Gardens* programme, they were so intrigued with the idea of eating seaweed that I invited each of them to come up with their own seaweed recipe. These are some of the results.

Donal Hamilton the cameraman decided on his failsafe nut roast which we paired with Alaria: full of crunch and flavour.

Be sure to serve it with the tomato sauce...

nut roast and tomato sauce

Seaweed used: Alaria
Serves 4 – 6

25g (1oz) ***dried Alaria,*** *snipped into 5mm (1/4 inch) pieces*
25g (1oz) butter and a dash of olive oil
2 large onions, diced
2 cloves garlic, finely chopped
250g (9oz) chestnut mushrooms, sliced roughly
225g (8oz) mix of hazelnuts, cashews or walnuts
115g (4oz) pine nuts
115g (4oz) ground almonds
2 eggs, lightly beaten
225g (8oz) breadcrumbs, preferably brown
2 tablespoons soy sauce
2 – 3 tablespoons lemon juice
2 teaspoons dried tarragon or 4 big sprigs fresh thyme
3 tablespoons parsley, chopped
1 sprig rosemary, chopped
1 teaspoon yeast extract (optional)
100 – 150ml (3 – 5fl oz) sea and land vegetable stock or Marigold bouillon

To prepare the Alaria

Soak Alaria in 300ml (1/2 pint) of warm water for 10 – 15 minutes then simmer briskly in a small covered saucepan for about 30 – 40 minutes until the midstem is soft.

1 Preheat the oven to 180°C/350°F/Gas 4. Grease, and line a 450g (1lb) tin with greaseproof paper allowing paper to make a 2.5cm (1 inch) collar above the top of the tin. Old butter wrappers work well.

2 Heat the oil in a pan and gently sauté the onions and garlic until soft and translucent. Add the mushrooms and cook for 4 – 5 minutes.

3 Remove from the heat and blend in a food processor. Place the mixture in a large bowl and set aside.

4 Place the hazelnuts and cashews into food processor and pulse until roughly chopped. Add the walnuts if using and pine nuts and pulse for a few seconds, again to chop roughly. The nuts taste better if they are not pulverised.

5 Scrape the nut mixture into the prepared mushroom mixture and add the ground almonds. Stir in the beaten eggs, breadcrumbs, soy sauce, lemon juice, herbs of choice and the yeast extract if using. It will be quite stiff. Add the softened Alaria with the cooking water and some of the stock. Mix well. Use more of the stock if needed to ensure it is well mixed.

6 Spoon the mixture into prepared tin and flatten with a palette knife. The mixture will come above the tin onto the greased collar of paper. This makes a high loaf which looks well for serving and cutting.

7 Bake for 30 minutes, covered with a layer of greaseproof paper. Remove paper and bake for a further 10 minutes until golden on top, and cooked through.

8 Serve warm with tomato sauce or cold for a picnic with tomato salsa and salad.

TOMATO SAUCE
Seaweed used: Nori, Alaria or duileasc
Serves 4 – 6

2 – 3 tablespoons seaweed of choice: nori, Alaria, duileasc
2 tablespoons olive oil
knob of butter
3 onions, chopped and diced
4 cans 400g (14oz) each of tomatoes, ideally a mix of cherry and plum
8 big sprigs thyme
6 garlic cloves
4 long sprigs of rosemary
4 big sprigs of basil
1 bay leaf
1 teaspoon sweet paprika

To prepare the seaweed

Soak seaweed for 5 minutes in cold water.
Drain and chop finely with a sharp knife.
Reserve soaking water for stock.
Alternatively, snip into 2.5 – 5mm (1 – 1/4 inch) pieces.

1 Heat the oil in a large saucepan and gently sauté onions in olive oil and butter until soft and translucent.

2 Place all the remaining ingredients into a saucepan and simmer for 1 hour over a very low heat. Remove bay leaf and rosemary sprigs. Blend using a hand blender.

3 Serve with grains, such as quinoa and basmati, or with nut loaf.

COOK'S TIP

Use fresh or frozen tomatoes as an alternative to canned.

marinated tuna steaks

Carole and Darryl both opted for tuna and, in particular, speedy ways of preparing it. Although the cooking is done quickly in this first recipe, the real flavours come through after only a little time spent marinating in the fridge. Get to know your fish seller at your local market to get the freshest tuna.

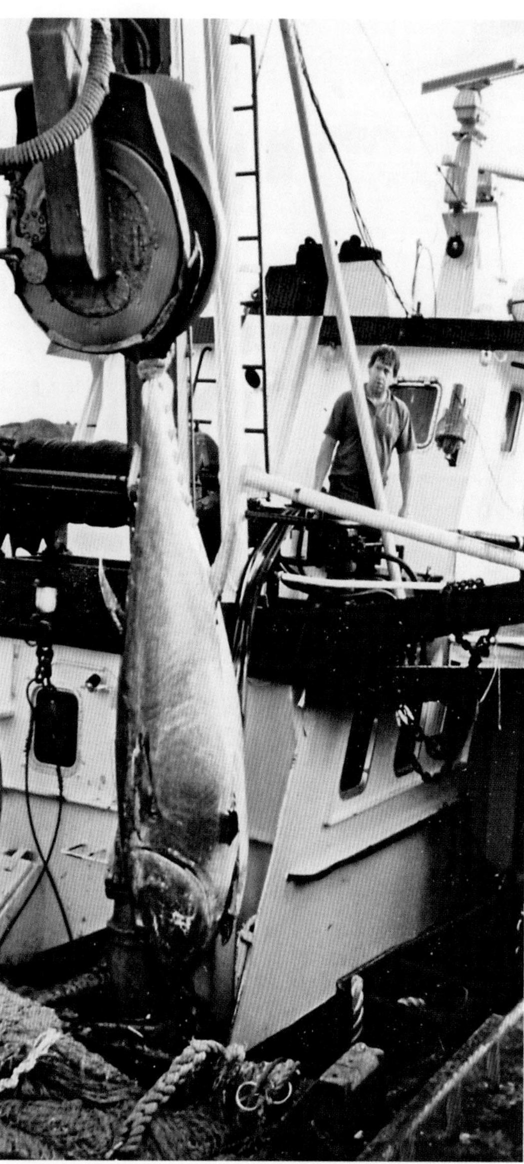

Seaweed used: Nori
Serves 2

2 fresh tuna steaks, each about 180g (6oz)
olive oil for cooking

MARINADE

1 tablespoon soy sauce or tamari
2 teaspoons brown sugar
1 clove garlic, minced
1 small knob ginger, grated finely
1 rounded teaspoon **ground nori,**
(see bookmark for preparation)

TO SERVE

4 sheets **nori,** ***toasted and cut into 2.5 – 5cm (1 – 2 inch) squares***

1 Combine all the marinade ingredients in a small bowl.

2 Using a small spoon rub the marinade all over the tuna steaks and set aside for 30 minutes or longer.

3 Heat a little oil in a pan over moderate heat and when hot place the steaks on the pan.

4 Sear the tuna for 1 minute. Turn and sear the other side for 1 minute. Remove from the pan.

5 Slice thinly and place small pieces on squares of nori. Serve with soy sauce for dipping.

Carole O'Kane, BBC Producer

Filming for BBC Northern Ireland's 'Secret Gardens' (L – R) Back row: Darryl Grimason, Prannie Rhatigan, Johnny Waters, Deke Thompson, Donal Hamilton. Front row: Carole O'Kane, Anke Lueddecke, Kate Waters

crispy tuna and pasta

Every cook needs a recipe like this one of Darryl's where the ingredients are to be found in most kitchen cupboards. Quickly prepared it has all the things in it that children love.

Seaweed used: Duileasc
Serves 4

300g (10oz) pasta spirals or twists
1 onion, chopped
1 clove garlic, chopped
olive oil
1 tin of tuna in oil or brine, drained
1 tin tomatoes, chopped
1 teaspoon tomato puree

TOPPING
225g (8oz) cheddar cheese, grated
28g or 1 pack of **duileasc,** ***snipped into 2.5cm (1 inch) pieces***

Preheat the oven to 180°C/350°F/Gas 4

1. Cook the pasta as per instructions on the packet.
2. Fry the onion and garlic in olive oil over gentle heat and add the tuna.
3. Add the tomatoes, tomato puree and cooked pasta to the onion, garlic and tuna and mix well. Transfer to a casserole dish and cover with cheese mixed with duileasc pieces.
4. Bake for about 20 minutes until the cheese has melted and browned slightly and the duileasc has become crisp. Serve at once with salad.

VARIATION

Prepare the duileasc crisps separately and serve on the side:

Snip the duileasc into 2.5cm (1 inch) pieces. Melt a knob of butter or use olive oil in a pan. Add the duileasc and fry for a minute or so until it turns green and smells of bacon. Remove with a slotted spoon and keep warm until the tuna and pasta bake is ready. The duileasc will continue to crisp up.

Darryl Grimason is the author of *Reading the Water – A life spent fishing*. Born to fish and forced to work, he is a TV reporter and presenter for BBC Northern Ireland.

Sushi

Making sushi is great fun for both adults and children. It doesn't have to be absolutely perfect with every grain in place. The important thing is that it tastes good. If children help to prepare their own food they are more likely to eat it... and it is a healthy option. It is also eminently transportable and can be easily packed into a lunch box for school, work or a picnic.

At this stage I have seen many sushi chefs make sushi. We were fortunate to see master chef ToJo, who is credited with inventing the California roll, in Vancouver one Christmas. We have also seen many masters in action in Japan.

There are some great sushi places in Ireland too; I invited Kappa Ya in Galway, our nearest sushi retaurant, to contribute a favourite recipe to the book.

I am not going to go into detail here with the precise Japanese names for each type of sushi, but will instead give you a very simple basic outline that will allow you to have fun using both Japanese and Irish ingredients and to create something you will want to prepare over and over again.

While very precise recipes exist, my attitude to sushi sometimes is to make 'cream of refrigerator' sushi whereby I open the fridge and use whatever leftovers I see to make a meal. This can be a mix of quinoa and basmati rice rolled with organic beef sausage and our own tomato relish... or teriyaki chicken with fresh lettuce from the garden... all wrapped in a sheet of seaweed... the combinations are endless. All you need is your imagination.

1 rice

Seaweed used: Kombu

Interestingly, sushi rice is never weighed but always measured in cups; the ratio being 2 cups of rice to 2 cups of water.

400g (14oz) (2 cups) sushi rice for authentic sushi, or use brown rice for more nutrients, or any grain of choice
450ml (16fl oz) (2 cups) of cold water
plenty of cold tap water for washing and soaking rice
*a piece of **kombu,** 10cm (4 inches) long*
a dash of mirin (a sweet rice wine similar to sake and used in cooking)

2 rice dressing/seasoning

Irish Version

3 dessertspoons lemon juice or half a juicy lemon
3 dessertspoons mirin
generous pinch of salt
1 scant teaspoon very dark sugar

or

Authentic Japanese Version

50ml (2 fl oz) rice vinegar
2 tablespoons sugar
1 teaspoon salt

3 to assemble and to serve

You need

*4 – 5 **nori sheets***
wasabi (a Japanese pungent root similar to horseradish only much stronger. Available as a paste or powder)
pickled ginger
soy sauce or tamari (wheat free soy sauce)

Choice of fillings

prawns, cooked plainly or pan–fried with chilli avocado, sliced thinly and soaked in lemon juice to retain colour
carrot, raw, grated finely or parboiled and sliced finely in lengths
raisins, plumped by soaking in lemon juice for 10 to 20 minutes
pine nuts
roasted red pepper, skinned and sliced into long thin slices
asparagus tips
spinach and mushrooms, tossed on a pan with olive oil and a pinch of nutmeg
sweet potato or any vegetable of choice, parboiled and cut into thin strips
seared salmon, or tuna – 1 minute on 1 side, turn, cover, and remove from heat for 10 minutes until cooked through
chicken, cooked, cooled, cut into long strips, and dressed with yoghurt and tarragon or paprika
crabmeat with a little home made mayonnaise
scrambled egg or Japanese omelette (see recipe on page 117)

4 equipment

sushi mat or folded tea towel
rice paddle or untainted clean wooden spoon
sharp knife
cutting board
damp cloth for cleaning knife

Hand washing bowl containing:
125ml (4fl oz) rice vinegar or cider vinegar
375ml (13fl oz) water (don't let this mixture drip onto the rice when making a roll)

a cloth to wipe sticky hands
platter for servings

directions...

1 cook the rice

Sushi rice can be prepared in many different ways and every Japanese person has a version of how to do it perfectly. Generally it takes about 1 hour to prepare and cook.

equal amounts of rice and water
***10cm (4 inch) piece of* kombu**
a dash of mirin

1 Rinse the rice and place in a large bowl of clean cold water. Allow to soak for 15 to 20 minutes or until the grains turn milky white. Drain in a sieve and set aside to dry for about 15 to 20 minutes.

2 Place in a wide heavy bottomed pot with a tight fitting lid. I find a glass lid is ideal for observing the cooking process. Add rice and water in equal amounts, for example 2 cups rice and a bare 2 cups of water.

3 Add kombu and mirin and bring to the boil over medium heat. Shake the pot.

4 Turn the heat to medium low and cook for about 5 – 8 minutes or until almost all the water is absorbed.

5 Turn heat to very low for another 10 – 15 minutes until rice is cooked. Set the covered pot aside for 10 minutes to allow the rice to set.

2 prepare rice seasoning

1 Choose one of the options listed om page 111. We prefer the Irish version which has vitamin C from the lemon and less sugar and salt.

2 Put the ingredients into a non–reactive bowl, such as ceramic, wooden or plastic and mix using a wooden or plastic spoon. Set aside until rice is ready. Using anything metal from here on can cause an unpleasant taste in the finished result.

3 prepare the wasabi

Use either a ready–made paste or add a little water to a teaspoon of dry wasabi and mix to a paste. Set aside for 10 minutes.

4 cool and dress the rice

1 When the rice is ready tip it into a Pyrex dish or wooden bowl and run the paddle through it. Have somebody fan the rice with a newspaper – children love this job, and it gets them out from under your feet.

2 While fanning, add the seasoning carefully – working it in while turning the rice to mix and cool it. You may not need all the seasoning. It takes 10 minutes to quickly cool the rice and give it a nice glossy sheen.

3 In Japan they have a special rice cooling fan for this job. Living in the breezy north west of Ireland we just open the nearest door or window.

COOK'S TIP

2 cups of uncooked rice yields about $3^3/_4$ cups cooked rice. Using about $^3/_4$ cup per roll you will make 5 medium sized rolls depending on the amount of other filling ingredients used.

Making a sushi roll

5 to make a sushi roll

Optional: Briefly toast the nori by placing in a hot oven for 30 seconds or under a grill until the colour changes to green, roughly 10 to 20 seconds. This is important if the sushi is prepared some time in advance of eating as it prevents the nori going soggy.

Place a sheet of nori on the mat, shiny side down and 20cm (8 inch) side at near edge of mat (the side closest to you).

Take about 1/2 – 3/4 cup of rice and spread evenly over nori, leaving the top, which is the farthest end from you, uncovered for 2.5cm (1 inch).

Over the first 1/3 of the area covered in rice, spread a smear of wasabi along the rice, going from left to right. Place the filling of choice end to end along the smear of wasabi. Don't use too much. For example, put a thin strip each of carrot and avocado followed by a sprinkle of some raisins and pine nuts. Add small strips of pickled ginger. Dab a little water on the end of the nori sheet to help it to stick. Roll up like a Swiss roll using the sushi mat to help the rolling process. Squeeze gently when completed.
Using a sharp knife cut the roll in half, then cut each piece in half and each piece again in half. This is an easy way to make 8 even–sized pieces.

Arrange cut side up on small plates. Serve with a little mound of pickled ginger and some dipping soy sauce. Some more wasabi can be added carefully.
Wasabi is very very hot stuff so please be careful.

growing up in japan

Our friend Yumiko tells us she often 'trims off both ends of the sushi roll and tastes them' because it evokes childhood memories of waiting for her mother to trim the rolls, and offer the 'royal' or special tasty morsel to the child helping in the kitchen… a bit like licking the bowl when our mother made a cake for us.

I packed a little sushi picnic for Yumiko for her journey when she was leaving and she said it reminded her of going to school: her mother used to arrange some sushi cut nice and small for school lunch. Yumiko showed us this zushi trick from her childhood which has become a firm favourite in our household, and certainly takes the ceremony out of sushi:

Te - mari - zushi

Te = hand, Mari = ball and Zushi = sushi

Temari is an old fashioned brightly coloured small ball that is a popular toy for young girls.

Put a square of cling film on the table. Place some rice on it and fillings of choice. Bring the 4 ends of the cling film together and swing and whirl the contents around over your head. Open the cling film and the contents will have formed a sushi ball. Great!

kappa–ya sushi

or 'gomoku zushi' japanese traditional roll

Run by Junichi and Yoshimi, Kappa Ya is a Japanese restaurant in the heart of Galway acclaimed by the Bridgestone Guide as 'boldly going where no Japanese cook in Ireland has ever gone before. So, fasten your safety belts, and unlock your culinary imaginations.'

For my purposes I wanted something simple and traditional that could be easily made at home. This is what they suggested: a specific recipe for 4 servings of 7 – 8 sushi pieces each...

2 cups sushi rice
2 cups of cold water
3 sheets nori
wasabi paste, tip of a teaspoon
55g (2oz) spinach
1 tablespoon sesame seeds
a dash of sesame oil
a pinch of salt
100g (3½ oz) mushrooms
pinch of sugar
carrot, half, grated finely, or cooked
115g (4oz) cooked prawns, chopped finely, thawed and well dried if frozen
Japanese omelette (see recipe on opposite page)

While Yoshimi was demonstrating her way of cooking rice she told me that there is an old saying in Japan: 'even if the baby is crying with hunger, don't open the lid on the pot of rice that is cooking.

I had bad old habits whereby I looked into the pot after the rice boiled and scraped down the bits of rice stuck to the sides.

'Fatal,' says Yoshimi.

She is Japanese so she knows. I stopped doing it.

To make fillings

Spinach

Blanch in boiling water for 30 seconds and then put into cold water. Drain, squeeze, and put in a bowl. Mix with sesame seeds, sesame oil and salt.

Mushrooms

Slice thinly and cook slowly with soy sauce and sugar for 5 to 10 minutes until it becomes dry.

Carrot

Slice finely and cook with a pinch of sugar and a dash of water until barely cooked. This takes five minutes.

1 Cook rice using one of the previously mentioned methods and use the authentic dressing.

2 Assemble as already described using about 1¼ cups of cooked rice per roll. These ingredients will make 3 very large rolls. Prepare as already described and slice each into 10 pieces.

COOK'S TIP

Use sliced radish in season for extra crunch and colour.

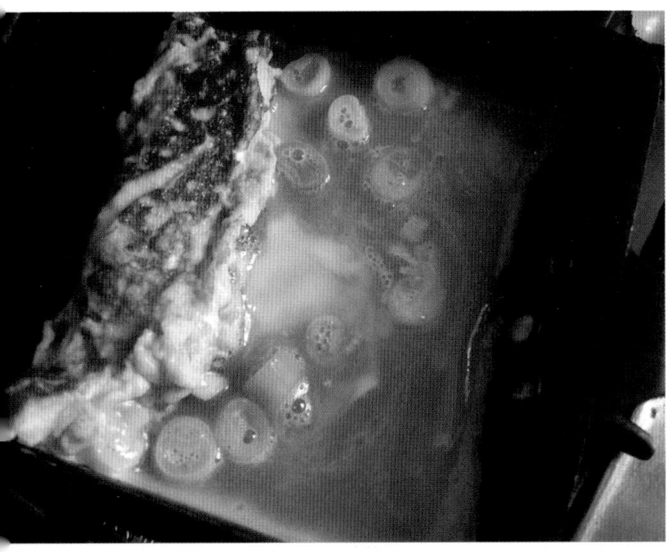

japanese omelette

To serve on its own or as part of a filling for sushi. Junichi demonstrated these for us.

3 eggs
1 tablespoon runny honey
1 shot of dashi
good sprinkle of salt
1/2 teaspoon soy sauce
1 spring onion (green onion), chopped finely

Prepare a special Japanese omelette pan if you have one. If not use a 450–900g (1 or 2lb) loaf tin. Warm the pan or loaf tin and rub with some kitchen paper dipped in oil.

1 Stir the eggs and honey in a bowl. Add all the rest of the ingredients and mix well.

2 Pour a thin layer of egg mixture onto the pan and allow to cook until set. Starting at the short end of the pan fold over 10cm (2 inches) of the cooked egg onto itself and keep folding until it is all folded at the other side of the pan. Pull the folded rectangle of egg across to the starting side of the pan.

3 Pour in another layer of egg. Repeat until all the egg is used up. It is like rolling a Swiss roll except it forms a rectangle, not a log. It will all be folded up in layers when done.

4 Remove from the pan and serve warm with a salad or cool and use slices as an additional sushi filling.

COOK'S TIP

Place a nori sheet on the egg mixture at the start of cooking for an interesting variation

drew rolls

Duika Burges Watson, originally from Tasmania now living in the UK, wrote her PhD on seaweeds and as a social geographer continues to be fascinated by the social history of seaweeds. She holds occasional sushi classes and parties in the Newcastle area and devised these egg and asparagus sushi rolls in honour of Kathleen Drew Baker – the Manchester scientist who discovered the crucial life–cycle phase for the nori seaweed, Porphyra, which led to farming nori in Japan, and to sushi consumption for everyone (see 'memories of sleabhac'on page 50).

The rolls have lots of crunch and freshness.

Seaweed Used: Nori
Makes 4 rolls

$^1/_2$ bunch fresh asparagus, 12 – 16 spears
4 nori sheets, toasted briefly
3 – 4 tablespoons cream cheese
4 teaspoons pesto
4 hard boiled eggs, mashed
4 tablespoons chives, chopped finely
4 teaspoons mayonnaise, home made or good quality

For a real mayonnaise with seaweeds recipe see page 252.

1. Chop off the ends of the asparagus and rinse under a cold tap. Place in a large saucepan and either steam briefly or cover with boiling water for 2 minutes, then rinse with cold water and drain well.

2. Place a nori sheet on a mat and spread $^3/_4$ – 1 tablespoon cream cheese evenly on the sheet.

3. Spread 1 teaspoon pesto across sheet from left to right. Arrange 3 – 4 asparagus spears, depending on size, over the pesto as for regular sushi. Mix the eggs and chives with the mayonnaise and spread $^1/_4$ of this over the asparagus. Dampen the edge of the nori sheet with a little water to help it stick. Roll up carefully and squeeze gently – then slice the roll into 6 – 8 pieces. Arrange cut side up on a serving plate and serve with a little extra pesto as a dipping sauce if desired.

raw food frank's simple sushi

Frank was another visitor to our house who had lots of wonderful ideas and recipes. I was thrilled to discover a new way of making sushi, substituting parsnip or cauliflower for the rice. By using either vegetable instead of rice, the end product is light, fluffy and full of flavour. This is a great alternative to conventional rice sushi and of course the humble parsnip gets unexpectedly elevated to new and dizzying heights.

Seaweed used: Nori

***nori** sheets*
400g (14oz) cauliflower florets, broken up or 400g (14oz) parsnip, diced
100g ($3\frac{1}{2}$ oz) walnuts, soaked in water for 2 – 4 hrs, drained, rinsed well and drained again
1 clove garlic
2 tablespoons freshly grated ginger
1 lime, juiced
salt to taste

Dipping Sauce
50ml (2fl oz) tamari or nama shoyu
2 tablespoons fresh lime or lemon juice
pinch of cayenne pepper

Filling ideas
fresh coriander, parsley or lettuce leaves
julienne of carrot, bell peppers, celery
avocado slices
sprouts
spring onions (green onions) sliced

Frank Giglio, chef and raw food workshop facilitator www.rawfoodfrank.wordpress.com

1 Process the cauliflower or parsnip in a food processor until broken into rice–sized pieces.

2 Place in a mixing bowl. Repeat the process with the walnuts. Add the walnuts to the mixing bowl and stir well to mix. Add ginger, lime juice and salt to taste. Mix well and set aside. This is the "rice".

3 Make the dipping sauce by stirring together the tamari or soy sauce, lime or lemon juice and cayenne pepper. Set aside.

4 Prepare fillings from the choice of fillings listed.

5 Place a sheet of nori on the mat, shiny side down and 20cm (8 inch) side at near edge of mat, the side closest to you. Take about $\frac{1}{4}$ – $\frac{1}{2}$ cup of the "rice" and spread evenly over nori, leaving the top, which is the farthest end from you, uncovered for 2.5cm (1 inch). Lightly pack the "rice" onto the sheets. Spread a little streak of wasabi across each roll.

6 Place a small amount of filling on top of the cauliflower or parsnip "rice" as you would for regular sushi. Carefully roll the nori sheet by hand or with the help of a sushi mat. Before completion, dab a little water on the end of the nori sheet. This will act as a glue once rolled. Slice into 6 – 8 pieces.

Can be eaten with more wasabi, dipping sauce or just on its own.

clambake

a gathering characterised by noisy sociability...

Clambakes

vary the world over and are normally associated with the beach. We decided to change the location to our garden as an experiment and were delighted with the results.

Debates continue about what goes into an authentic clambake. Our solution is to cook what we and our guests enjoy eating. Some of our friends salivate at the thought of lobster generously brushed with garlic butter; some are vegetarian and make straight for our organic salads, and others like nothing more than a perfectly cooked free range chicken. This recipe for a clambake with a selection of favourite salads and breads will feed 25 people. Focaccia is always a great choice. The secret of a successful clambake is to prepare everything in advance. Fruit salad with brown bread and duileasc ice cream, or a birthday cake, depending on the occasion, is the perfect ending.

You will need...

- ***a spade, metal garden rake and 1 or 2 long handled shovels***
- ***tinfoil – wide and strong like you use for cooking a turkey at Christmas***
- ***100 sea or granite river stones, each about the size of a large fist. These are stocked in most garden supply shops. Old oven bricks can also be used***
- ***1 barrowful of old dry timber, heavy logs are ideal***
- ***3 bushels of seaweed (a bushel is about the size of a laundry basket), bladder or egg wrack is perfect***
- ***12 potatoes wrapped individually in tinfoil***
- ***6 – 8 lobsters, placed in freezer for 30 minutes before using***
- ***1 – 2 free–range chickens, halved and wrapped in muslin***
- ***onions with a dollop of hoisin, individually wrapped in tinfoil***
- ***3kg (7lb) of clams, bagged in muslin tied with string***
- ***4kg (about 9lb) of mussels, bagged in muslin tied with string***
- ***12 sweet corn in husks if possible, wrapped in muslin***
- ***12 – 14 sweet potatoes, individually wrapped in tinfoil***
- ***6 – 12 ramekin dishes of garlic butter***

1. Choose a spot in the garden where a hole can be dug safely and easily. Dig a circular hole 50cm (about 1 foot 8 inches) deep x 90cm (about 3 foot) in diameter. Keep the first upturned sods aside to replace when finished. Line the hole with tinfoil and allow the foil to come out beyond the sides of the hole for 30 cm (1 foot) all around.

2. Line the hole with one layer of the sea or river stones. Put in a few extra at the bottom if there are any left over. Place some dry logs in the lined hole and light the fire. Burn a good fire for one and a half to two hours in the open pit. When the fire dies down rake it over with a steel garden rake and take out most of the cinders with long handled shovels. Be really careful, as the stones are red hot at this stage.

3. Place a 7.5 – 10cm (3 – 4 inch) layer of damp to wet bladder wrack over the base of the hole. Place the items that take the longest cooking time – the potatoes, chicken halves and onions – on the bladder wrack. Put a 5cm (2 inch) layer of seaweed over this.

4. Place the lobsters on top and put another layer of seaweed 5cm (2 inches) thick over them. Then place the sweet corn, clams and mussels, and the sweet potatoes on top.

5. Cover with a thick layer of seaweed about 7.5cm (3 inches). Cover the pit with more sheets of tinfoil and use the overlying edges of foil to make a complete seal. Twist the foil into place. Place the remainder of the seaweed on top. Finally put the ramekin dishes of garlic butter near the heat to warm.

6. Appoint a responsible person to supervise the cooking pit at all times as children playing and chasing each other could well run over the hole and be injured.

COOK'S TIP

Talk to your local licenced harvester about getting a supply of fresh seaweed for the occasion.

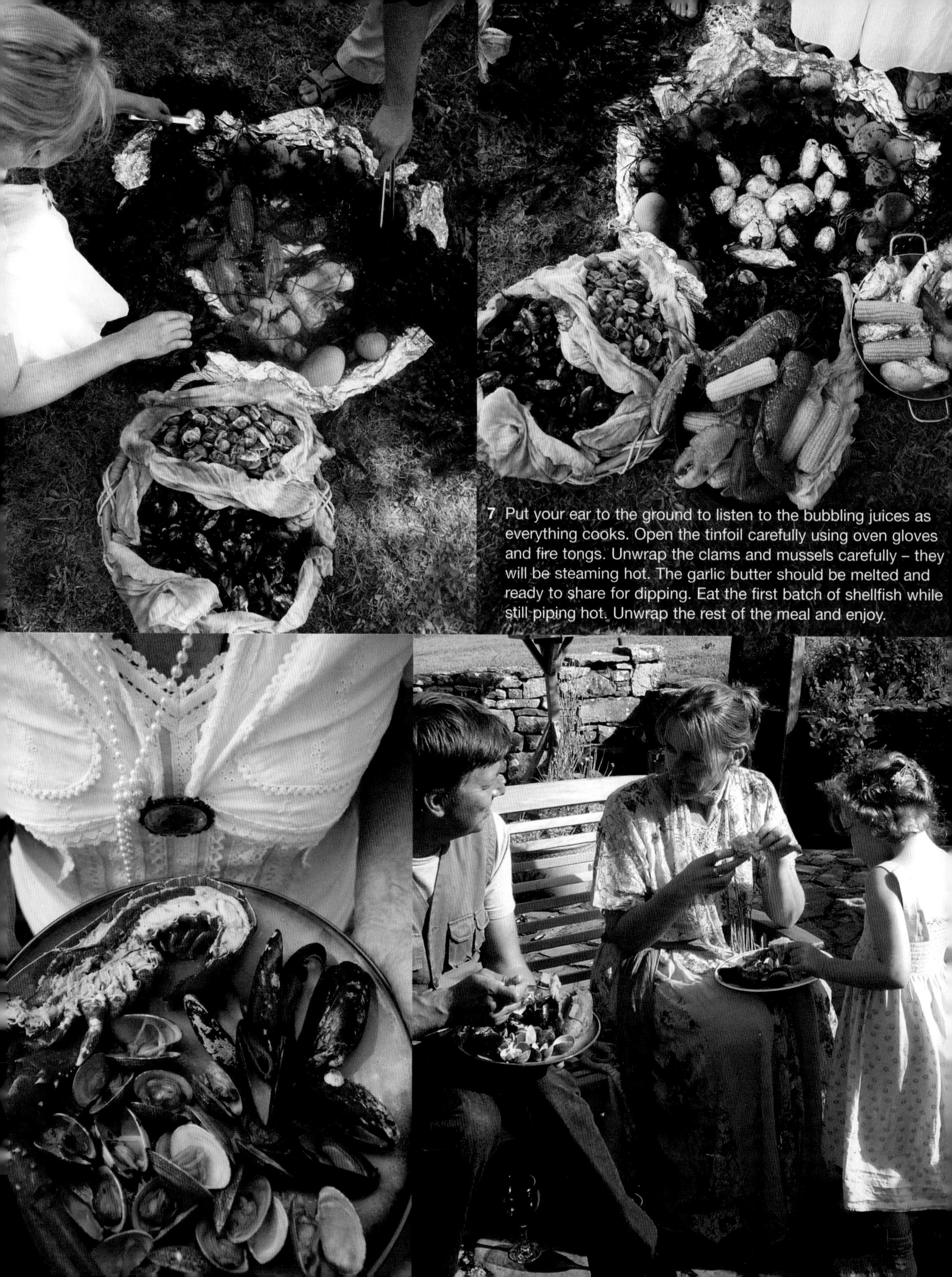

7 Put your ear to the ground to listen to the bubbling juices as everything cooks. Open the tinfoil carefully using oven gloves and fire tongs. Unwrap the clams and mussels carefully – they will be steaming hot. The garlic butter should be melted and ready to share for dipping. Eat the first batch of shellfish while still piping hot. Unwrap the rest of the meal and enjoy.

8 When the party is over put the seaweed in the compost heap. Recycle the tinfoil. Save the stones for the next time. Fill the hole and replace the sods on top. One week later it will be as if nothing was ever there. We tried leaving the hole open and covering it with a wooden board but it just filled with rainwater. It is easier to dig it out on each occasion.

inishmurray island lobster

from Granny Waters

Mary Anne Mannion learned how to make this dish in New York, where she worked as a cook between 1890 and 1909 in one of the 'Big Houses', before returning to Innishmurray to take care of her mother.

Apparently she was an excellent cook and referred to this dish as a 'goulash', reflecting the ethnic mix in New York at the time. It has been handed down in the Waters family for over a century.

Mary Anne married Michael Waters who also returned from New York because his father who was the King of the island had died in 1908. They were reluctant to leave New York.

This recipe was contributed to the book by their grandson Michael Waters, Johnny's brother. Neither seaweed nor cheese was used in the recipe of the day but have been added here as a variation. With the exception of sleabhac, the people of Innishmurray used seaweed to feed cattle – especially calves to give them a shiny coat for the market.

Seaweed used: Bladderwrack
Serves 4

25g (1oz) flour
25g (1oz) butter
600ml (1 pint) milk
4 eggs
2 lobster
Salt and pepper to season
Cheese to taste
Nori to taste

1. Make a white sauce with milk, butter and flour. Hard boil eggs and quarter them.
2. Cook/steam the lobster, in bladderwrack for added flavour, and shell it.
3. Chop lobster into bite sized pieces, season with salt and pepper.
4. Mix the eggs, white sauce and lobster pieces gently together and serve.

Modern addition
Mix some cheese with flaked nori and put it on top. Place in the oven until the cheese melts.

AGA
1 2 3 4 5
KEEP TIGHTLY
CLOSED.

main courses

meat fish and poultry

turbot steamed over bladderwrack
with oysters, sea lettuce and samphire
from Richard Corrigan

Remarkably, Lindsay House, London, run by this award winning chef, has retained its Michelin star for ten successive years.

'I still like the anticipation, the waiting for foods in season. Respect for food, even the humblest carrot is important.'

Seaweed used: Bladderwrack, sea lettuce
Serves 3

turbot, scored across and left on the bone
*2 handfuls **bladderwrack** to steam turbot*
3 oysters
knob of butter
*1 handful **sea lettuce**, rinsed in cold water, steamed until just soft and chopped finely*
squeeze of lemon
chives, snipped
mashed potato
olive oil
1 bunch samphire, steamed and lightly salted with sea salt

1. Nestle the turbot into a bed of bladderwrack and steam, covered, for 15 minutes.
2. Open the oysters and strain the juice into a small pot with a knob of butter. Add the steamed sea lettuce, a squeeze of lemon and a few chives. Stir briefly over moderate heat to melt the butter, add the oysters and set aside.
3. Place the mashed potato on the bottom of a large, deep serving bowl and drizzle with olive oil. Arrange the samphire next.
4. Add a few of the bladderwrack tips used to steam the turbot, and place the turbot on top.
5. Carefully pour the sea lettuce sauce containing the 3 oysters over the turbot and serve.

Bentley's Oyster Bar and Grill.
www.bentleysdublin.com

Turbot, above. *Brill, opposite.*

black bream steamed over seaweed
with a fennel butter sauce

from Rick Stein

'Nothing is more exhilarating than fresh fish simply cooked.'
Rick Stein, Seafood Chef

Seaweed used: Bladderwrack
Serves 4

4 x 225g (8oz) black bream, cleaned and trimmed
750g (1½lb) fresh bladderwrack seaweed
salt and freshly ground black pepper

For the fennel butter sauce
200g (7oz) unsalted butter
½ fennel bulb, trimmed and thinly sliced
40g (1½oz) onion, thinly sliced
½ small garlic clove, chopped
150ml (5fl oz) fish or chicken stock
1 tablespoon white wine
2 tablespoons Pernod
2 teaspoons lemon juice
2 egg yolks
3 tablespoons chopped fennel herb

substitute hake if black bream is difficult to get

From Rick Stein's Seafood
Published by BBC Worldwide Ltd

1. Season the fish inside and out with a little salt and pepper. Wash the seaweed and spread it over the base of a sauté pan large enough to hold the fish in a single layer (if you don't have a pan large enough, use two). Add 300ml (10fl oz) of water, put the fish on top and cover with a tight-fitting lid. Set to one side.
2. For the fennel butter sauce, melt 25g (1oz) of the butter in a pan. Add the fennel, onion and garlic and fry for 5 minutes until soft but not browned. Add the stock, white wine and some salt and pepper and simmer for 15 minutes until the vegetables are very soft and most of the liquid has evaporated.
3. Spoon the mixture into a liquidizer and leave to cool slightly. Then add the Pernod, lemon juice and egg yolks. Melt the rest of the butter in a clean pan. As soon as it begins to bubble, turn on the machine and blend the contents for 1 minute. Then slowly pour in the hot melted butter to make a hollandaise-like mixture. Pour the sauce into a bowl and stir in chopped fennel herb and some seasoning to taste. Keep warm.
4. Place the pan of fish and seaweed over a high heat and, as soon as some steam starts to leak from underneath the lid, turn the heat down and steam for 5 minutes until the fish are cooked through. Without lifting the lid, take the pan of fish to the table, together with the fennel butter sauce. Remove the lid so your guests can appreciate the aroma and serve with some plain boiled potatoes.
5. Serve at once.

seafood paella

Alaria and sea spaghetti add the final layer of seafood flavour to this seafood dish. Great for a special occasion and even more idyllic if you can cook it outdoors...

Seaweed used: Sea spaghetti, Alaria
Serves 4

2 – 4 tablespoons olive oil
1 – 2 tablespoons butter
1 medium onion, chopped finely
4 – 6 cloves garlic, sliced finely
450g (1lb) long grain rice, white
4 – 5 teaspoons ***sea spaghetti****, dried and ground, (see bookmark)*
2 – 3 teaspoons turmeric, or 1 teaspoon crushed saffron
1 litre (1¾ pints) vegetable stock
125g (4¼ oz) garden peas
1 red pepper, diced

Selection of fish
2 medium squid, cut into strips
24 mussels, 6 per person, scrubbed and beards removed
12 tiger prawns, 3 per person, split with a knife to butterfly, or
24 clams, rinsed under running tap water or, a mix of shellfish and crab claws in season

To serve
parsley, chopped
1 teaspoon ***Alaria****, dried and ground*
2 organic lemons and / or limes, quartered

1 Heat half the olive oil and half the butter in a large frying/paella pan over moderate heat, add the onion and fry gently for about 2 minutes. Add the garlic and cook for a further 2 minutes. Remove with a slotted spoon and set aside.

2 Add the rice, sea spaghetti and turmeric, if using and mix well. If using saffron add with the stock.

3 Return the onion and garlic to the pan and add the vegetable stock. Reduce the heat and cook slowly for 10 – 15 minutes, adding the peas and red pepper towards the end of the cooking time.

4 When the rice is almost cooked, place the remaining butter and oil into a separate pan over moderate heat. When hot, add the squid and cook for 2 – 3 minutes. Remove with a slotted spoon and add to the rice dish.

5 Add the prepared mussels to the pan and cook until they open, then transfer to the rice dish.

6 Cook the split prawns or clams and add to the cooked rice dish. Mix gently.

Recipe collected in old Spain by Donegal medics Paul and Bella Stewart.

COOK'S TIP

Arrange the quartered lemons and sprinkle with parsley and Alaria. Serve from the paella pan in the centre of the table and leave extra Alaria and parsley in small dishes for sprinkling.

smoked haddock with chives and baby vegetables

from Hugo Arnold

'The idea is to use spices to season, to enhance, to build the dish. Too often we home cooks think only of salt. Seaweed can and does do a similar job. Go on, experiment.'

Hugo Arnold, journalist, cook and restaurant consultant

Seaweed used: Kombu/kelp
Serves 2

225g (8oz) smoked haddock
1 tablespoon Chinese chives, chopped finely (Regular chives can be substituted although they lack the garlic kick of Chinese chives)
a large pinch of black pepper
250g (9oz) ramen noodles
1 litre ($1^{3}/_{4}$ pints) miso soup, (see page 29) or use 3 tablespoons of white miso paste
55g (2oz) baby sweet corn
55g (2oz) courgettes
large handful of watercress
25g (1oz) ***kombu,*** *soaked in warm water for (5 minutes, drained and sliced finely*
12 pieces menma, drained, rinsed well and dried with kitchen paper – these are pickled bamboo shoots which can be bought canned. Use water chestnuts or seasonal vegetables if unavailable

1 Place the haddock, skin side down, into a saucepan, cover with water, put the lid on and bring to the boil.

2 Simmer for 5 minutes or until opaque all the way through. Remove the fish from the water.

3 Gently flake the fish, removing any bones and skin. Add the Chinese chives and black pepper and set aside.

4 Cook the noodles in a large pan of boiling water for 2 – 3 minutes until just tender. Drain thoroughly, refresh under cold water and divide between two bowls.

5 Heat the miso soup in a saucepan until boiling, then add the baby vegetables and courgettes and cook for three minutes, or until tender.

6 Ladle the soup and vegetables over the noodles and top with the watercress and haddock, kombu and menma.

mackerel coated in honey, seaweed and wholegrain mustard

Anyone who grew up or spent time by the sea will remember the great taste of grilled or pan–fried mackerel. Just one mouthful can transport people back to childhood, forgotten summer evenings spent fishing, or those two weeks in August in the cottage by the seaside...

This is my husband Johnny's speciality.

Seaweed used: Alaria
Serves 4

Coating – enough for 8 medium fillets:
2 tablespoons honey
*1 tablespoon **Alaria flakes***
1 tablespoon whole grain mustard, whiskey flavoured if possible
8 mackerel fillets, 2 medium sized per person

COOK'S TIP

A sweet acidic jam or sauce works really well with mackerel. Keep some gooseberries in the freezer or use a sharp cranberry sauce if you have frozen cranberries left over from Christmas.

Preheat grill setting at 150°C/300°F/Gas 2

1 Mix the honey, seaweed, and mustard in a small bowl and set aside.

2 Place the mackerel fillets skin side down on grill pan. Place under the grill for 2 – 3 minutes or until the flesh turns white. Remove the pan and turn fillets to skin side up. Cook until the skin bubbles and crisps up. This will take about 3 – 4 minutes.

3 Remove the pan from the grill, and turn fillets once more to skin side down. Using a teaspoon coat the flesh side with the mixture. Replace under the grill and cook for a further 2 minutes.

4 Serve at once, on its own or with a rocket salad and gooseberry sauce.

crisp oven baked quick fish

Devised by Johnny's sister Frances in an effort to get her son to eat fish, this crisps up beautifully and became a much requested dinner.

Seaweed used: Nori or mixed seaweeds
Serves 2

2 portions of any white fish, filleted: monkfish, haddock, cod, plaice, lemon sole
well–seasoned flour for dredging
55g (2oz) rice crispies, crushed roughly
1 – 2 tablespoons ***nori*** *or* ***mixed seaweed,*** *ground or flaked*
olive oil
1 egg, beaten

Variations

Omit the flour and roll fish in salted ground mixed seaweed, then into egg, then rice crispies with or without nori…really great.

Use a mix of half – seasoned flour and half – mixed seaweeds to dredge fish and proceed as above.

Set the oven to very hot 230°C/450°F/Gas 8. Brush a baking tray with olive oil and place in the centre of the oven to heat.

1 Wash and dry the fish then dredge in the flour and shake off excess.

2 Mix the rice crispies and seaweed together and spread out on a flat plate. Set aside. Roll the fish in beaten egg to coat evenly making sure all of the fish has some egg on it.

3 Roll the egg–dipped fish in the seaweed and rice crispie mix to coat evenly.

4 Place on the hot baking tray, replace the baking tray in the oven and bake for 15 – 20 minutes. The coating will turn golden when cooked.

5 Remove and serve at once. A green salad and a sweet chilli dipping sauce work well as an accompaniment.

COOK'S TIP

A chunky piece of fish will take a longer cooking time while a small fillet will cook faster.

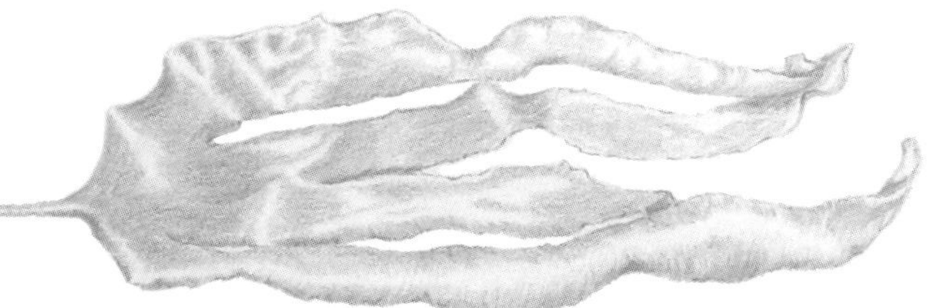

kelp wrapped grilled fish with egg sauce

The kelp adds a subtle flavour to the fish while protecting it from over cooking. White fish with egg and parsley white sauce is a dish my mother cooked particularly well, taking the best from the flavours of organic eggs, fresh fish, and our own milk and parsley. Also a favourite of Stefan Kraan's, Manager of the Irish Seaweed Centre.

Seaweed used: Kelp

Blades of kelp, ***fresh or dried, size depends on the size of the blades, use 1 small to medium blade per 1 fish fillet. A large blade can be split to do 2 fillets***

Choose a thick white fish, for example pollack, 1 portion per person

1. If using dried kelp, rehydrate by soaking in tepid water for 10 minutes or until supple enough to bend. Remove, and dry off excess water with kitchen towel.
2. Wrap the blade or blades around the fish and grill as you normally grill. Flavours of kelp will go into the fish.
3. Open the blades and serve with a squeeze of lemon and sweet chilli dipping sauce or a parsley and hard – boiled egg white sauce.

COOK'S TIP

If the blades of kelp are not burned you can eat a little of the kelp too or crumble a little of the toasted blades of kelp over the fish.

WHITE SAUCE

25g (1oz) flour
25g (1oz) butter
600ml (1 pint) milk
1 or 2 eggs, hard–boiled and cut into wedges
1 tablespoon parsley chopped finely
1 tablespoon mixed sea vegetables

1. Melt the butter over a moderate heat in a saucepan.
2. Stir in the flour and cook for 1 minute.
3. Add the milk gradually and whisk to eliminate lumps.
4. Cook, stirring continually until the sauce thickens. Add the remaining ingredients and stir to mix.
5. Serve with kelp wrapped fish and wedges of lemon.

25m/m

kedgeree

Kedgeree is a supper everyone wants to go home to after working up an appetite on the shore.
This version is warming and traditional and adapts extremely well to the addition of nori. Use organic eggs where possible.

Seaweed used: Nori
Serves 4 – 6

450g (1lb) smoked haddock, undyed if possible
150ml (1/4 pint) milk
2 eggs, hardboiled and cut into small wedges
225g (8oz) cooked brown short grain rice: approximately 150g (5oz) uncooked will yield this amount
1/4 teaspoon ground nutmeg
juice of 1 lemon
zest of 1/2 lemon
4 heaped teaspoons nori, flaked
pinch of sea salt
generous pinch cayenne pepper
50ml (2 fl oz) cream
15g (1/2 oz) butter
chopped parsley for garnish

To prepare nori see bookmark.
Preheat the oven 180°C/350°F/Gas 4.
Butter a deep ovenproof dish.

1 Place the haddock into a saucepan with the milk and poach gently for 5 – 7 minutes. Allow to cool slightly. Remove the fish from the saucepan and reserve the milk. Skin the fish and flake with a fork. Check for bones. Place the flaked fish and the eggs into the prepared dish.

2 Mix the rice, nutmeg, lemon juice and zest in a bowl and stir in the nori flakes. Add the salt and cayenne pepper and mix well.

3 Spoon the spiced rice mixture over the fish, spreading evenly.

4 Add the cream to the reserved milk to make 200ml (7fl oz) in total and pour over the dish. Dot with butter, cover the dish and bake in the centre of the oven for 30 minutes.

5 Garnish with chopped parsley.

SALMON VERSION

Use 225g (8 oz) salmon, cooked and flaked. Proceed as above but do not add lemon juice or nutmeg. Instead chop an onion and cook in a little oil until transparent. Mix salmon, rice, onion, egg, nori, salt and cayenne pepper. Sprinkle with parsley.

brown trout
with marsh samphire

from Darina Allen

'A fat brown trout is a rare treat nowadays, if it's not an option rainbow trout are available in virtually every fish shop. This combination is surprisingly delicious and very fast to cook.

If dill is difficult to find use a mixture of fresh herbs.'

Darina Allen, Ireland's best known food ambassador

Serves 4

225 – 275g (8 – 10oz) marsh samphire*
large knob of butter to coat samphire
4 fresh trout
salt and freshly ground pepper
25g (1oz) butter
175ml (6fl oz) single cream
1.5 – 2 tablespoons fresh dill, chopped finely

***Note on samphire**

Not a seaweed but a marsh plant that comes into season in the spring and can be cooked like asparagus.

The name is an alteration of the earlier sampiere from early French (herbe de) Saint Pierre or St Peter's herb.

1. Wash the marsh samphire well.
2. Bring a large saucepan of water to the boil, add the samphire, and return to the boil for 3 or 4 minutes, drain.
3. While the samphire is cooking, melt the large knob of butter. Add the melted butter to the drained samphire and keep warm.
4. Gut the trout, fillet carefully, wash and dry well. Season with salt and freshly ground pepper.
5. Melt the butter in a frying pan, fry the trout fillets flesh side down until golden brown. Turn over on to the skin side, add the cream and freshly chopped dill. Simmer gently for 3 or 4 minutes or until the trout is cooked. Taste the sauce to check the seasoning and serve immediately with marsh samphire.

VARIATION

Pan-grilled brown trout. Gut and fillet the fish as above. Season with salt and freshly ground pepper. Drizzle with extra virgin olive oil. Cook on a preheated grill pan for a few minutes on each side. Serve on a hot plate with a wedge of lemon, marsh samphire and parsley butter over the top.

fillet of brill with sea spaghetti and saffron risotto

Piero Melis was raised in Sardinia and has always had an interest in using seaweeds.

This Mediterranean touch is what makes his restaurant, 'The Courthouse Tavern' tucked away in Kinlough, Co. Leitrim, a great dining choice and earned the establishment an entry in the Bridgestone Guide.

Piero's recipe blends seaweeds with saffron which reminds him of his sunny childhood in the Mediterranean.

Seaweed used: Sea spaghetti, mixed seaweeds
Serves 4

55g (2oz) ***sea spaghetti***
100ml (3½ fl oz) extra virgin olive oil
1 shallot, chopped finely
20g (¾ oz) ***mixed seaweeds*** *chopped finely*
250g (9oz) Arborio rice
600ml (1 pint) of fish stock
1 small sachet/about 5g saffron
25g (1oz) of salted butter
½ bunch of flat leaved parsley
4 large fillets of brill, seasoned with salt and pepper
1 clove of garlic, chopped finely
1 small dry chilli

Dressing
1 tablespoon olive oil
1 teaspoon lemon juice

COOK'S TIP

Dried sea spaghetti swells up to approximately 10 times in volume when rehydrated.

To Prepare the sea spaghetti

Soak in cold water for about 2 hours.
Remove from water, drain, and dry with kitchen paper.

1. In a saucepan over medium heat, shallow fry the shallot in half the olive oil for 1 minute, then add the mixed seaweed and fry for a further minute.
2. Add the rice and cook slowly adding the fish stock ladleful by ladleful, stirring all the time. Repeat until all the stock has been added to the rice, a process that takes roughly 20 minutes, stirring with each ladleful. Add the saffron towards the end of cooking.
3. Add the butter and parsley, stirring all the time until the risotto develops a nice creamy texture.
4. In a separate pan fry the brill for 1 minute on each side.
5. in a third pan heat the rest of the olive oil and gently fry the garlic and chilli. Add the drained sea spaghetti and fry for about 3 minutes.
6. To serve, use the spaghetti seaweed as a bed for the brill and serve the risotto on the other side of the plate. Drizzle oil and lemon dressing over the fish and serve immediately.

For the Oil and Lemon Dressing:

Blend olive oil and lemon juice.

mediterranean baked fish

This dish subscribes to the theory that fine simple ingredients, cleverly put together, produce great meals. Winner of a national healthy recipe competition in 1999, this recipe comes from the kitchen of Catherine Gallagher, and was also published in *Healthy Food Magazine* in 2000. Once tasted, it comes as no surprise that Catherine has more than once been awarded 'Best Cook' at the leading Irish Agricultural Show held in Tullamore.

Seaweed used: Mixed seaweeds
Serves: 3 – 4

340g (12oz) firm white fish such as cod or monkfish, skinned
salt and red pepper
1 lemon, juiced
2 teaspoons olive oil
1 medium onion, chopped
1 clove garlic, chopped
1 small courgette, chopped
1 green pepper, sliced
55g (2oz) mushrooms, sliced
2 heaped tablespoons, **mixed dried seaweeds**
1 tablespoon parsley, chopped
1 tablespoon dried mixed herbs or 2 tablespoons fresh mixed herbs to include rosemary, marjoram and fennel
3 medium tomatoes, chopped
1 lemon, quartered for garnish
extra parsley for garnish

Preheat the oven to 160°C/325°F/Gas 3.

1. Rinse the fish under cold water and pat dry, then season with salt, red pepper and lemon juice. Set aside.
2. Heat the olive oil in a pan and cook the onions over moderate heat for 1 minute until softened a little. Add the garlic, courgette, pepper, mushrooms and seaweed and cook for 1 minute.
3. Stir in the parsley and mixed herbs and place the vegetables into a casserole dish. Arrange the tomatoes on top of the vegetables.
4. Place the fish on top of the tomatoes and cover with a lid. Bake in the oven for 25 – 30 minutes.
5. Serve hot, garnished with lemon and chopped parsley. Baked potatoes or basmati rice and a small salad complement the Mediterranean theme perfectly.

COOK'S TIP

If using a heavy casserole dish add on extra time for cooking.

Catherine Gallagher is a houseparent with the Learning Disability Services.

pan–fried salmon
with ginger, nori and hoisin glaze

from Domini Kemp

This dish is so delicious served on top of Domini's 'Champ with Mixed Seaweeds' (see page 82) that it just had to be included.

Seaweed used: Nori
Serves 4

1 tablespoon olive oil
4 salmon fillets, about 175g (5 – 6 oz) each, skin removed
2 tablespoons hoisin sauce
*2 teaspoons **ground nori**, mixed to a paste with a little lime juice or water. 1 sheet of **nori** equals 2 teaspoons (see bookmark)*
knob of ginger, peeled and sliced finely
knob of butter and freshly ground red pepper
salt

1. Heat the olive oil in a large frying pan until moderately hot.
2. Gently place the salmon in the pan and fry for about 4 minutes before turning to cook on the other side. If the salmon sticks to the pan, lower the heat and fry for an extra minute or so. The salmon will release itself from the pan when it has started to cook.
3. Meanwhile stir the hoisin into the nori paste. Using a fish slice, turn the salmon over and add the nori/hoisin paste, ginger, butter, salt and pepper to the pan. Cook for 30 seconds to cook the ginger then baste the salmon and lower the heat.
4. Cook another 3 to 4 minutes at reduced heat until done. The salmon will flake easily when cooked.
5. Remove from the heat and serve on top of the champ.

fish pie

The ingredients for this pie resemble every mother's wish list: fresh fish, carrots, spinach, cheese, eggs... served up in a creamy sauce with crispy pastry or mashed potatoes.
Created by parents Donal and Anna who say there's just never any left over!

Seaweed used: Duileasc
Serves 4

1½ tablespoons olive oil
1 onion, chopped finely
1 celery stick, chopped finely
2 carrots, chopped finely
spinach – two fresh handfuls
300ml (½ pint) milk
125ml (5fl oz) of cream
115g (4oz) cheddar cheese
1 tablespoon Dijon mustard
Juice of ½ lemon
15g (½oz) duileasc, rinsed and snipped
few twists of red pepper
500g (1lb 2oz) smoked fish, haddock
500g (1lb 2oz) cod
3 eggs, hard–boiled
1 sheet ready–rolled puff pastry
egg to glaze

Preheat oven to 200°C/400°F/Gas 6 and grease a large casserole dish.

1 In a large pan or pot, heat the oil over moderate heat, add the onions and fry gently until softened. Add the celery and carrots and cook for about 4 minutes.

2 Add the spinach and cook until tender.

3 Stir in the milk and cream and bring to the boil, then add the cheese, mustard and lemon juice, duileasc and pepper, stirring gently to mix.

4 Cut the fish into chunks and place in a casserole dish.

5 Cut the eggs into quarters or slices and place on top of the fish. Pour the vegetable mixture on top.

6 The pastry can be placed on top of the dish or cut into shapes and placed on top of the mixture. Brush the pastry with egg and bake in the oven for 20 – 30 minutes or until the pastry has risen and the fish is cooked.

COOK'S TIP

Mashed potato can be used instead of pastry.

Recipe from Donal Conaty and Anna Galligan, who opted to move their family to the north west some years ago, and now live right on the coast in County Sligo.

prawns with land and sea spaghetti

from Eithna O Sullivan

Sea spaghetti comes into season around St Patrick's day and turns green when cooked – a fun dish to celebrate the national holiday.

Seaweed used: Sea vegetables, sea spaghetti
Serves 4

*20 – 30g dry weight **sea spaghetti** or approximately 250g if using fresh*
250g (9oz) organic spaghetti
1 – 2 tablespoons grape seed oil
2 shallots or 1 small onion, peeled and chopped finely
2 cloves garlic, peeled and chopped finely
1 red chilli, deseeded and chopped
500g (1lb 2oz) jumbo peeled cooked prawns de-shelled, fully thawed if from frozen and very well dried
1 teaspoon Thai 7 spice for stir-fry
25g (1oz) flat leaf parsley, chopped
25g (1oz) coriander, leaves and stems, chopped
a dash oyster sauce
sea salt
*1 handful mixed **sea vegetables,** soaked in hot water to barely cover for 2 – 3 minutes*
extra coriander and parsley to garnish

Eithna O Sullivan,
Chef and cookery instructor

1. Cook the sea spaghetti in a pot with plenty seasoned water for 15 minutes or until al dente.
2. Cook the spaghetti in a separate pot of seasoned water for 10 – 12 minutes or until al dente.
3. Heat the oil in frying pan over moderate heat, and sweat off onions and garlic. Add chilli and cook for 1 minute. Add the prawns, seasoning, herbs, oyster sauce and salt to taste. Stir until the ingredients are heated through and well mixed, about 2 – 3 minutes.
4. Drain the spaghetti and sea spaghetti and place in a warmed serving dish.
5. Add the contents of the frying pan, spices, seasoning, mixed sea vegetables and their hot soaking water. Stir gently to mix, check seasoning and serve on warm plates sprinkled with chopped coriander and parsley.

VARIATION

Try Kate's favourite which is a spaghetti bolognaise recipe of your choice and a mix of spaghetti and sea spaghetti as above.

COOK'S TIP

600g (1lb 5½ oz) of prawns serves 5 adults and small garden peas can be added as an extra vegetable portion. Cut down/omit chilli if cooking for children.

pollack with chilli sauce

The ultimate fast food fish supper, mouth–watering and on the table in minutes.

Seaweed used: Duileasc
Serves 1

3 tablespoons olive oil
1 onion, chopped roughly
10 – 15g (1 heaped tablespoon) ***duileasc,*** *chopped*
1 medium sized or half a large fillet of pollack or other firm whitefish, skinned, rinsed, patted dry and well seasoned with salt
1 heaped tablespoon sweet chilli sauce

COOK'S TIP

Don't over cook the onion – leave some bite in it.

1 Heat one tablespoon of the oil in a heavy pan over moderate heat. Add the onion and cook for about one minute.

2 Add the duileasc and cook for a further minute and a half. Remove and keep hot.

3 Add the rest of the oil and when hot place the fish in the pan. Cook for 2$^1/_2$ minutes and turn over. Place the chilli sauce on top of the fillet.

4 Cook for approximately 4 minutes or until done. Remove from the pan and cut into bite sized pieces.

5 Serve with onions and duileasc. Add some extra chilli sauce if desired.

Goes well with chipped sweet potato and garden peas.

steamed pot of mussels

Created in response to a request for steamed mussels without the standard garlic sauce, this duileasc cream sauce has become an established favourite. Although this recipe has the finesse of a restaurant standard, it is not difficult to recreate in your own kitchen.

Seaweed used: Duileasc Serves 1

700g (1$^1/_2$ lb) mussels, washed, scrubbed, beards removed
$^1/_2$ shallot chopped finely
50ml (2fl oz) white wine
50ml (2fl oz) fish stock
25ml (1fl oz) double cream
1 tablespoon ***duileasc,*** *chopped finely*
1 tablespoon parsley, chopped finely

1 Heat a large pan at high temperature. Add mussels, shallot and white wine. Cook for 3 – 5 minutes or until all the mussels have opened. Discard any unopened mussels.

2 Strain for any pieces of shell and return the liquid to the pan. Add the fish stock and stir to heat.

3 Add the cream, seaweed and parsley. Cook for an additional 2 – 3 minutes.

4 Serve with warm crusty bread.

from Shaun Paul Brady,
Irish chef working in Chicago

pollack with chilli sauce

green rice prawn stir-fry

This is one of those meals where everyone asks for the recipe. It is substantial and tasty with a great texture, and is literally prepared in minutes once the rice is cooked.

It is really important to dry the prawns thoroughly before adding to the dish, if not, the salty water can interfere with the taste of the finished product.

One of the great one pot meals!

Seaweed used: Alaria
Serves 3 – 4

*1 teaspoon ground **Alaria***
*1 teaspoon ground **mixed seaweeds** (see bookmark)*
250g (9oz) uncooked rice, brown or white
1 tablespoon olive oil
350g (12½ oz) cooked or thawed spinach
150g (5 oz) cooked prawns, well drained and dried in kitchen paper
2 teaspoons fish sauce
2 tablespoons tamari
pinch of sea salt
1 teaspoon soya sauce
2 tablespoons cream (optional)

1. Cook or steam the rice as normal. Set aside.
2. Heat the oil in a large frying pan over moderate heat, add the rice and cooked spinach and mix to combine.
3. Stir in the prawns, then add the rest of the ingredients except the cream. Cook for 2 to 3 minutes, mixing well.
4. Reduce the heat, and warm the ingredients thoroughly for about 4 to 5 minutes. This will take longer if using frozen spinach or cold rice from the fridge.
5. Remove from the heat, stir in the cream, if using, and return to the heat for 1 minute.

Serve on warmed plates.

Adapted from a recipe by Joe McHugh, uillean piper.

COOK'S TIP

It is important to retain the moisture and heavy texture of the dish. Adding the cream at the end generally restores the moisture balance, but if you don't want to use cream, add a little olive oil or water. The cream gives a little taste of luxury, and is great for special occasions.

oyster and guinness beef pie with sea spaghetti

from Máirín Uí Chomáin

Máirín is a broadcastor and native Irish speaker who is a leading expert on Irish food and author of *Irish Oyster Cuisine*.

Including sea spaghetti in this recipe raises this surf and turf combination from satisfying to supreme. 'Great depth and delectable combination of flavours,' was the verdict from the test kitchen.

Seaweed used: Sea spaghetti
Serves 4 – 6

2 tablespoons plain flour
sea salt
twist of freshly ground black pepper
700g (1½ lb) rib beef, cubed
2 tablespoons sunflower oil
1 – 2 onions, chopped finely
225g (8oz) mushrooms, chopped
425ml (15fl oz) Guinness
1 tablespoon Worcestershire sauce
***10 – 15g (¼ – ½oz) sea spaghetti,** rinsed in cold water and soaked for 5 minutes*

12 oysters, shells removed, juices strained and reserved

200g (7oz) ready made puff pastry

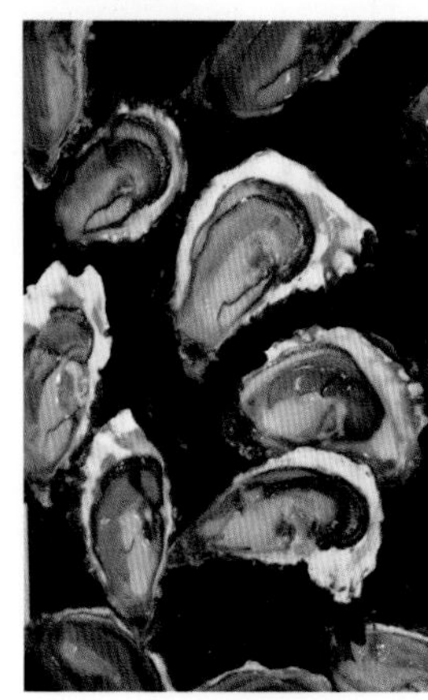

1. Season the flour with salt and pepper and toss the beef in it.
2. Heat the oil in a large, heavy frying pan. Once hot, add the beef to the pan a little at a time and seal. Be careful not to overcrowd the pan as this will only create a stewing process. Remove the beef from the pan.
3. In the same pan fry the onions and mushrooms until soft and then return the meat to the pan. Add the Guinness, Worcestershire sauce, sea spaghetti and oyster juices and season with salt and pepper. Mix well, cover and simmer until the meat is tender, about 1½ hours. Remove from the heat and allow to cool completely. Add the oysters.
4. Preheat the oven to 200°C/400°F/Gas 6 and grease a deep pie dish.
5. Pour the mixture into the pie dish. Cover with the pastry, leaving a slight overhang around the edge of the dish. Crimp the edges firmly and cut an air vent in the centre of the pastry.
6. Bake in the centre of the oven for 15 minutes. Reduce the heat to 180°C/350°F/Gas 4 and bake for a further 30 minutes until the meat is heated through.
7. Serve hot with a green salad or baked potatoes.

Reflets de France
MOUTARDE A L'ANCIENNE
AUX GRAINES ET AU VIN BLANC AOC DE
Bourgogne

barbecued chicken and braised rice

An unusual recipe in that the marinade cooks with the chicken, resurfacing as a flavoursome sauce, so there is no waste.

Seaweeds used: Sea spaghetti, Alaria
Serves 6

One large free range chicken, portioned

Marinade

300ml (1/2 pint) hot stock, vegetable and seaweed or chicken
5 tablespoons tomato ketchup
3 tablespoons cider vinegar or lemon juice
3 tablespoons honey or brown sugar
1 tablespoon soya sauce or tamari
3 teaspoons* sea spaghetti, *ground roughly

To prepare the marinade

Mix all the marinade ingredients in a large jug.

1 Place the chicken in an ovenproof dish and cover with the hot marinade. When cool place in the fridge for 1 – 3 hours or longer.

2 Preheat the oven to 190°C/375°F/Gas 5. Remove from the fridge and cover dish with foil. Allow the dish to warm slightly – don't put it straight from the fridge to the oven. Cook for 1 1/4 hours.

3 Remove from the oven and take off the foil cover. Pour the bulk of the marinade into a saucepan and put the uncovered chicken back into the oven to brown and crisp, about 30 minutes.

3 Meanwhile bring the marinade to a rolling boil over moderate heat and boil uncovered until it reduces and thickens to a sauce. Tilt the saucepan and carefully pour away the excess fat floating on top of the marinade.

4 Serve with or over the chicken.

Braised Rice

1 tablespoon olive oil
$^1/_2$ medium onion
370g (13oz) long grain brown rice
1 heaped teaspoon ground Alaria
5 – 6 green cardamom pods, seeds removed and ground finely
800ml (27fl oz) water or seaweed stock
2 tablespoons raisins
flaked almonds, toasted (optional)

1 Heat the oil in a saucepan until moderately hot

2 Add the onion and fry gently until soft, then add the rice and fry for 2 – 3 minutes mixing in the Alaria and cardamom after about 2$^1/_2$ minutes.

3 Add the water/stock and raisins to the saucepan and bring to the boil. Cover and simmer gently for about 15 minutes or until all the water is absorbed.

4 Fluff gently with a fork and serve with a sprinkle of toasted almonds on top.

COOK'S TIP

Cardamom is best stored in pod form because once the seeds are exposed or ground they quickly lose their flavour. About 10 whole pods equals 1$^1/_2$ teaspoons of ground cardamom.

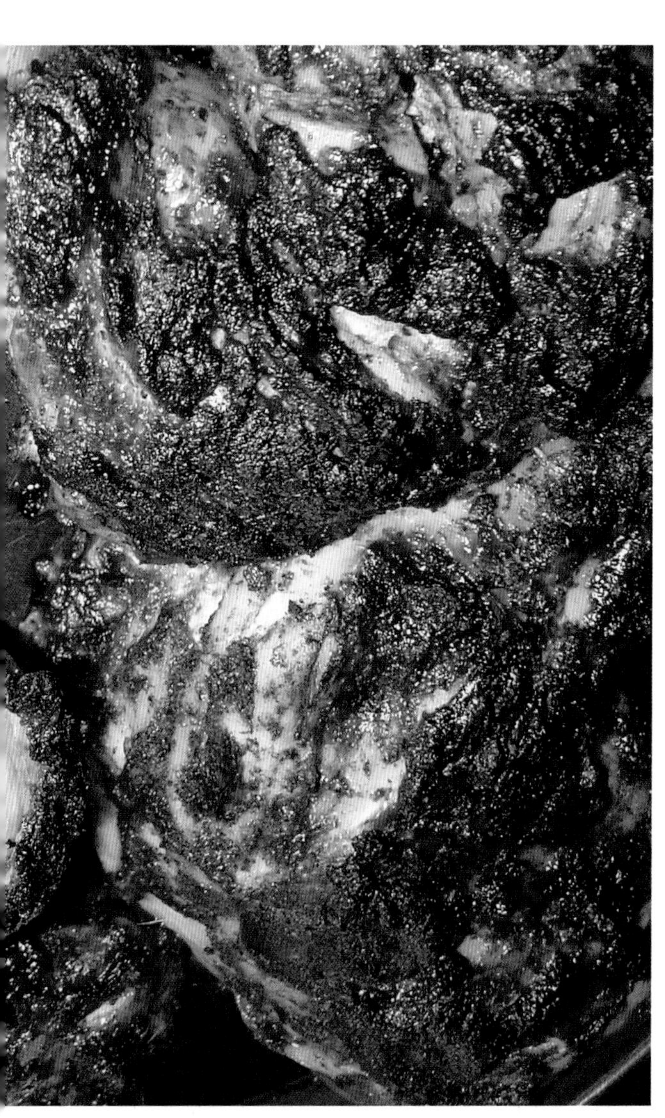

Top of the list of favourite dinners from my neighbours, Anne and Philip Waters, as voted by their five children.

malaysian honey chicken with an irish twist

A Malaysian friend came up with this one years ago. After the initial garlic shock, yes, it's three to four bulbs, the recipe quickly became integrated into our culinary repertoire, where it has remained, unchallenged, as King of the Garlic dishes.

Great with basmati fried rice (see recipe on page 163).

Seaweed used: Alaria
Serves 4

Marinade sauce

3 – 4 tablespoons sesame seed oil
2 – 3 onions, thinly sliced and chopped
3 – 4 bulbs not cloves garlic, minced finely
two thirds of a jar of runny honey
3 – 4 tablespoons dark soy sauce
*3 – 4 tablespoons ground **Alaria** mixed with 3 tablespoons cold water*
1 free range chicken, cubed, bones and skin discarded or 4 large portions of chicken, cubed

To prepare ground Alaria see bookmark

To prepare the marinade and chicken

1. Heat the sesame oil in a frying pan over a low – moderate heat. Gently fry the onions until softened.
2. Add the garlic and gently fry in oil until fragrant. Remove from the heat and cool slightly.
3. Add the honey, soy and seaweed paste to the onions and garlic and stir to combine. Allow to cool.
4. Place the cubed chicken in an ovenproof dish or roasting tin and pour over marinade. Marinate for a minimum of 1/2 hour or overnight if possible.
5. Preheat the oven 190°C/375°F/Gas 5.Cover the chicken dish with tinfoil and bake 45 minutes.
6. Remove the foil and bake until crispy.

Serve with salad, and basmati or fried rice.

fruity rice with lamb

Packed with fruity flavours and fresh herbs, the dish can be prepared without the lamb as a rice accompaniment and served hot or cold. It refrigerates well and far from reappearing as a leftover, it benefits from fridge time, and emerges as a succulent and flavour-infused rice salad. Stir in 2 teaspoons of sunflower oil to refresh.

Seaweed used: Nori Serves 4

300g (10oz) lamb chump steaks, organic for best flavour, cubed
2 rounded teaspoons ***nori,*** *flaked*
700ml (23½ fl oz) light vegetable stock
3 tablespoons olive oil
1 spring onion, chopped
2 teaspoons of freshly grated ginger
2 cloves garlic, chopped finely
250g (9oz) wild rice mix
½ teaspoon ground coriander
6 dried apricots, chopped, unsulphured
25g (1oz) sultanas
25g (1oz) chopped dates
1 papaya, peeled and cut into bite sized pieces
40g (1½ oz) toasted almonds, flaked
1 tablespoon fresh parsley
handful of fresh coriander, chopped

Marinade
1 tablespoon soy sauce
2 tablespoons olive oil
1 heaped teaspoon ***nori flakes***
1 tablespoon red wine (optional)
1 teaspoon wholegrain mustard
1¼ teaspoons runny honey
2 tablespoons olive or sunflower oil for cooking

To prepare the marinade

1. Combine the ingredients together in a large bowl and stir well.
2. Coat lamb with the marinade, cover and place in the fridge for an hour minimum, preferably longer.

To prepare the rice

1. Add the nori to the vegetable stock and stir well. Heat the oil in a large heavy bottomed saucepan. When bubbles appear in the oil, add the spring onion and fry for 30 seconds.
2. Add the ginger and garlic and stir on moderate heat for 2 minutes. Add the rice, ground coriander and stock to the pan, making sure all the nori flakes from the bottom of the stock jug are added, and stir.
3. Add the dried fruit, stir, cover the saucepan and cook on moderate heat for 30 minutes or until the liquid has evaporated and the rice is cooked.
4. While the rice is cooking prepare the meat. In a frying pan heat the oil until just bubbling, remove the pan from heat, and add the meat. Do this in two batches, as frying too much meat will give a stewing effect, and the lamb is better slightly crisped. Seal, fry until browned, remove with a slotted spoon and set aside.
5. When the rice is cooked, remove from the heat and add the cooked meat, papaya, toasted almonds, parsley and coriander. Stir gently to combine and serve.

COOK'S TIP

If preparing the rice dish as a cold salad, allow it to cool, then fridge immediately. Rice should not be refrigerated more than once. Add the fresh herbs and papaya just before serving or cook the rice without the lamb and serve with marinated grilled lamb chops.

beef in guinness with sea herbs

A quick and easy to prepare casserole which is good enough to serve when entertaining. Use shin or chuck steak for real economy, and organic meat where possible, and savour the great combination of Guinness and seaweed.

Seaweed used: mixed sea vegetables or duileasc, sea lettuce and nori
Serves 4 – 6

25g (1oz) plain flour
sea salt and pepper
1kg (2lb 3½oz) stewing steak, cubed
2 tablespoons ***mixed sea vegetables***
2 cloves garlic, crushed
1 can Guinness
4 onions, chopped
6 carrots, diced
1 small turnip, diced
water

Recipe from fashion cosultant, Stella McGroarty.

1. Season the flour with a little salt and pepper, toss the meat in it and place in a casserole dish with the mixed sea vegetables and crushed garlic.
2. Pour in the Guinness, cover and leave in the fridge for 2 hours. This tenderises the beef and allows the flavours to infuse.
3. Preheat the oven to 160°C/325°F/Gas 3.Remove from the fridge, add the vegetables and enough water to almost cover the ingredients. Cover the casserole and cook in oven 2½ hours or until the meat is tender. Check after 1½ hours as some cuts vary in cooking time.
4. Serve with boiled new potatoes, brown rice or crusty bread.

COOK'S TIP

The flour is used to thicken the stew. Use rice flour if preferred.

beef stew

'I love this recipe as it is simple and easy, and reminds me of my mother. It is great on a nippy fall evening, when the days are becoming shorter. I often cook it when my sisters and I get together, and we enjoy the stew with the rest of the red wine from the recipe!'
– Martha

Seaweed used: kelp, mixed seaweed
Serves 4

3 tablespoons olive oil
1kg (2lb 3½oz) stewing beef, cut into 2.5cm (1inch) cubes, excess fat removed
1 teaspoon ground cumin
1 teaspoon chilli powder
1 teaspoon sea salt
½ tablespoon ground kelp
2 tablespoons chopped ***mixed seaweeds***
80ml (3fl oz) full bodied red wine, (not cooking wine)
500 – 600ml (about 1 pint) chicken or vegetable stock
1 medium onion, chopped coarsely
2 cloves garlic, chopped coarsely
4 carrots, peeled and sliced on diagonal
500g (1lb 2oz) green beans

1. Heat the oil in a large pot over moderate heat and brown the beef in two batches. After the second batch is done, return the first batch to the pot and add the spices and seaweeds. Cook for 5 minutes.
2. Add the wine and stir well. Add 500ml stock initially, onions and garlic, cover the pot and simmer for 1 hour, checking occasionally to see if more stock is needed.
3. Add the carrots, cover and simmer for 30 minutes. Check for tenderness. Add the green beans and cook for another 10 – 15 minutes.

Serve with brown rice or by itself.

COOK'S TIP

2 sliced Portobello mushrooms can be added with the carrots for extra texture.

Martha Mosko D'Adamo, President and CEO of North American Pharmacal.

beef curry with egg fried rice

This delicious curry is low on preparation time and cooks itself. Ideal for a working at home day; you work, it cooks, and you can meet up over a glass of wine in the evening.

Seaweed used: Sea spaghetti
Serves 4 – 6

1 – 2 tablespoons olive oil
500g (1lb 2oz) organic beef, cubed
2 large onions or 6 shallots totalling a weight of 200g, chopped finely
4 – 6 cloves garlic, chopped finely
1 heaped tablespoon Patas madras medium curry paste
1 tin organic plum tomatoes, chopped, or equivalent in frozen tomatoes, thawed and chopped
1 tablespoon tomato puree
*15g (1/2oz) dry **sea spaghetti**, broken into 2.5cm (1 inch) pieces or 75g (2 1/2oz) fresh*

1 Heat the oil in a heavy based saucepan over medium heat and brown the meat. Add the onion and garlic and cook for a further 2 minutes.

2 Add the curry paste and stir well for half a minute, then cook for a further minute. Add the tomatoes, puree and sea spaghetti and bring to the boil uncovered, stirring occasionally.

3 Cover and simmer for 2 – 3 hours or until the meat is meltingly tender.

Serve with Basmati rice, or egg fried rice see recipe opposite.

COOK'S TIP

If you have an Aga, transfer to a casserole dish at step 3 and put in the bottom oven overnight.

egg fried basmati rice

Serves 4

4 tablespoons olive oil
4 eggs
675g (1$^{1}/_{2}$ lb) of cooked basmati rice, hot or cold

COOK'S TIP

Patas curry paste was recommended to us many years ago by a Malaysian foodie friend, Rabin, who said it was almost as good as his own homemade curry paste, or even as good as his Granny's finest award winning curry pastes but we had to promise never to tell her that...

The rice is fried in 2 batches in the pan.

1. Heat 2 tablespoons of oil over moderate heat in a heavy based frying pan. When hot, crack in 2 eggs and stir the eggs through the oil, breaking them up with a spatula.
2. When the egg mixture is on the point of setting add in half of the rice and stir to mix the egg through the rice. Cook until the rice is heated through – about 2 minutes.
3. Remove, keep warm and repeat with the other half of the rice.

Serve with vegetables on the side. Carrots and green beans work well.

venison
with figs port, chocolate and sea spaghetti

The tastes and colours of the winter kitchen combine wonderfully in this warming mix of figs, ruby red port, dark chocolate, sea spaghetti and venison. A handful of frozen elderberries can be added to the pot instead of half the dried fruit, and makes a delicious variation. I always have them in the freezer to ward off winter colds... use them if you can.

This is Johnny's winter speciality.

Seaweed used: Sea spaghetti Serves 4 - 6

1 – 2 tablespoons olive oil,
675g (1½ lb) venison, cubed
3 onions, chopped roughly
½ head garlic, chopped finely
1 tablespoon Patas medium curry paste
1 tin tomatoes or cherry tomatoes
Porcini mushrooms – full fist
2 sprigs of thyme
1 bay leaf
3 – 4 dried prunes, chopped
2 – 3 dried figs, chopped
2 carrots, diced (optional)
15g (½ oz) sea spaghetti, roughly broken up
100ml (3½ fl oz) port
15g (1 full square) of cocoa 70% cooking chocolate

1 Heat 1 tablespoon of olive oil in a saucepan over high heat and seal and brown the meat in batches. Set aside.

2 Add the remaining olive oil to the saucepan and gently cook the onions and garlic over moderate heat for 2 minutes.

3 Add the curry paste and stir well to cook and burst the flavours. Return the meat to the saucepan and stir to coat with onion and spices.

4 Add the tomatoes, porcini mushrooms, thyme and bay leaf. Stir in the prunes, figs and carrots if using. Bring to the boil, add the sea spaghetti, cover and set aside to simmer for 1 – 1½ hours.

5 Add the port and chocolate towards the end of cooking and mix gently.

Serve with mashed root vegetables.

moroccan tagine of lamb, apricot and nori

with
- herby lemony quinoa
- organic salad leaves with dressing
- cumin and chilli roasted sweet potatoes with duileasc

This has everything you need for a nourishing and warming menu; seaweed, organic salad and side dishes included.

Created by Siobhán Morris, organic and speciality food consultant, the main dish has Moroccan overtones, but has evolved over time into this sumptuous concoction which literally slow cooks itself.

Choose the freshest and most varied selection of organic leaves you can, including edible flowers.

Quinoa has a high protein content, thus supplementing the red meat protein amounts, and also contains calcium. Without the sweet potatoes this will feed 5 – 6 people. Steamed broccoli with garlic and ginger also make a good side dish with the tagine.

For the first hour or so of cooking, the tagine looks disturbingly unpromising – grey and watery. But then something magical happens as the apricots break down and the sauce thickens to a rich, glossy, gloopy consistency.

Seaweeds used: Alaria, duileasc, nori
Whole Menu serves 9 adults easily

Test kitchen comment:
Great for a large family gathering

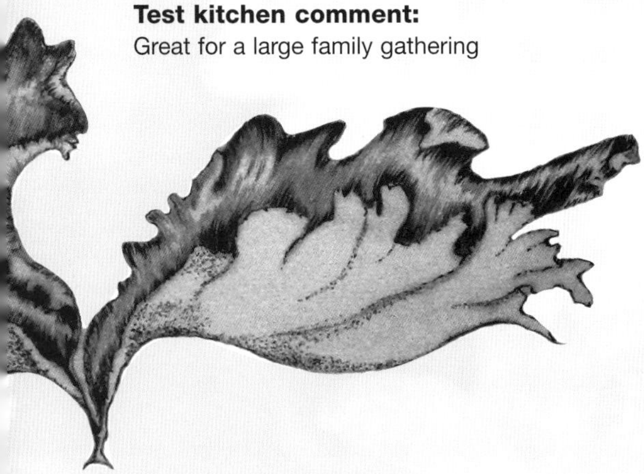

A NOTE ON QUINOA

- Pronounced *keen – wah* it is one of the oldest grains on the planet and was at one time the primary grain of the Incas.
- It has 17% protein and is also very high in calcium. It has a bitter protective coating that needs to be well washed off by rinsing and rubbing with the fingers for a minute under cold running water. It is also a very small grain so use a fine meshed sieve to prevent grains from escaping.
- Once cooked, little halos become visible in the grains which is a fascination for children. Use in place of rice for a welcome change or better still use half brown basmati rice and half quinoa for a lovely mix of grains.

COOK'S TIP

Chilli flakes in the sweet potatoes may be too hot for children.

ingredients

TAGINE

olive oil for frying
2 – 3 onions, sliced quite roughly
2 teaspoons ground cinnamon
2 teaspoons ground cumin
good pinch of saffron
good pinch of chilli flakes, or powder
2 – 3 garlic cloves, chopped roughly
2 – 3cm fresh root ginger, diced or a teaspoon of dried ground ginger
1.5kg (3 1/2 lb) of cubed lamb for casseroling / slow cooking
1 litre (under 2 pints) hot water
1 teaspoon organic vegetable stock powder such as Marigold
sea salt and cracked/freshly ground red pepper
500g (1lb 2oz) dried unsulphured whole apricots
1 sheet of nori, crumbled finely

method

To prepare the tagine

1 Heat a little olive oil in a large frying pan and fry the onions over moderate heat for a few minutes to soften. Sprinkle the dried spices over the onions and stir. Add the garlic and fresh ginger and stir over the heat for about 30 seconds.

2 Add the lamb. You may need to do this in 2 – 3 batches. Cook the lamb for a few minutes to coat in onion/spice mixture. Transfer the batches to heavy based saucepan or casserole dish while you fry the rest. Transfer all the contents of the frying pan, lamb and onions, to a large saucepan or casserole dish.

3 Add a litre/a little less than 2 pints of hot water, or enough to just cover the lamb, and stir in the vegetable stock, a good pinch of salt and a few twists of red pepper. Put the lid on and bring to a steady rolling boil. Once the pot begins to bubble, turn the heat to low and simmer for at least an hour. If time allows, turn lower and simmer longer, an hour and thirty minutes is ideal.

4 Occasionally check to make sure there is plenty of liquid and give a gentle poke with a spoon so that nothing is sticking. Prepare the sweet potatoes if using as a side dish.

5 Stir in the apricots about half an hour before the dish is cooked.

6 About 15 minutes after adding the apricots, stir in the nori, and start preparing the quinoa.

Longer cooking time will improve this dish especially if meat is casserole quality.

HERBY LEMONY QUINOA

400g (14oz) organic quinoa
Cold water
1 teaspoon ***ground Alaria***
2 teaspoons organic vegetable stock powder such as Marigold
pinch of saffron or 1/2 teaspoon turmeric
a couple of handfuls of whatever fresh herbs are available
juice of half an organic lemon

ORGANIC SALAD LEAVES

Mixed salad leaves to serve 6 – 9

CUMIN AND CHILLI ROASTED SWEET POTATOES WITH DUILEASC

4 – 6 sweet potatoes, peeled and chopped into large chunks
2 – 3 tablespoons olive oil
pinch of chilli flakes
1 teaspoon of cumin seeds.
1 teaspoon ***duileasc,*** *flaked*

ORGANIC SALAD DRESSING

3 – 4 tablespoons of extra virgin olive oil
juice of an organic lemon
2 teaspoons of honey
a large pinch of cumin seeds

To prepare the herby lemony quinoa

1. Rinse the quinoa very well under cold water. Place in a saucepan and add exactly twice the volume of cold water.
2. Bring to the boil, add the Alaria, and then simmer for 15 minutes or until the little 'c' in the grains is visible. If you have measured your water properly there will be no problem, but if you find it is turning to mush, drain a little of the water away. If it starts to crackle and stick, top up with some extra water.
3. If you want to turn the quinoa a vivid, warm yellow, add about 1 teaspoon of vegetable stock, half way through the cooking when the water is hot, along with a pinch of saffron or some turmeric.
4. Finely chop all the herbs together. Use anything seasonal – parsley, sage, thyme, coriander, dill, chervil, basil. Rosemary is not a good choice as it is too strong. Alternatively, just parsley can be used.
5. Just before serving stir the lemon juice and the herbs through the quinoa. It will be a delicious yellow moist mixture heavily flecked with green. The more herbs the better.

To prepare cumin & chilli roasted sweet potatoes with duileasc

Preheat the oven to medium 180°C/350°F/Gas 4

Place these in the oven just after adding the apricots to the tagine.

Place the potatoes into a roasting tray and add olive oil, chilli flakes, duileasc and cumin seeds. Toss the potatoes in the oil and spices with your hands and roast in the oven for 20 – 25 minutes.

To prepare the organic salad leaves and dressing

Wash and dry the salad leaves. Put the dressing ingredients in a jar with a lid and shake.
Toss the salad leaves in the dressing in a very large salad bowl or 2 medium sized bowls.

To serve

Place everything on the table and invite guests to help themselves.

THE TEDDY BEARS

PICNIC

If you go down to the woods today..

You'll be very lucky to get there and back without a downpour, given a typical Irish summer. That said, we can have the most idyllic of blue sky days with near tropical soft winds warming the sand, and long balmy evenings just made for eating outside.

Kate loves picnics, and so any al fresco dining is a picnic for us. Her favourite is a spur of the moment affair when we pile ourselves and some food into Johnny's Orkney Longliner boat and head along the North Sligo coast to what we have always called the 'Magic Beach'.

Every Teddy Bear will agree that a planned picnic is the ideal, but will also agree that spontaneity is a huge asset in dealing with the Irish climate. The real secret to the picnic is a mix of both. A picnic basket with non–perishable essentials at the ready is handy; cutlery, drinking utensils, and a selection of small and medium sized Tupperware containers with lids can all be packed on standby on the rainy day of your choice. All you need do is rapidly transfer the components of your chosen feast into the containers at high speed, and off you go. Picnic rugs and a wind tent, even a few beers for thirsty grown up bears, can all be pre–packed.

Try and include a good selection of fruit and vegetables. Watermelon is really refreshing and loved by children, but is heavy to carry, so just bring a small amount, wrapped in Clingfilm. And a fork. Cherry tomatoes are great, and lots of water and fruit juice is essential.

For those of you who believe in weather forecasts, baking something from the delightful selection of cookies and biscuits in this section can be done in advance.
If it rains on the day, take all your teddy bears into the sitting room, seat them comfortably and just have the picnic there. Rain battering on the windows gives a picnic a whole new dimension. Believe me, Kate, the Teddys and I have done it regularly.

gingerbread and seaweed people

Gingerbread men with no added sugar! The dough is sweetened with molasses and banana, and no sugar–fuelled children makes the picnic all the sweeter... ask any Teddy Bear.

Seaweeds used: nori, sugar kelp
Recipe makes 25 – 30 depending on size

115g (4oz) butter, softened
85g (2 generous tablespoons) molasses
1 – 2 ripe large bananas
1 egg, beaten
2 – 3 teaspoons ginger powder
1 teaspoon fresh ginger, grated – optional
2 teaspoons allspice
1 – 2 tablespoons ***nori****, ground or flaked*
a generous pinch of ***sugar kelp***
1 tablespoon good quality cocoa powder
1/2 teaspoon baking powder
325g (11oz) plain flour or white spelt flour plus extra for kneading and rolling

Decorations
Good quality dark chocolate drops and buttons

1 Place the softened butter and molasses in a large mixing bowl and cream with a fork or wooden spoon. Mash the banana and add to the mixture with the egg. Mix well together.

2 Add the spices, seaweeds and sifted cocoa powder and mix well. Add the baking powder to the flour. Work in 1/4 of the flour with a wooden spoon until well combined. Add the next 1/4 and work until also well combined. Get your little helpers to assist with the mixing and kneading.

3 Tip in the remaining weighed flour and use your hands to gather into a dough. You will need to add a little extra flour to rub all the dough from your hands and from the side of the bowl. Once all the dough is together in a ball, knead lightly. Add flour if necessary so that there is no stickiness. Wrap in clingfilm and chill in the fridge for 2 hours or overnight.

4 Unwrap and leave for 20 minutes to soften a little so it will be easy to roll out.

5 Preheat the oven to 180°C/350°F/Gas 4. Grease some baking trays.

6 Roll the dough to a thickness of 4 to 5mm (1/4 inch). Cut into lots of shapes with a variety of cutters. Decorate. Bake large shapes together if possible, as they need a bit longer in the oven. Small thin biscuits will cook very quickly. Generally 10 to 12 minutes will cook all sizes but watch them carefully – they burn easily. Cool on the baking trays to firm up and then transfer to a wire tray.

sea spaghetti cookies
with honey and lemon, almonds and white chocolate chunks

Moist and chewy with interesting flavours.
Every Teddy Bear loves them.

Seaweed used: Sea spaghetti
Makes 16 very large or 32 small cookies

***8 – 10g (1/4 oz) sea spaghetti**, rehydrated for 10 minutes in enough warm water to cover it*
55g (2oz) butter
2 generous tablespoons runny honey
2 tablespoons pear concentrate
1 teaspoon vanilla extract
juice of 1 organic lemon
1 egg, beaten
160g (5 1/2 oz) white spelt flour
160g (5 1/2 oz) ground almonds
1 teaspoon baking powder
125g (4 1/2 oz) white chocolate, roughly chopped, or chunks
85g (3oz) almonds, flaked

To prepare the sea spaghetti

Place the sea spaghetti into a small saucepan with a little of the soak water, cover and simmer for 10 minutes or until soft. Remove the sea spaghetti from the saucepan, chop finely and place in a mixing bowl. Reserve the cooking water in a small bowl and use the saucepan to melt the butter.

Preheat the oven to 180°C/350°F/Gas 4.
Grease some baking trays.

1. Add the honey, pear concentrate, vanilla extract and lemon juice to the sea spaghetti. Mix well. Add the melted butter and egg.
2. Mix the flour, ground almonds and baking powder together in another bowl and fold into the sea spaghetti mixture. Add a little of the reserved soaking water if the dough is too stiff.
3. Stir in the white chocolate and flaked almonds. Put teaspoons of the mixture onto a baking tray and bake for 10 minutes until just browned at the edges. Bake for an extra 5 – 7 minutes if opting for the large cookies. Allow to cool on the baking tray to set fully.

Sprinkle with calendula flowers (pot marigold) if you have some in your garden

---

COOK'S TIP

Not all children like the lemon flavoured cookies. You can make a batch using 60ml of soak water instead of lemon juice if baking specifically for children.

coco's cookies

Baking these sweet and simple cookies with children is a great way of introducing seaweed into their cookery repertoire. Always popular at parties too!

Seaweed Used: Alaria, sugar kelp
Makes about 40 little cookies

125g (4 1/2 oz) butter
50g (1 3/4 oz) brown Demerara
3 tablespoons water
1 tablespoon almond essence
1 tablespoon vanilla extract
250g (9oz) flour
25g (1oz) cocoa
1 teaspoon baking powder
2 teaspoons ***Alaria*** *and 1 teaspoon* ***sugar kelp,*** *both finely ground or*
3 teaspoons ***Alaria****, finely ground*

To decorate
Icing sugar
about 55g (2oz) melted white chocolate

WELL COVERED KELP

Just as we ensure that our children are well covered with sun screen when the sun is out, the huge macrocystis kelp parents do something similar.

They release phlorotannins into the water on a hot day to protect the baby kelp. Phlorotannins are great at protecting against the harmful effects of ultraviolet radiation.

Recipe from Grit Glass, musician.

Preheat the oven to 180°C/350°F/Gas 4.
Grease a baking tray

1. Melt the butter in a small saucepan over moderate heat and stir in the sugar. Mix well and allow to cool a little. Add the water, almond essence and vanilla extract and transfer to a mixing bowl.
2. Sift the flour, cocoa and baking powder into the butter mixture in the mixing bowl. Stir in the Alaria and sugar kelp and mix well to combine.
3. Roll the dough into little balls using a teaspoon and your hands. If it's hard to roll, place in the fridge for 5 to 10 minutes. Place the balls on the prepared baking tray and bake for about 12 minutes.
4. Remove from the oven, place in a bowl and sift a little icing sugar over them. Using a teaspoon drizzle a little white chocolate over them for an extra special effect.

COOK'S TIP

For adults only, as children could choke on a whole nut: Put a whole hazelnut into the centre of each cookie for a surprise centre. Crushed hazelnuts can be added to the cocoa balls for an extra crunch.

hanna's little jammy jewel cookies

Great for childrens' parties because they are little more than bite sized, and therefore less likely to be discarded half eaten.
Use different colour jams to create a sparkling and attractive array for the party table.
These little cookies are traditionally made in the Thuringian region of East Germany and this recipe was handed down to my friend Grit from her German granny, Hanna.

Seaweed used: Sugar kelp, nori
This recipe makes about 60 tiny cookies

240g (8½oz) butter
3 egg yolks
75g (2½oz) icing sugar
370g (13oz) flour
*3 teaspoons **nori**, ground*
*1 teaspoon **sugar kelp**, ground*

A selection of jams
strawberry, blueberry or blackcurrant, and apricot give a nice mix of colours and work very well together
Icing sugar to decorate

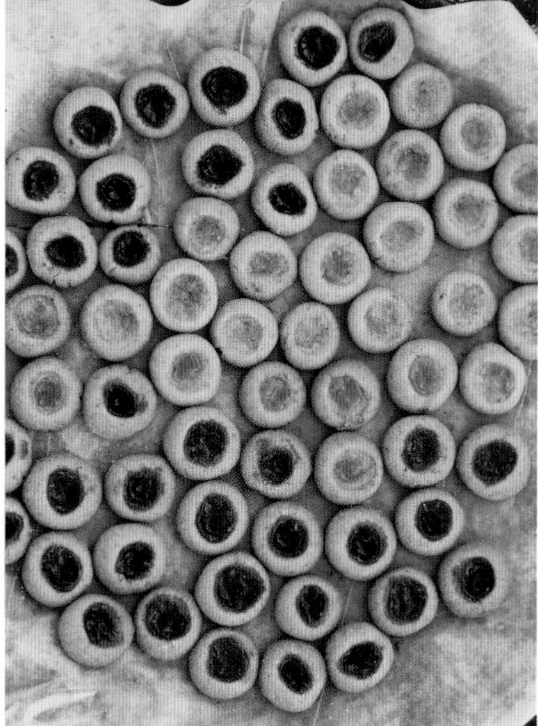

Preheat the oven to 180°C/350°F/Gas 4 and grease 2 baking trays
(To prepare the seaweed, see the bookmark.)

1. Melt the butter in a small saucepan and set aside to cool slightly. Add the egg yolks to the butter and mix well to combine.
2. Transfer this mixture to a small mixing bowl.
3. Sift in the icing sugar and flour to the butter and egg mixture. Add the ground seaweed and mix well to combine.
4. Scoop out teaspoons of the mixture and roll into little balls. Place these onto the baking tray and flatten slightly. Using your little finger make dents in the balls to hold the jam and using a small teaspoon insert a small amount of jam into each hole.
5. Place the trays in the oven and bake for about 15 minutes or until just turning golden at the edges. Allow another 5 minutes if necessary depending on the size of the cookies.
6. Remove from the oven and cool on a wire rack. When cooling sift a little icing sugar over the cookies.

COOK'S TIP

The cookies keep well in an airtight box and are easily transported for picnics.

walnuts and nori
chocolate brownies

The flavour of the nori pairs brilliantly with the chocolate and also does a superb job in keeping the brownies moist and dense. You will never make them any other way.

Seaweeds used: Nori
Makes 16 small brownies

4 – 5g (1 sheet) ***nori,*** *torn and soaked in a few tablespoons of tepid water, mixed to a paste using a fork and set aside*
55g (2oz) butter
100g (3½ oz) chocolate 70 % cocoa
1 tablespoon cocoa powder
100ml (3½ fl oz) milk or rice milk
150g (5oz) dark brown sugar or molasses sugar
1 teaspoon vanilla extract
3 eggs, beaten
150g (5oz) spelt flour
1½ teaspoons baking powder
175g (6oz) walnuts, roughly chopped
85g (3oz) plain chocolate, broken roughly

Preheat the oven to 180°C/350°F/Gas4.
Butter a 20 – 22.5cm (8 – 9") square tin.

1. Melt the butter and 70% cocoa chocolate in a large glass bowl set over a saucepan of gently simmering water.
2. Stir in the cocoa powder, half the milk and nori with soaking water. Mix well.
3. Stir in the molasses or brown sugar, the other half of the milk and vanilla extract. Allow to cool and add the eggs.
4. Mix the spelt and baking powder in a bowl and add to the chocolate mixture. Stir in the walnuts and plain chocolate. Add another drop of milk if too dry.
5. Pour into the prepared tin and place in the oven. Bake for 20 minutes. Check to see that the top has formed a light brown crust and has started to crack. The edges should be firm and the centre look a little underdone. It is better this way as it will continue to cook and set when it comes out of the oven.
6. Cool in the tin and cut into squares.

COOK'S TIP

Add 55g (2oz) dried cherries or goji berries instead of 55g (2oz) of the walnuts for even more added luxury.

Rated as the best brownie maker in the area, this recipe comes from Esther Waters, Kate's cousin.

rice crispie buns with attitude

This is a really sneaky way of getting fruit, nuts and seaweed into children – that is if the adults don't get to them first. Make some with white chocolate too for contrast and fun.

Seaweed used: Alaria
Makes 30 buns

8 – 10g (1 level tablespoon) ***Alaria,*** *ground (see bookmark)*
300g (10½ oz) dark or plain chocolate
125g (4½ oz) rice crispies
25g (1oz) figs, 2 medium sized figs, chopped finely
100g (3½ oz) raisins or sultanas
75g (2½ oz) walnuts, chopped
25g (1oz) flaked almonds
Honey (optional)

COOK'S TIP

For a change use toasted hazelnuts instead of walnuts.

Lay out 30 medium sized paper bun cases.

1. Break the chocolate into a bowl and stand the bowl over a saucepan of barely simmering water and allow to melt. Don't let the water touch the bowl.
2. Remove from the heat and fold in Alaria, rice crispies, fruit and nuts, stirring to ensure the chocolate covers all the ingredients.
3. Taste the mixture. If using dark chocolate and making it for children with a very sweet tooth you might like to mix in a little honey at this stage.
4. Spoon into the paper cases and allow to set at room temperature or in the fridge. Store in an airtight container.

breads and cakes

baking with spelt flour

'Just remember you have just 4 minutes from when you add the dry to the wet ingredients to make a dough. The gluten is fragile and the cake won't rise if the flour is mixed for too long...'

- Spelt is an ancient grain similar to wheat and possibly the ancestor to modern wheat. It is very easy on the digestive system. White spelt bread is more nutritious than white wheat bread. However it is wise to add a little brown spelt to the recipe for the extra fibre that is so important for a healthy digestive system.

- The gluten in spelt is very fragile and therefore it is important not to over–mix the dough or the bread won't rise. Here is a tip I have learned through bitter experience: I discovered that answering the phone or the door while in the middle of mixing the wet and dry ingredients causes the gluten to collapse and results in rock hard bread. From the moment the liquid comes in contact with the spelt flour you have about 4 minutes to mix to a dough. Once mixed it can be treated like ordinary wheat flour.

- One way of making the 4 minute deadline is to set a timer, and don't allow yourself to get distracted. 4 minutes is plenty of time to mix the ingredients into a dough.

big sweet sultana sleabhac* scone

This is a traditional way of making bread where a big scone or round of bread is marked into wedges before baking. Traditionally made on St Patrick's Day in our family, you will find yourself making this regularly.

It is quick, easy and delicious. Get into the habit of keeping ground nori in a sealed container and avoid the delay of having to dry and grind the seaweed. You can then have the bread in the oven in minutes.

Seaweed used: Sleabhac* also called nori
Serves 8

2 tablespoons ***nori flakes*** *(see bookmark)*
100ml (3 1/2 fl oz) milk
4 eggs, beaten
225g (8oz) sultanas
Zest of 1 organic lemon
Drop of lemon essential oil, optional
450g (1lb) white spelt flour plus extra, see note on using spelt flour
4 rounded teaspoons baking powder
115g (4oz) butter

*** nori, porphyra, laver**

COOK'S TIP

For a lighter scone consistency, handle the dough as little as possible.

Preheat the oven to 200°C/400°F/Gas 6.
Grease and flour one baking tray.

1. Pour the milk into a measuring jug and beat in the eggs. Add the sultanas, nori, lemon zest and lemon oil if using. Set aside. This allows the sultanas to plump up.
2. Mix the flour and baking powder together in a mixing bowl. Rub in the butter with your fingertips until the mixture resembles coarse breadcrumbs. Make a well in the centre of the bowl
3. Stir the wet mixture into the dry ingredients, reserving a little of the egg/milk mixture, and gently form into a soft, but not sticky dough. Use extra milk if too dry.
4. Turn out onto a floured surface and form into a circle, over 5cm (2 inches) high, with your hands. Transfer to the baking tray and with a sharp knife cut deeply into 8 wedges. Push any sultanas into the dough so they don't burn when cooking. Brush the dough with reserved egg/milk liquid.
5. Bake in the centre of the oven for 20 – 30 minutes, until golden. Serve warm with a little butter on the same day. Can be frozen, just make sure it is completely cold before wrapping.

duileasc and cheese scones

These have become my signature scone and people who attend my seaweed courses expect to taste or make a batch.

Seaweed used: Duileasc
Makes 20 – 22 small scones

40g (1½ oz) ***duileasc,*** *toasted and crumbled (see bookmark)*
Olive oil, for frying
2 onions, chopped very finely
2 garlic cloves
450g (1lb) plain flour
1 tablespoon baking powder
2 level teaspoons mustard powder
¼ teaspoon cream of tarter
¼ – ½ teaspoon cayenne pepper
85g (3oz) butter, softened
225ml (8fl oz) milk
1 egg, beaten
85g (3oz) strong sheep or goats' cheese or a strong cheddar, for example Mount Callan, grated
25g (1oz) strong cheddar, grated, as above or a smoked cheese, or Parmesan, for sprinkling

COOK'S TIP

To avoid re–rolling the dough, shape it into a square. Brush with reserved milk and egg mixture and sprinkle cheese on top. Using a large cleaver or knife cut the dough into 2.5cm (1 inch) lengths across and then down making a grid of scones each about 2.5cm (1 inch) square. Transfer the scones to the baking tray to bake as above.

Preheat the oven 210°C/410°F/Gas 6½.
Lightly grease one large baking tray.

1 Heat the oil in a pan, add the onions and garlic and fry gently over moderate heat for 3 minutes until softened and transparent. Add the crumbled duileasc towards the end and mix gently to combine. Set aside to cool.

2 Sift the flour and baking powder into a mixing bowl. Stir in the mustard, cream of tartar and cayenne pepper. Dice and rub in the butter with your fingertips until the mixture resembles fine breadcrumbs. Make a well and pour in the milk and egg, reserving a little. Mix gently to combine. Stir in the cheese, and the cooled onion and duileasc mixture.

3 Turn the dough onto a floured surface and flatten by hand or with a rolling pin, to a thickness of just over 2.5cm (1 inch).

4 Using a 3.5cm (1½") round diameter cutter stamp out scones and place on the baking trays. These scones are very small in diameter, but very high

5 Brush with the reserved milk and egg mixture and sprinkle cheese on top.

6 Bake in the oven for 12 minutes until golden. Remove and cool slightly on a wire rack. Best served warm with butter.

memories of duileasc

I spell it this way as in the Republic of Ireland it is pronounced with a rolling 'l' sound

Of all the edible seaweeds growing along the Irish coastline, duileasc is certainly among the best documented historically. It is thought that the people of the Mesolithic Era (c.9000 – 4000 BC) used edible seaweeds along with fish and shellfish. Large areas of shell deposits 'middens' have been excavated in the coastal areas where they lived. Sligo (Sligeach, meaning shelly) has some fine examples. This suggests that the builders of Newgrange, (c.3200 BC) were already familiar with seaweeds in their diet.

The Brehon Laws, a complicated and comprehensive set of laws covering all aspects of Irish law were already old by the time they were first written down in the 5th century, and have been described as covering all aspects of Irish life from 'bee–keeping to tree–keeping to sea–keeping.' The section specific to legal affairs is known as the 'Crith Gabhlach' and mentions duileasc by name as a condiment to be served with bread, whey milk and butter. It was also served with roast fowl.

18th Century Scottish and Irish immigrants to North America clearly associated duileasc with the taste of home, and often had small parcels of it sent to them, despite the fact that it has always grown well off the shores of North America, particularly in the area of the Bay of Fundy.

19th century historian Robin Flower recounts how boatmen in the Blasket Islands chewed it constantly, while women kept a supply in their pockets and Dr. Browne, visiting Belmullet, Co Mayo in the 1880s describes how the women in the area, 'attended to all of the housework and the needs of their children, helped in the fields and on the bog and gathered and dried carraigín and dileasc'. This was sold in the neighbouring town – to where the women walked, barefoot, as they were expected to save their boots for market days and holidays – for two shillings a stone. The men, on the other hand, suffered under no such hardship.

The Auld Lammas Fair, in Ballycastle, Northern Ireland, was first held in 1606, and represents an unbroken four centuries of dulse (duileasc) trading in the province. Visitors to the fair, held on the last Monday and Tuesday in August every year, are often surprised to see the prominence and amount of 'dulse' on sale in market stalls.

Duileasc fried in a little butter, crisped, and eaten between two slices of white bread is a favourite in Northern Ireland, while further down the coast, in Sligo, Beezie McGowan remembers her mother harvesting creathnach, which is the same plant but believed to be a sweeter version of duileasc, and either serving it with boiled potatoes and bacon, or making it into a delicious soup with mussels, also harvested from the shore, in season.

Beezie herself recalls bringing it to school in the 1920s, dried, in a small paper bag, to be eaten as a relished snack. There wasn't a lot of it, but she always tried to bring a bit as a treat for school pals, with whom it was very popular. This I find fascinating as I hope to see this happen again in the future where duileasc is so prized and valued by the Irish that it is treated in the way Japanese people treat nori by using it as a normal lunchtime food for school children. Poppy Hunt and her sister, both from Sligo, state their favourite method of cooking duileasc is to boil it in milk or water and eat it as a vegetable.

Among the seaweed lore up and down the coast, the story of the Worm Rock in County Sligo stands out. Parents whose children were suffering from thread or pin worm could collect creathnach from the rock when it became uncovered during a good spring tide, boil it, and give the liquid to the afflicted child. Because the creathnach from this rock, and only this rock had the cure of the worms, many parents took the risk of getting cut off by the tide to quickly harvest from it. Beezie says the cure always worked, and as research shows creathnach /duileasc, Palmaria palmata to contain kainic acid which is anti–helmintic (kills worms), her memory serves her correctly.

In Wales it is used by some vets to prevent animals from getting worms and we give it to our dogs for the same reason. It is much harder to get our cats to eat duileasc! Interestingly, in conversation with Thierry Chopin, Professor of Marine Biology, University of New Brunswick, I learned that people around the Mediterranean Sea and Japan also use another red algae, Digenea simplex, as a source of kainic acid for worm treatment.

Duileasc harvested in early summer is a softer and saltier seaweed compared to the duileasc harvested in Autumn. Traditionally the summer harvest is enjoyed over the summer months while the autumn harvest is kept for the winter.

two traditional soda breads

white soda bread with duileasc

Duileasc was traditionally incorporated into breads and many Irish households bake a version of soda bread, often referred to as 'a cake of bread'.

My mother, Shelagh, like so many people, bakes bread without measuring anything. She can eyeball the ingredients while chatting and turn out a perfect cake each time.

To turn out really good cakes of bread, you have to have a baker's hand, something akin to a green thumb in gardening. I had to follow her every move to see exactly what amounts she uses and what she does.

Here it is...

Seaweed used: Duileasc
Makes 1 very large round loaf of bread

20 – 25g (1oz) ***duileasc,*** *rehydrated for 10 minutes in a little water, drained well and chopped finely*
900g (2lb) plain white flour or white spelt flour
1½ teaspoons bread soda
pinch of salt
350ml (12fl oz) sour milk or butter milk or yogurt, or a mix of all three
300ml/10fl oz water

COOK'S TIP

When replacing the bread in the oven for the final few minutes, place it upside down on the tray.

Preheat oven 200°C/400°F/Gas 6.
Lightly grease and flour a baking tray.

1. Sieve the flour, bread soda and salt into a large bowl.
2. Add the duileasc to the jug of combined measured liquids (milk and water).
3. Make a well in the centre of the bowl and gradually pour in the liquids containing the duileasc, mixing the dough as quickly and as gently and as little as possible. Use a little more milk or water if necessary.
4. When the dough comes together carefully scrape it onto a baking tray and pat it gently into a round shape. With a sharp knife cut a deep cross in it.
5. Place in the oven and bake for about 45 – 50 minutes until the crust has browned and it looks cooked. Remove, quickly turn over and tap the base; when perfectly cooked, bread will sound hollow when the base is tapped. Return to the oven for a few more minutes if necessary until cooked fully.

Cool on a wire rack.

brown soda bread with oatmeal and duileasc

'Start off with 1 teaspoon of duileasc and see how you like the result. Add a tablespoon or more as you acquire a taste for it and reduce the salt to a pinch, if any at all.'

The common way to eat dulse in Canada is to put it in a paper bag and leave it on the dashboard of the car... it gets soft and can be eaten as a tasty snack.

Seaweed used: Duileasc
Makes a 2lb loaf

450g (1lb) stone–ground whole meal flour or whole meal spelt, (see note on using spelt flour on page 182)
100g (3½ oz) oatmeal
½ teaspoon salt (optional)
2 teaspoons dried unwashed ***duileasc,*** *crushed or chopped finely, (see bookmark)*
55g (2oz) brown sugar or 1 teaspoon molasses
125g (4½ oz) plain white flour or white spelt flour
1 teaspoon heaped bread soda
450ml (¾ pint) buttermilk
1 egg, beaten
to sprinkle: sesame or poppy seeds optional

Preheat the oven to 180°C/350°F/Gas 4.
Lightly flour a 900g/2lb loaf tin

1. Put the brown flour, oatmeal, salt, duileasc and brown sugar, if using in a large mixing bowl.
2. Sieve the white flour and bread soda into the bowl and mix well.
3. Make a well in the centre, add the buttermilk, egg, molasses if not using brown sugar, and mix well again.
4. Spoon into the prepared loaf tin, sprinkle with seeds, if using, and bake for about 50 minutes or until hollow when tapped.

Regina Kiernan, a colleague of mine, learned how to bake this great loaf while helping out as a student in the kitchen of the local convent.

yogurt for baking bread

My mother kept a pet cow so we would have a supply of pure and fresh butter, cream, milk and buttermilk when we were growing up. The cow had her own special single–cow milking machine which was a great source of mirth for the local farmers who had big herds.

After many years the commitment to morning and evening milking became too much for my mother and she had to give it up, though very reluctantly.

The cow was replaced by a yoghurt/buttermilk plant which remained in the kitchen press and did not require milking twice a day. As long as it was washed and fed fresh milk every 4 – 5 days it stayed alive and produced yoghurt.

We often killed it by accident and had to start again or get some starter from neighbours. It is easy to do and a great source of fermented milk for making bread. Either ask around to see if anybody has a plant or start your own...

25g (1oz) fresh yeast
500ml (17½fl oz) boiled and cooled to barely warm water.
25g (1oz) white sugar
500ml (17½fl oz) barely warm milk

1 Blend the yeast with a little of the water. Add the sugar to dissolve and the rest of the water and milk.

2 Pour into a Pyrex jug or bowl that has been well rinsed and scalded with boiling water, and cover. Place in a warm location like a kitchen press.

3 Check the plant each day until it ferments and smells like yogurt or buttermilk. This process will depend on the temperature of the press, but it should be complete in 2 – 3 days.

4 Using a plastic sieve and a wooden or plastic spoon, strain off the liquid into a bowl. The firm white plant, resembling cottage cheese will remain in the sieve.

5 Clean off all the residual milk by running it briefly under the cold tap. Rinse the jug in boiling water and warm some more milk. Tip the washed plant into the warm milk, cover and set aside as before, in the press.

6 Every day or so you can strain the plant and collect the yogurt. The plant will grow as the weeks pass and will benefit from being halved and shared with friends every time it gets too big. Just remember to feed and wash it at least every 4 – 5 days, always rinse and scald the jug in boiling water, and don't use metal which can kill it – always wood or plastic.

THE BLACK CAT
Clearwater Beach
Florida

duileasc spelt seed bread

A recipe from Gerry Harrington. Great with his soup on page 25.

Seaweed used: Duileasc
Makes 1 loaf

340g (12oz) brown whole meal spelt flour
2 teaspoons baking powder
55g (2oz) pumpkin seeds
55g (2oz) sunflower seeds
55g (2oz) sesame seeds
15g (½oz) duileasc, chopped finely
300ml (½ pint) water, plus extra if needed
2 tablespoons olive oil

Preheat oven to 230°C/450°F/Gas 8.
Prepare a circular baking tin, 20cm (8") diameter by flouring well.

1. Mix flour and baking powder together in a large mixing bowl. Add seeds and duileasc and mix well.
2. Form a well in the centre and add the water and olive oil to make a wet dough.
3. Knead briefly in the bowl. Remember to work quickly as the gluten is fragile in spelt flour. See note on spelt flour, page 182.
4. Tip the dough into the prepared tin and bake for about 45 minutes. Test with a large needle and if the dough does not stick to the needle the bread is baked. Check by tapping on the base for a hollow sound. Remove from the tin and cool on a wire rack.

using yeast

spelt yeast bread with duileasc or mixed seaweeds

LONG METHOD

This method is also used for making focaccia (See recipe on page 196) and can also be used to make the spelt bread.

Mix all the yeast with some of the water and flour and set aside until doubled in size. You can leave it overnight in an unheated room if you prefer. Then add in the rest of the liquid, fold in the flour and knead for 5 minutes or longer if possible.

Allow to double in size again. Punch back, shape and allow to rise before putting into the oven.

As making this bread takes some effort, make double the amount and freeze the loaves.

Here is the exact method:

a selection of bread tins, for example 2 x 900g (2lb) and 1 x 675g (l ½ lb)
1.5kg (3½ lb) white, half white and half wholemeal or all wholemeal spelt flour
700ml (1¼ pints) tepid water
1 heaped tablespoon of honey or molasses; honey keeps the bread white, molasses darkens it
25g (1oz) fresh yeast or 2 sachets, dried
300ml (½ pint) tepid water, approximately, depending on flour used
1 egg, beaten
1 tablespoon olive oil
40 – 50g (1½ – 2oz) ***duileasc*** *or* ***mixed seaweeds*** *chopped finely*
1 teaspoon sea salt

1. Mix half the flour with 700ml of the water, honey and all the yeast. Beat to combine for 1 minute. Cover and set aside until doubled in size, or overnight.
2. Add 300ml (½ pint) water, egg, olive oil, the rest of the flour, the duileasc and the salt. Mix well and add a little more water if necessary to make a stiff dough.
3. Knead for 6 minutes. Cover and set aside in a warm place to double in size.
4. Knock back and shape into 2 or 3 loaves.
5. Half fill well oiled bread tins and allow to rise, covered with spare upturned tins for 20 minutes in a warm place. Preheat the oven to 220°C/425°F/Gas 7
6. Bake for 40 – 45 minutes. A larger loaf will take a little longer to cook.
7. Tip out of tin and check if baked. The base will sound hollow when cooked. Cool on a wire tray.

using yeast

a quicker version of making spelt yeast bread

This makes 1 x 800g (1½ lb) loaf.

Oil a 1½ lb or 2lb loaf tin depending on what you have available.

The loaf will rise high over the smaller sized loaf tin and have a gentle curve in the larger sized tin.

1 tablespoon honey
300ml (½ pint) tepid water
500g (1lb 2oz) white spelt flour
a pinch of salt
1 egg, beaten
1 tablespoon olive oil
*20g (¾ oz) dry weight **duileasc** or **mixed seaweeds**, chopped*
1 teaspoon/sachet dried yeast

1. Dissolve the honey in 100ml (3½ fl oz) of hot water. Add the remaining 200ml (7fl oz) of cold water and stir.
2. Sift the flour and salt into a large mixing bowl.
3. Make a well in the centre and pour in the water containing the honey, the egg, olive oil, duileasc and yeast. Using a wooden spoon stir quickly to combine. The dough will come together and using your hand, knead well. Add a little more flour if it is too wet.
4. Oil the sides of the bowl and cover the bowl with cling film. Set aside in a warm place and allow to double in size. This will take about 1 hour.
5. Knock back and knead briefly. Shape into a loaf and put into the prepared tin. Put an empty tin of the same size upside down over the dough and set aside in a warm place again to rise. Use a large bowl if you don't have a tin. After 30 – 40 minutes the dough should have doubled in size. Preheat the oven to 220°C/435°F/Gas 7.
6. Place in the oven and bake for 40 – 45 minutes. Remove, tap the base to check if baked, and cool on a wire rack.

COOK'S TIP

Brush with beaten egg for a golden crust just before the dough rises for the second time.

spelt 'one rising' yeast bread

This is the fastest way of making a yeast loaf that I know of!

1 teaspoon/sachet dried yeast
1 teaspoon raw cane sugar
300ml (1/2 pint) hand hot water
450g (1lb) white or wholemeal spelt flour
(A mix of half and half is good)
1/2 teaspoon sea salt
2 heaped tablespoons* duileasc *or
***mixed seaweeds,* chopped**
1 tablespoon olive oil

Oil a 900g (2lb) loaf tin.

1 Dissolve the yeast and sugar in the measuring jug of water. Leave in a warm place for 5 – 10 minutes until it forms a frothy head.

2 In a large mixing bowl mix together the flour, salt and seaweed. Leave this bowl in a warm place while waiting for the yeast to froth.

3 Add the frothed yeast mixture to the dry ingredients and add the olive oil.

4 Mix all the ingredients together to form a dough ball. Add a little extra flour if the dough is too sticky. Turn onto a floured board and knead well.

5 Shape into a loaf and place in the prepared tin. Allow to rise in a warm place for about 30 minutes or until doubled in size. Preheat the oven 220°C/435°F/Gas 7.

6 Bake for 35 minutes or until the bottom of the loaf sounds hollow when tapped. Cool on a wire rack.

COOK'S TIP

At the end of step 4 allow the dough to rise for about 20 minutes. Knock back, shape into a plait and allow to rise for 30 minutes. Bake.

Mairead Higgins, social worker and organic gardener who rises and bakes her yeast bread in a north Leitrim cottage powered by water, wind and sun.

focaccia

Bernadette O'Shea ran her highly acclaimed and award winning 'Truffles' pizza restaurant for many years in Sligo town. This is a recipe she gave me from her classic *Pizza Defined* cookbook, into which I incorporate a mix of different seaweeds.

Every so often when the basil and tomatoes are plentiful in the garden we invite friends over, take down Bernadette's book, crank up the Aga to max and set to work making her wonderful pizza creations to order.

Always a memorable success.

Seaweed used: Duileasc and sea lettuce or mixed seaweeds
Serves 10 – 12

DOUGH

350ml (12fl oz) lukewarm water
20g (3/4 oz) fresh yeast or 1 tablespoon dried yeast
560g (1lb 2oz) strong white flour
3/4 teaspoon salt
50ml (2fl oz) olive oil
2 – 3 heaped tablespoons ***duileasc***
1 heaped tablespoon ***sea lettuce*** *or 3 – 4 heaped tablespoons* ***mixed seaweeds,*** *rehydrated in just enough cold water to cover them for 10 minutes, squeezed dry and chopped*

To make the Dough

1. Pour 175ml (6fl oz) of the warm water into a large mixing bowl which must be large enough to hold the dough when doubled in bulk.
2. Add the yeast and stir to dissolve.
3. Add 150g (5oz) of flour and stir quickly and vigorously in the one direction until very well combined in a smooth batter.
4. Cover the bowl tightly with cling film and let it stand for a minimum of 25 minutes or up to 3 hours in a draught–free area.
5. After rising remove the cling film, sprinkle on the salt, pour over the oil, a further 175ml (6fl oz) of lukewarm water and gradually add the final 410g (13oz) flour in a folding motion until completely incorporated.
6. Knead. Place in an oiled bowl and brush the dough with oil. Cover with a damp cloth.
7. Allow about 2 hours to double in bulk. Punch down the dough. Add the seaweeds to the dough and knead for a few minutes to incorporate fully.

FOCACCIA TOPPING

2 – 3 very ripe tomatoes, thinly sliced
1/2 teaspoon salt
2 – 4 cloves garlic, minced
2 tablespoons olive oil
6 basil leaves, finely julienned
25g (1oz) Parmesan, grated
2 heaped tablespoons mixed seaweeds, prepared as above but chopped finely
olive oil to drizzle when cooked

To make the focaccia

Preheat the oven to maximum temperature.
Oil a 23cm (9") pan, square or round.

1. Press the dough into the pan. Cover the pan with cling film and allow the dough to rest for 30 minutes.
2. Dimple the dough with your fingers. Place the tomatoes in a single layer on top and sprinkle over all the other ingredients.
3. Bake in the preheated oven for about 20 minutes.
4. Serve warm, drizzled with olive oil, or a flavoured oil, or the oil from sun dried tomatoes.

carrot and duileasc loaf

This recipe was sent to me by Stefan Kraan and is the 'signature bread' of the Irish Seaweed Centre, Galway, Ireland. Quick and easy, it is a nice introduction to cooking with duileasc.

Seaweed used: Duileasc
Makes 10 – 12 slices

25g (1oz) ***dried duileasc***
115g (4oz) butter, melted
4 eggs, beaten
1 large carrot, grated
A pinch of sea salt
50g (1¾ oz) castor sugar (optional)
250g (9oz) plain white flour
1½ teaspoons baking powder
A little milk if necessary

To prepare the duileasc

Soak it in fresh water for 5 minutes.
Remove, dry with kitchen paper and chop finely.
Reserve soak water

Preheat oven 190/375/gas 5.
Grease and line a 675g (1 ½ lb) loaf tin.

1. Combine the butter, eggs, duileasc, carrots and salt in a mixing bowl. Add the sugar if using.
2. Sieve the flour and baking powder into the mixture, folding gently. If mixture is dry add a little milk or soak water.
3. Pour into the tin and bake for 50 – 55mins. Remove and cool in tin on wire rack. Slice and serve with butter.

Recipe originally comes from Jim Morrissey, one of the authors of *A Guide to Commercially Important Seaweeds on the Irish Coast.*

courgette and walnut loaf

..another great way to use up courgettes lurking in the garden in the height of the summer.

Seaweed used: Alaria
Makes 10–12 slices

2 teaspoons ***Alaria,*** *ground,*
to prepare see bookmark
450g (1lb) plain flour
2 heaped teaspoons baking powder
½ teaspoon allspice
1 teaspoon cinnamon
3 eggs, beaten
85g (3oz) dark molasses sugar
1 tablespoon molasses
1 teaspoon vanilla extract
115g (4oz) butter, melted (optional)
see cook's tip
400g (14oz) courgettes, grated
225g (8oz) walnuts, roughly chopped

Preheat oven to 180°C/350°F/Gas 4.
Grease 2 x 900g (2lb) loaf tins or 2 x 450g (1lb) tins.

1. Sift the flour, baking powder and spices into a mixing bowl. Set aside.
2. Beat the eggs, sugar and molasses in a large mixing bowl. Add the Alaria and vanilla. Fold in half of the flour mixture. Stir in the melted butter if using. Fold in the remainder of the flour mixture.
3. Stir in half the courgette and half the walnuts. Mix well. Gently fold in the remainder of the courgette and walnuts.
4. Pour into the prepared tins and bake for 45 minutes in the centre of the oven.
5. Turn out and cool on wire rack.

COOK'S TIP

Substitute olive oil for melted butter, or the butter can be omitted entirely. It turns out perfectly, but won't stay fresh for as long.

ginger nori biscotti ideal for dunking

The zest of ginger and spices and the rich flavour of nori combine wonderfully well in these biscuits, which can be hard, for dunking, or soft and chewy, depending on the final bake. Easy to make and very popular with children as a little 'something' with a warm drink.

Seaweed used: Nori
Makes 35 – 45 slices

2 tablespoons/2 sheets ***ground nori,*** *(see bookmark)*
280g (9½oz) flour
1¼ teaspoons baking powder
¼ teaspoons bread soda
115g (4oz) dark sugar
3 teaspoons ground ginger
1 teaspoon allspice
170g (6oz) almonds – chopped coarsely
2 large eggs
55ml (2fl oz) molasses
Zest of 1 organic lemon
1 teaspoon vanilla extract
1–3 tablespoons of milk, if necessary

Preheat oven to 180°C/350°F/Gas 4. Grease and line two baking trays with greaseproof paper.

1 Sift the flour and baking powder into a large bowl and add the bread soda, nori, sugar, ginger and allspice. Stir in the almonds and set aside.

2 Beat the eggs in a large mixing bowl and add molasses, lemon zest and vanilla. Gradually add the dry ingredients to the egg mixture. Add milk if it is too dry.

3 Turn out onto a very lightly floured work surface and divide into two. Shape each piece into a log 25cm (10 inches) long and 2.5cm (1 inch) wide. Place both logs onto baking tray and bake in centre of oven for 30 – 35 minutes until they are firm to the touch. Transfer to a wire rack and cool for 10 minutes.

4 Peel off the greaseproof paper and place the logs on a cutting board. Using a serrated bread knife, cut each log into diagonal slices 1.5cm (¾ inch) wide, like cutting French bread.

5 Return to baking tray arranged cut side down. No greaseproof paper is needed this time. Bake for a further 20 minutes for a really dry and hard biscotti for dunking or 10 minutes for moist and chewy biscotti.

6 Transfer to wire rack. The biscotti will harden as they cool. Store in an airtight container.

Noleen Boyle, College of Tourism, Killybegs, Co Donegal, expertly makes biscotti

drop scones with duileasc

A fast and reliable recipe, great as an accompaniment to chowder or fish cakes.

Seaweed used: Duileasc
Makes 16

340g (12oz) flour
1 teaspoon baking powder
1/2 teaspoon sea salt
55g (2oz) melted butter
450ml (3/4 pint) milk
2 eggs
pinch of herbs
twist of red pepper
25g (1oz) chopped ***dried duileasc***
olive oil for cooking

1. Beat all the ingredients to a smooth batter or process in a blender.
2. Heat a heavy pan with a little olive oil.
3. Drop tablespoons of batter onto the hot oil. Cook until golden underneath. Turn and cook the underside briefly. Remove and keep warm.
4. Repeat until all the batter is used up.

Recipe from Elizabeth Studenski, Feng Shui consultant.

banana and Alaria loaf

Ripe bananas regularly come on sale in supermarkets everywhere, and this is your opportunity to team them with Alaria and make this moist succulent bread which is perfect for every occasion, especially breakfast.

Seaweed used : Alaria
Makes 10 - 12 slices

20g (3/4 oz) dried Alaria, snipped into 5mm (1/4 inch) pieces
2 eggs
115g (4oz) sultanas
2 tablespoons honey
a drop of rum (optional)
85g (3oz) butter, melted
2 tablespoons sugar, raw cane
225g (8oz) plain flour, sifted
2 well rounded teaspoons baking powder
450g (1lb) bananas, about 3 medium to large

To prepare the Alaria
Soak the Alaria in a saucepan with 300ml (1/2 pint) of water for 20 minutes. Place on a low heat and simmer, covered, for 40 minutes or until the mid stem is soft. Allow to cool slightly.

Preheat oven to 180°C/350°F/Gas 4.
Grease and flour a 900g (2lb) loaf tin.

1. Beat the eggs in a small mixing bowl. Soak the sultanas in the eggs to allow them to plump up.
2. Add honey, and rum if using, to the seaweed and cooking liquid.
3. Melt the butter in a saucepan, stir in the sugar and allow to cool slightly. Add the honeyed seaweed and liquid, and the soaked sultanas in egg mixture.
4. Mix the flour and baking powder in a large bowl. Add a large tablespoon of this to the wet mixture and mix well. Gently fold in the remaining flour mixture.
5. Stir in the mashed bananas. Spoon the mixture, which should be of a soft dropping consistency, into the prepared tin. Bake in the centre of the oven for 90 minutes. Remove and cool in the tin on a wire rack for 10 minutes.
6. Remove from the tin and allow to cool completely before serving with or without butter.

carrot, nori and sugar kelp cake

Rich and moist with a nutty texture, this cake has had a presence at every major gathering I've been at over the last 20 years, and is still requested. Where a sumptuously textured crowd pleaser is called for, this is the cake to bake.

I learned how to make this fantastic carrot cake from Kathleen Greaney, whom I stayed with while working in Boston one summer. When I got back to Ireland, I experimented with the seaweeds, resulting in this great combination of flavours.

Seaweeds used: nori, sugar kelp
Makes 20 portions or 40 finger food portions

Cake

8 – 12g (1/3 - 1/4 oz)/2 – 3 ***nori sheets****/2 – 3 heaped teaspoons* ***nori flakes***
1 teaspoon ***ground sugar kelp,*** *(see bookmark)*
600ml (1 pint) light olive oil or sunflower oil
225g (8oz) dark brown sugar
5 eggs
450g (1lb) white flour
3 heaped teaspoons baking powder
1 rounded teaspoon bread soda
675g (1 1/2 lb), carrots, grated
150g (5oz) walnuts, chopped roughly

Preheat oven 190°C/375°F/Gas 5.
Oil a large roasting tin 37 1/2 x 25 x 6cm (15 1/2"x 10" x 2 1/2 deep) with a little of the olive oil/sunflower.

1. Mix the oil and sugar together in a large mixing bowl. Beat in the eggs one at a time with a whisk or electric hand mixer.
2. Sift the flour, baking powder and bread soda into another bowl and set aside.
3. Fold the flour into the egg mixture. Add the carrots, walnuts, sugar kelp and nori and mix.
4. Pour the cake mixture into the prepared tin. Bake for 50 minutes until risen and browned. Cover with parchment paper to prevent further browning.
5. Bake for a further 10 minutes or until the cake starts to come away from the sides or an inserted skewer comes out moist but clean. Remove from the oven and leave to cool in the tin.

Topping

4 heaped teaspoons butter, softened
225g (8oz) cream cheese, full fat
2 teaspoons vanilla extract
100g (3 – 3 1/2 oz) icing sugar, sifted, to taste

To prepare the topping

1. Mash the butter in a bowl. Mash the cream cheese and combine with butter and vanilla. Sieve in the icing sugar and stir until completely mixed.
2. Spread over the top of the cooled cake with a palette knife. Decorate with edible flowers if you wish.

Variation

I use 30g/7 – 8 nori sheets/2 1/2 heaped tablespoons ground or flaked Irish nori plus 1 extra egg and an extra 3oz of sugar. Omit 30g of the flour if using this amount of seaweed.

Mug method

An easy way to make this big cake is to find a mug that has a capacity of 450ml (3/4 pint) and use the 'mug method' which is:

1 1/2 mugs of light olive oil or sunflower oil
1 scant mug of dark brown sugar, use 1 heaped mug if using the extra amount of nori
5 eggs, use 6 eggs if using the extra amount of nori
2 mugs flour, scant if using the extra amount of nori
3/4 mug of walnuts
2 heaped teaspoons baking powder, use 3 heaped teaspoons if using the extra amount of nori
2 heaped teaspoons bread soda
3 mugs of grated carrots.

old fashioned seed and sugar kelp cake

My mother learned how to make this cake from her mother, who was also a great baker. The distinctive taste of caraway seeds has marked special occasions in our house for as far back as I can remember, and the combination of seeds and sugar kelp works deliciously in this old fashioned Madeira recipe.

Seaweed used: Sugar kelp
Makes 12 – 18 portions

*2 heaped teaspoons **sugar kelp**,*
(see bookmark)
225g (8oz) butter, softened
115g (4oz) castor sugar
4 large eggs
340g (12oz) spelt or plain flour, sifted
1 teaspoon baking powder
½ teaspoon vanilla extract
2 teaspoons caraway seeds
2 tablespoons milk may be required

COOK'S TIP

Use little greaseproof cake tin liners if you can get them, they save time cutting and fixing the exact greaseproof size into tins.

Preheat oven 180°C/350°F/Gas 4.
Grease and line the base and sides of a 20 – 22½cm (8 – 9") round, deep cake tin with greaseproof paper.

1. Place the butter and sugar in a bowl and cream until light and fluffy.
2. Add the eggs one at a time beating well. If mixture shows signs of curdling add a little flour.
3. Stir the baking powder and sugar kelp into the flour, then add the flour to the egg mixture together with the vanilla extract, caraway seeds, and enough milk to make a fairly soft cake mix.
4. Turn into the prepared cake tin and bake in the centre of the oven for 50 minutes. It may need another 10 minutes or until a wooden skewer inserted into the centre of the cake comes out clean.
5. Cool in the tin.

layered chocolate walnut squares

Once asked by the youngest daughter of a colleague to bake something for her school cake sale fund raiser, I baked these. I knew they were a winner when she and her friends hid them away for themselves and got her mother to send money to the cake sale instead.

Just remember you have to prepare and assemble the 3 layers before placing them into the oven to cook.

Seaweed used: Alaria
Makes 16 – 20 squares

Layer 1

2 teaspoons Alaria, ground finely. (see bookmark)
1 tablespoon milk
115g (4oz) butter
25g (1oz) cocoa powder
175g (6oz) dark brown sugar
150g (5oz) plain flour
1 teaspoon baking powder
2 eggs
1 teaspoon vanilla extract
85g (3oz) walnuts

Layer 2

170g (6oz) cream cheese
55g (2oz) butter, softened
55g (2oz) castor sugar
1 egg
1 tablespoon milk
½ teaspoon vanilla extract
2 tablespoon plain flour
¼ teaspoon baking powder

Layer 3

1 – 2 teaspoons nori, ground finely. (see bookmark)
115g (4oz) dark chocolate, grated finely

Preheat oven to 190°C/375°F/Gas 5.
Grease and line a 22.5cm (9") square tin.

Layer 1

1. Measure the milk into a small bowl, stir in Alaria and set aside.
2. Melt the butter in a large saucepan. Stir in the cocoa and sugar and remove from the heat.
3. Sift the flour and baking powder into the melted butter mixture
4. Add the eggs one at a time and beat well. Add the milk soaked Alaria, vanilla and walnuts and mix well to combine. Spread the mixture evenly into the prepared tin and set aside.

Layer 2

1. Put cream cheese, butter, sugar, egg, milk and vanilla in a food processor on medium setting.
2. Mix the flour and baking powder together. Spoon into processor and continue blending until the mixture is smooth and almost white. Spread this mixture evenly over the chocolate mixture already in the tin.

Layer 3

Dust a layer of nori evenly over the white mixture in the tin. Dust grated chocolate over the nori.

To Bake

Place in the centre of the oven for 45 – 55 minutes until risen. Allow to cool in the tin. Turn out and cut into squares.

COOK'S TIP

Almonds can be used successfully instead of walnuts.

nori and no flour chocolate cake with lemon curd topping

This magnificently indulgent chocolate cake loses absolutely nothing by being wheat free, and is guaranteed to delight people who have wheat on their avoid list.

I first saw it being baked when visiting Elspeth Semple in Scotland, and worked on the recipe back in my kitchen to discover that it pairs magnificently with nori. Serve very small portions as this really is a rich offering.

Seaweed used: Nori
Serves 15 – 20

2 sheets nori, prepared as paste
225g (8oz) plain chocolate
115g (4oz) butter
125g (4½ oz) castor sugar
200g (7oz) ground almonds
4 eggs, separated

To prepare the nori

Soak nori sheets in tepid water for 5 – 10 minutes. Remove and squeeze out excess water with hand or a sieve. Tear and stir nori into a paste. Set aside.

Preheat the oven to 180°C/350°F/Gas 4

Line and grease the base of a spring form tin 7½" square or 22cm (8½") round

1. Break the chocolate into pieces and place in a bowl over a saucepan of gently simmering water. Allow to melt. Add the nori paste. Remove from heat and allow to cool slightly.
2. Put the butter and sugar into a large mixing bowl and beat until light and fluffy. Stir in the ground almonds, egg yolks and melted chocolate with nori paste.
3. Whisk the egg whites until stiff and fold into the butter, eggs and chocolate mixture.
4. Spoon into the prepared tin and bake for 50 – 55 minutes until firm to touch.
5. Remove from the oven, leave to settle for five minutes, then turn onto a wire rack to cool. The cake will sink slightly while cooling.

Topping

55g (2oz) butter
85g (3oz) plain chocolate
5 tablespoons lemon curd or favourite jam

To prepare the topping:

1. Melt butter and chocolate in the bowl placed over the saucepan of simmering water. Remove from heat and allow to cool slightly.
2. Spread the lemon curd over the cake followed by the runny chocolate butter topping. It doesn't matter if it runs down the sides in places.
3. Serve in small slices.

Elspeth Semple, historical researcher and writer.

moist triple ginger and guinness cake

This took a long time to get absolutely right. I was working from two incomplete recipes, one from Maura Waters, my mother in law, and one from a friend's grandmother. By version ten I was happy with it, and entered it in the local agricultural show where it received the ultimate stamp of approval in the form of first prize.

Seaweed used: Nori
Serves 8 – 10

***2 sheets nori** (8 – 10g), prepared as a paste*
130ml (4½ fl oz) warm water
225ml (8fl oz) Guinness stout
225ml (8fl oz) molasses
1½ teaspoons bread soda
3 large eggs, beaten
115g (4oz) granulated raw cane sugar
100g (3½oz) dark brown sugar
175ml (6¼fl oz) light olive oil or sunflower
1½ tablespoons ginger root, grated
215g (7½ oz) plain white flour or white spelt flour
1½ teaspoons baking powder
2 tablespoons ginger, ground
1 teaspoon ground cardamom (see note, page 156)
¾ teaspoon cinnamon, ground
¼ teaspoon cloves, ground
4 pieces crystalised ginger, sliced for decoration

To prepare the nori:

Soak nori sheets in tepid water for 5 – 10 minutes. Remove and squeeze out excess water with hand or using a sieve. Tear and stir nori into a paste. Set aside.

1 Pour the Guinness into a large saucepan, add the molasses and bring to the boil. Remove from heat.

2 Sprinkle in the bread soda. This will cause the mixture to foam up very high. Cover with a lid and set aside. Allow the mixture to cool and the foam to disappear. This can take up to half an hour.

3 Preheat oven to 180°C/350°F/Gas 4. Grease 22½x12½cm (9 x 5") loaf tin with greaseproof paper

4 Transfer the cooled Guinness, molasses and bread soda mixture to a large mixing bowl. Beat in the eggs, both types of sugar and the oil. Add the nori and freshly grated ginger.

5 Sieve the flour and baking powder into another bowl and add in the remaining dry spices. Add the dry ingredients to the wet mixture, a little at a time, mixing thoroughly.

6 Pour the cake mixture into prepared tin and bake for one hour. Don't open the oven during cooking as this will cause the cake to flatten completely.

7 Remove from the oven and leave to settle for 10 minutes. Remove from the tin and cool completely on a wire rack. Decorate with crystalised ginger.

8 Can be served warm or cold.

desserts and puddings

blueberry crisp rice cobbler

Blueberries are bursting with healthy goodness. I make this dessert from blueberries that we pick ourselves on Derrynavilla Blueberry Farm in Ireland and freeze for winter use.

For maximum benefit blueberries are best eaten uncooked, either just fresh or in smoothies from frozen, but they also make a great cooked dessert now and then.

Derrynavilla Blueberry farm won the Irish Food Writers' Guild Award in 2009 for their innovative Blueberry Tonic and Preserves.

Seaweed used: Nori
Serves 6

2 tablespoons ***nori,*** *flaked or finely ground, (see bookmark)*
125g (4¹/₂ oz) rice flakes
225ml (8fl oz) milk or rice milk
55g (2oz) butter, softened
80g (2³/₄ oz) plain flour
50g (1³/₄ oz) walnuts, chopped roughly
25g (1oz) flaked almonds
40g (1¹/₂ oz) ground almonds
¹/₂ teaspoon arrowroot
75g (2¹/₂ oz) brown sugar
2 teaspoons vanilla extract
¹/₄ teaspoon allspice
1 tablespoon lemon juice
250g (9oz) blueberries

1 Soak the rice flakes in a bowl in the milk or rice milk for about 30 minutes, until softened.

2 Preheat the oven to 190°C/375°F/Gas 5, and grease a 25 – 30cm (10" – 12") flan dish.

3 Rub the butter into the flour until the mixture resembles coarse breadcrumbs. Stir in walnuts, ground and flaked almonds, arrowroot and sugar and mix well.

4 Stir in the rice flakes, then add vanilla extract, allspice, nori and lemon juice and mix gently together.

5 Spoon half the mixture into the flan dish. Scatter the blueberries on top and spoon over the rest of the mixture. This keeps the blueberries from drying out during baking.

6 Bake in the oven for 20 minutes or until golden.

7 Serve with natural yogurt, custard (see recipe on page 215) or cream and fresh blueberries.

COOK'S TIP

This dish was also made with rice milk and spelt flour and worked very well. Blackcurrants can be used instead of blueberries.

brown bread and duileasc ice cream

Brown bread ice cream, properly made, is a great anytime treat, popular with young and old and a perfect finale for both winter and summer feasts. In this version which comes from Georgie, a colleague from my hospital days, the characteristic blend of smooth cream and slightly grainy breadcrumbs is given more texture with the addition of duileasc.

I use up to 40g (1½ oz) duileasc when cooking for my own family. Start with the lower amount in this recipe and see how your guests enjoy that before using larger amounts.

Seaweed used: Duileasc
Serves 6

15–20g (½ – ¾ oz) ***duileasc,*** *ground finely (see bookmark)*
20ml (1½ tablespoons) water
20g (¾ oz) brown sugar

For the caramelised brown breadcrumbs

115g (4oz) brown bread, crumbled roughly (a heavy brown bread works best)
50g (1¾ oz) brown sugar

For the ice cream

115g (4oz) meringues, or 8 half meringues
700ml (23½ fl oz) whipping cream
duileasc, prepared as instructed
caramelised breadcrumbs, prepared as instructed
100g (3½ oz) almonds, flaked and lightly toasted
25ml/1 shot of whiskey or brandy or Baileys (optional)

To prepare the duileasc

Place it in a small saucepan with the water and sugar. Cover with a lid and heat on a very low heat for 15 minutes or until the duileasc is soft and has absorbed the water. Leave to cool.

To prepare the caramelised breadcrumbs

Preheat oven to 180°C/350°F/Gas 4

1. Spread the breadcrumbs out on a baking tray and sprinkle with sugar.
2. Place in the oven for 10 to 15 minutes. Turn the crumbs over often until the sugar melts and caramelises, turning the mixture golden. Watch carefully, especially towards the end as the breadcrumbs can burn very quickly. The breadcrumbs can also be prepared under the grill or in a heavy–based pan.
3. Allow to cool, then crush with a rolling pin to make rough breadcrumbs.

To prepare the ice cream

1. Place the meringues in a plastic or brown paper bag and crush gently with a rolling pin.
2. Whip the cream until it forms soft peaks and fold in the meringues.
3. Fold in the prepared duileasc, caramalised breadcrumbs and almonds. Mix well together and add whiskey, brandy or Baileys if using.
4. Spoon the mixture into a glass freezer proof dish. Cover and place in freezer for 4 hours or until firm.
5. Remove the ice cream from the freezer 30 minutes before serving. Delicious with fresh fruit.

USING A CUSTARD TO MAKE THE ICE CREAM

Custard

1 vanilla pod, split, or 1 teaspoon vanilla extract
300ml (1/2 pint) milk
1 egg
3 egg yolks
75g (2 1/2 oz) icing sugar
1 teaspoon arrowroot
1 tablespoon brandy

***duileasc** prepared as for brown bread and duileasc ice cream (see recipe opposite)*

300ml (1/2 pint) whipping cream
caramelised brown bread prepared as for brown bread and duileasc ice cream (see recipe opposite)

COOK'S TIP

You can make a double duileasc ice cream by using breadcrumbs made from the duileasc brown bread (see recipe on page 188). For custard to accompany any other recipe omit seaweed and brandy.

To prepare the custard

1. Place the vanilla pod and seeds or vanilla extract into a saucepan and allow to infuse with the milk.
2. Whisk the egg, egg yolks and sugar in a large bowl until pale and smooth. Add the arrowroot to the egg mixture and combine well.
3. Heat the milk infused with vanilla to just below boiling point, and stirring with a wooden spoon, pour the hot milk into the egg mixture. Return the mixture to the saucepan and heat gently, stirring frequently, until it thickens and coats the back of a wooden spoon. Allow to cool.
4. Remove the vanilla pod. Don't throw it out as it can be used to make vanilla sugar by rinsing and drying it, then placing it in an airtight jar of castor sugar.
5. Stir in the brandy and prepared duileasc, and allow the mixture to go completely cold.

To prepare the ice cream

1. Whip the cream in a separate bowl until it forms soft peaks and fold into the cold custard.
2. Fold in the breadcrumbs and spoon the mixture into a glass freezer proof dish.
3. Cover and place in freezer for 4 hours or until firm.

御抹茶

green tea and nori ice cream
topped with melting sugar cinnamon rolled sea lettuce

I first encountered this interesting ice cream in Japan, and spent a long time trying to recreate it when I got home. Green tea powder, (yamakaen), gives a deep green colour and intense flavour, and is available from the Asian Market in Dublin, and from Asian stores worldwide. The sea lettuce garnish was added by Rathlin Islander Benji McFaul.

Prepared in advance and served in tall glasses, this elegant ice cream will bring any meal to a sophisticated close.

Seaweed used: Nori, sea lettuce
Serves: 6 – 8

Ice Cream

1 heaped tablespoon ***nori flakes,*** *(see bookmark) mixed with 2 – 3 tablespoons water*
1 Crunchie bar
125g (4½ oz) meringues
700ml (23½ fl oz) cream
1 heaped tablespoon good quality green tea powder
100g (3½ oz) flaked almonds
25ml (1fl oz) brandy, optional

1. Crush the Crunchie bar and meringues in a plastic or paper bag with a rolling pin to resemble breadcrumbs or crush between 2 sheets of greaseproof paper.
2. Whip the cream until it forms stiff peaks. Sprinkle the green tea powder over the cream and fold in gently. Add the meringues, nori and almonds and fold again. Add brandy if using.
3. Spoon the mixture into a glass freezer-proof dish.
4. Cover and place in freezer for 4 hours or until firm.

COOK'S TIP

Ice cream can be prepared in advance and stored for up to 6 months in the freezer.

Sea lettuce garnish

Sea lettuce garnish is on the menu of The Manor House, Rathlin Island – the only inhabited Island off Northern Ireland.

1 tablespoon fine sugar
½ teaspoon ground cinnamon
1 handful ***sea lettuce leaves,*** *washed and drained*
1 – 2 tablespoons olive oil

1. Place the sugar and cinnamon in a brown paper bag, shake to mix and set aside.
2. Dry the sea lettuce completely, by patting it dry with kitchen roll.
3. Heat the oil until hot in a pan, and shallow fry the sea lettuce leaves for a few seconds.
4. Drain on dry kitchen roll and using a kitchen tongs, toss the fried sea lettuce into the bag of prepared cinnamon sugar to coat.
5. Arrange over the ice cream and serve immediately. Melts in your mouth.

GREEN TEA FOR GOOD HEALTH

- Research has shown that because of its action on repositioning methyl groups in the body, green tea is very beneficial to health. The research looks very positive, specifically on the anti cancer properties of 2 cups of good quality green tea taken daily.

Born on a farm in Northern Ireland, Noel McMeel grew up appreciating the delicate balance between the turning seasons and the produce of the land. This became the cornerstone upon which his international career as a chef is built, and the fare from his kitchen is guaranteed to be creative, natural and in tune with local ingredients.

baked oat crumble

with bushmills whiskey and apple custard and a dulse* and yellaman ice cream

from Noel McMeel

Noel's contribution is firmly rooted in one of the great traditions of Northern Ireland; the Auld Lammas Fair, held the last Monday and Tuesday in August since 1608, in Ballycastle, Co. Antrim. Local produce, including dulse, has been on sale there for 4 centuries, and the fair itself, now a big event, is well documented in song and story.

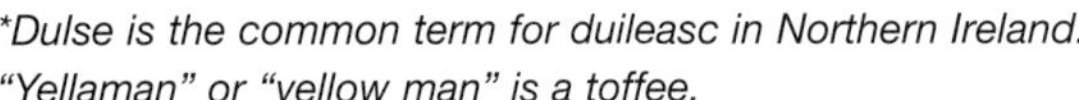

**Dulse is the common term for duileasc in Northern Ireland.*
"Yellaman" or "yellow man" is a toffee.

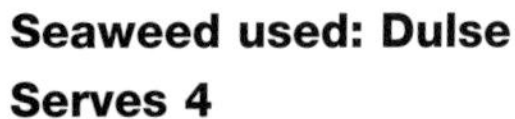

Seaweed used: Dulse
Serves 4

Apple Custard and Ice Cream
9 medium egg yolks
250g (9oz) castor sugar
1 vanilla pod, split lengthways
1 litre (1 3/4 pint) whipping cream
200g (7oz) bramley apple, diced
juice of 1/2 lemon
100ml (3 1/2 fl oz) Bushmills whiskey
100g (3 1/2 oz) yellaman
100g (3 1/2 oz) **dulse**

Crumble
100g (3 1/2 oz) plain flour
50g (1 3/4 oz) porridge oats
1 teaspoon ground **dulse**, *see bookmark*
75g (2 1/2 oz) salted butter
50g (1 3/4 oz) castor sugar

Tuile biscuit garnish
100g (3 1/2 oz) plain flour
100g (3 1/2 oz) icing sugar
1 egg white
100g (3 1/2 oz) melted butter at 37°C

Dulse garnish
8 pieces of **dulse**, *each 7.5 – 10cm (3 – 4 inches) long*
200g (7oz) sugar
1 tablespoon water

Yellaman
4 tablespoons butter
340g (12oz) brown sugar
4 tablespoons golden syrup
1 tablespoon water
1 teaspoon vinegar
2 teaspoons baking soda

Yellaman is thick and sweet,
And much tradition lies behind it;
For centuries at Lammas Fair
In Ballycastle, you would find it.

To make this toffee, first you melt
The butter in a heavy pan;
Add sugar, syrup, vinegar,
And start to boil your Yellaman.

Now put the baking soda in –
You'll find that it will foam and froth;
So take a spoon and rapidly
Keep stirring up the bubbling broth.

Now pour it in a well–greased tin;
Cool, then break in bits to eat.
You'll soon know why, at Lammas fair,
The Yellaman was such a treat.

To test it, take a spoonful up
And in cold water let it fall:
It's ready if the mixture turns
Into a crisp and brittle ball.

To prepare the custards and yellaman ice cream

1. Put the egg yolks and 200g (7oz) of the castor sugar in a bowl. Scrape the vanilla seeds from the pod, add them to the bowl, and mix together by hand with a whisk.
2. Add the vanilla pod to the cream and bring to the boil. Add to the egg mixture, remove vanilla pod and mix thoroughly.
3. Divide the custard into two halves. Cool one half rapidly over a bowl of ice, and chill in the fridge for 10 – 15 minutes.
4. Preheat the oven to 165°C/325°F/Gas 3.
5. Place the diced Bramley apple in a saucepan with the remaining castor sugar and the lemon juice. Poach gently for 3 to 4 minutes, then place in the bottom of four 12cm (5") moulds or cups.
6. Add the whiskey to the custard and mix, then pour the unchilled custard on top. Place in a deep pan, pour in warm water to come halfway up the sides of the moulds, then bake au bain marie for 30 minutes or until the custards are just set – they should wobble like a jelly when tapped. Remove from the oven, leave to cool, then put in the fridge. Keep the oven on.

To prepare the crumble

Put all the crumble ingredients into a food processor and blitz quickly. Spread out on a baking sheet and bake at the same temperature as the custards for 10 – 15 minutes until golden. Leave to cool.

To complete the ice cream

Mix the chilled custard and yellaman and chopped dulse, churn in an ice cream machine until thickened, then decant into a container and freeze.

To prepare the tuile biscuit garnish

1. Mix the flour and the sifted icing sugar together, add the egg white and beat to a smooth paste, then add the melted butter bit by bit and refrigerate for 20 minutes. Use as and when required.
2. Put teaspoons of the mixture onto a baking tray and bake for 5 – 10 minutes at 180°C/350°F/Gas 4 until golden at the edges.
3. Cool and keep in an airtight container. The uncooked mixture will keep for 1½ weeks in a fridge.

To prepare the dulse garnish

1. Put the sugar and water into a small saucepan and allow it to turn into a syrup over gentle heat. Increase the temperature and using a tongs immerse one to two of the dulse pieces in the syrup until crisped and sweetened.
2. Remove, and repeat until all the dulse is done.
3. Garnish each dessert with two pieces of dulse.
4. To serve, top the chilled whiskey custards with the crumble. Garnish with tuile biscuits, cracked yellaman dust, crisped dulse and yellaman ice cream.

banoffi pie on a nori walnut base

An old favourite with a new twist. Be sure to use sweetened condensed milk as unsweetened doesn't turn into toffee.

A feature of this interesting version of banoffi pie is the use of sweetened condensed milk to make a toffee sauce. The tin is boiled briskly for two hours. When it cools, you have toffee!

If you intend to make a lot of banoffi pie, then consider preparing a few tins together and storing them in a dry place. Once the condensed milk is ready, this impressive dessert is quickly prepared. It benefits from an hour or so in the fridge before serving.

Seaweed used: Nori Flakes
Serves 4 – 6

1 can sweetened condensed milk
225g (8oz) walnuts
*3 teaspoons **nori**, flaked or ground finely (see bookmark)*
1 tablespoon liquid such as pineapple juice may be required
675g (1½lb) firm bananas, 3 medium
juice of 1 lemon or 1 lime

Topping

550ml (22fl oz) whipping cream or custard
*½ teaspoon **nori flakes** or **finely ground nori***
chocolate, grated

Preparing the Toffee

Place the unopened can of sweetened condensed milk in a large saucepan of water. Make sure the top of the can is covered with water. Replace the lid. Bring to the boil and continue to boil briskly for 2 hours. Don't let water drop below top of can, check every ½ hour or so. The can may explode if the water level drops and the can dries out. Allow to go cold before opening. The heating process turns the condensed milk into toffee.

1 Crush the walnuts finely in a food processor and when completely crushed add 2 teaspoons of nori and pulse again. Add a tablespoon of liquid such as pineapple juice, if needed, to bring the mixture together. The nori and walnuts will stick together.

2 Using the back of a tablespoon, press the walnut and nori mixture into the base of a 22.5 – 24cm (9 – 10") lightly greased or lined loose bottomed tin or flan dish. Sprinkle base with remaining teaspoon of nori.

3 Open the can and spread the cold toffee made from condensed milk over the base, reserving a little. This can be difficult as the nori sticks to the toffee. Dot the toffee in spoonfuls and then join the dots with a knife. Refrigerate if making ahead of time.

4 When ready to serve, slice the bananas lengthways, squeeze lemon or lime juice over them to prevent them going black. Arrange the banana slices on the toffee. Drizzle the reserved toffee over the bananas.

5 Spread whipped cream or custard on top of the bananas.

6 Mix grated chocolate and toasted nori flakes together and sprinkle over top of pie.

Note from the test kitchen
Use a mix of walnut and biscuit/butter base for an interesting variation

---

COOK'S TIP

The walnut base is not as firm as the conventional biscuit and butter base used in the cheesecake recipe on page 239, but it is the healthier option and tastes great.

chocolate fudge pudding

This delicious pudding recipe which I got from Duigi Mercer, a teenage chef, withstood vigorous testing, and will perhaps encourage other young chefs to experiment with seaweed cooking.

Seaweed used: Nori
Serves 4 – 6

Pudding

150g (5oz) butter, softened
150g (5oz) plain white flour
1/2 teaspoon baking powder
1 tablespoon nori, ground
150g (5oz) runny honey
3 eggs, beaten
25g (1oz) chocolate powder

To prepare the pudding

1 Lightly grease a 1.2 litre (2 pints) pudding basin.

2 Place all the pudding ingredients in a mixing bowl and beat until well combined and smooth.

3 Spoon the mixture into the prepared basin and level the top with a spoon. Cover with a disc of greaseproof paper and tie with string. The pudding can be steamed with or without the lid of the bowl, but ideally use a lid.

4 Steam for 1 1/2 to 2 hours until the pudding is cooked. It will be springy to the touch.

Sauce

100g (3 1/2 oz) dark chocolate
125ml (4fl oz) sweetened condensed milk
a pinch of nori
4 tablespoons double cream

To prepare the sauce

1 Break the chocolate into small pieces and place in a small pan with the sweetened condensed milk. Heat gently and stir continuously until the chocolate melts.

2 Add the nori and stir well. Remove the pan from the heat and stir in the cream.

3 Serve immediately by turning the pudding onto a serving plate and pouring a little of the chocolate fudge sauce over it to coat lightly. The remaining sauce can be served separately.

COOK'S TIP

See instructions on how to steam a pudding on page 248.

chocolate fondant with nori

A sumptuous dessert, served with a scoop of ice cream to each diner is a perfect end to a meal. Dario moulds are small cylindrical metal or plastic moulds with slightly sloping sides, used for cooking puddings or to set desserts.

Seaweed used: Nori
Serves 8

*8g **nori flakes** or 2 sheets **nori***
butter for greasing
1 – 2 tablespoons cocoa powder
100g (3½ oz) chocolate, 70% cocoa solids
115g (4oz) butter, unsalted
2 whole eggs
2 egg yolks
60g (2¼ oz) castor sugar
7g (1 tablespoon) plain white flour
8 ovenproof Dario moulds of the size used for rum, baba, timbale or crème caramel, volume 100ml

---

COOK'S TIP

To be really sure that the fondants behave dramatically, spoon the mixture into the moulds until half full, place one large or two small dark or milk chocolate buttons in the centre and top up the mixture as before.
The chocolate will melt and is guaranteed to ooze out deliciously.

To prepare the nori

1. Place 2 nori sheets on a shallow dish and soak for 5 minutes in tepid water. Remove. Using your hands or a fine sieve squeeze out excess water. It is important that excess water is removed in this recipe, otherwise it will impair the final flavour.
2. Tear and mash into a paste. Set aside.

To prepare the fondant

Preheat oven to 180°C/350°F/Gas 4 and place a baking tray in the oven to heat. Grease 8 moulds with butter and dust lightly with cocoa powder.

1. Break the chocolate into a bowl and add the butter. Stand the bowl over a saucepan of barely simmering water and heat gently until melted. Don't let the water touch the bowl. Add the nori paste to the chocolate and mix gently. Leave on a very low heat.
2. Whisk the eggs, yolks and sugar in a large bowl until thick and pale. Whisk in half the chocolate nori mixture and continue whisking for one minute. Add the remainder and whisk again.
3. Fold the flour in gently. The mixture can be refrigerated at this point until ready to use.
4. Spoon the mixture into the prepared moulds, up to ⅞ full, place on heated baking tray and bake in centre of oven for 15 minutes until the tops are springy. (If you have made this ahead of time and placed it in fridge you will need to increase the cooking time to 20 minutes.)
5. Remove from the oven and tip the cooked fondant out of the Dario mould onto a serving plate and serve immediately with a scoop of brown bread ice cream or cream and a few raspberries scattered on the side if in season. If cooked properly each mould will ooze some molten lava chocolate with nori from the centre.

gooseberry cobbler tart

Grit Glass is a great baker and has a magic way with gooseberries. When choosing fruit for this dessert, choose the big red cooking berries, soft to the touch, the kind that come into their own around mid July. The dessert cooks slowly, and needs about 2 hours after cooking for the flavours to settle. Perfect for a lazy summer's day, when you can let the slow cooking scent of a garden fruit tart waft through your house, promising a treat to come.

Seaweed used: Sugar kelp, sea spaghetti, Alaria or nori Serves 10 – 12

Custard Topping

900ml (1 1/2 pints) milk
50g (1 3/4 oz) dark Demerara sugar
65g (2 1/4 oz) custard powder
5 eggs
2 teaspoons vanilla extract
25g (1oz) ***ground sugar kelp,*** *or a mix of* ***ground sea spaghetti*** *and* ***Alaria*** *or* ***nori***
800g (1lb 12oz) gooseberries, topped and tailed, fresh or frozen. If frozen remove from freezer at least 30 – 60 minutes before using
a little extra sugar to sprinkle

1 Prepare the custard topping first, as it needs time to cool. Heat 700ml (23 1/2 fl oz) milk in a medium saucepan.

2 In a jug, mix the sugar and custard powder into the remaining 200ml of cold milk.

3 Stir the cold mixture into hot milk, stirring continuously until the mixture thickens to a custard.

4 Remove from the heat and allow to cool down. Whisk in the eggs one at a time, add vanilla and seaweeds and stir.

COOK'S TIP

Placing the dish on a warmed baking sheet helps to cook the pastry in the bottom of the tin properly and evenly.

Dough

250g (9oz) soft butter
20g (3/4 oz) dark Demerara sugar
5g (2 teaspoons) dried yeast
300g (10oz) flour

To prepare the dough

Preheat the oven to 160°C/325°F/Gas 3 and place a baking sheet in the oven to heat.
Oil a tin, 28 x 35cm (11" x 14")

1 Cream the butter and sugar in a bowl.

2 Add the yeast, then sift the flour into the mixture – a little at a time and knead the dough.

3 Take two thirds of the dough and using fingers, spread it to about 5mm (1/4 inch) thickness, to cover the base of the tin. Prick the dough lightly several times with a fork and set aside in a warm place to rise for 20 minutes. Place the gooseberries on top.

4 Pour the custard mix over the gooseberries, then dot the remaining third of the dough over the gooseberries and custard by taking little pieces of dough, flattening them in your hand and placing them decoratively on top. The fruit will peep through the spaces. Sprinkle with Demerara sugar and place on the preheated baking tin, in the centre of the oven.

5 Bake for about 1 hour. Check the baking progress after 20 – 30 minutes. If the dough is baking too fast and likely to burn, cover the dish with tinfoil and continue to bake for the remaining 30 – 40 minutes, remembering to remove the foil during the final 10 – 15 minutes of baking time. Otherwise, leave in the oven uncovered for the 30 – 40 minutes, or until dough is golden and gooseberries bubbling. Allow to settle down for 1 – 2 hours. Serve with a little ice cream.

memories of carraigín

***Chondrus crispus* and *mastocarpus stellatus.* Also known as carrageen moss, carragheen, carraigín, Irish moss, jelly moss, cosainin carriage, mousse d'Irlande. *Mastocarpus stellatus* is also known as cluimhin chait**

"The name 'carrageen' was introduced around 1830 and probably came from Carrigan Head in Co. Donegal in north–western Ireland. 'Carrigan' or 'carrageen' is a common name throughout Ireland. There does not appear to be a standardised spelling."

PROFESSOR MIKE GUIRY

Looking North West from our house across Donegal Bay we can see the sheer 595 metre cliffs of Slieve League, at the bottom of which lies Carrigan Head, Ceann an Charraigín.

Carraigín means 'little rock', a description that aptly sums up the steadfast and unshakable position this delicate sea plant has traditionally held in Ireland for many generations. Prepared in kitchens throughout the country to relieve sore throats, coughs, colds and chest problems, it was an equally valuable source of finance to coastal dwellers, who harvested feverishly during the equinox spring tides, so the crop could be spread to dry and bleach in the March winds and rain and be ready for sale a few weeks later.

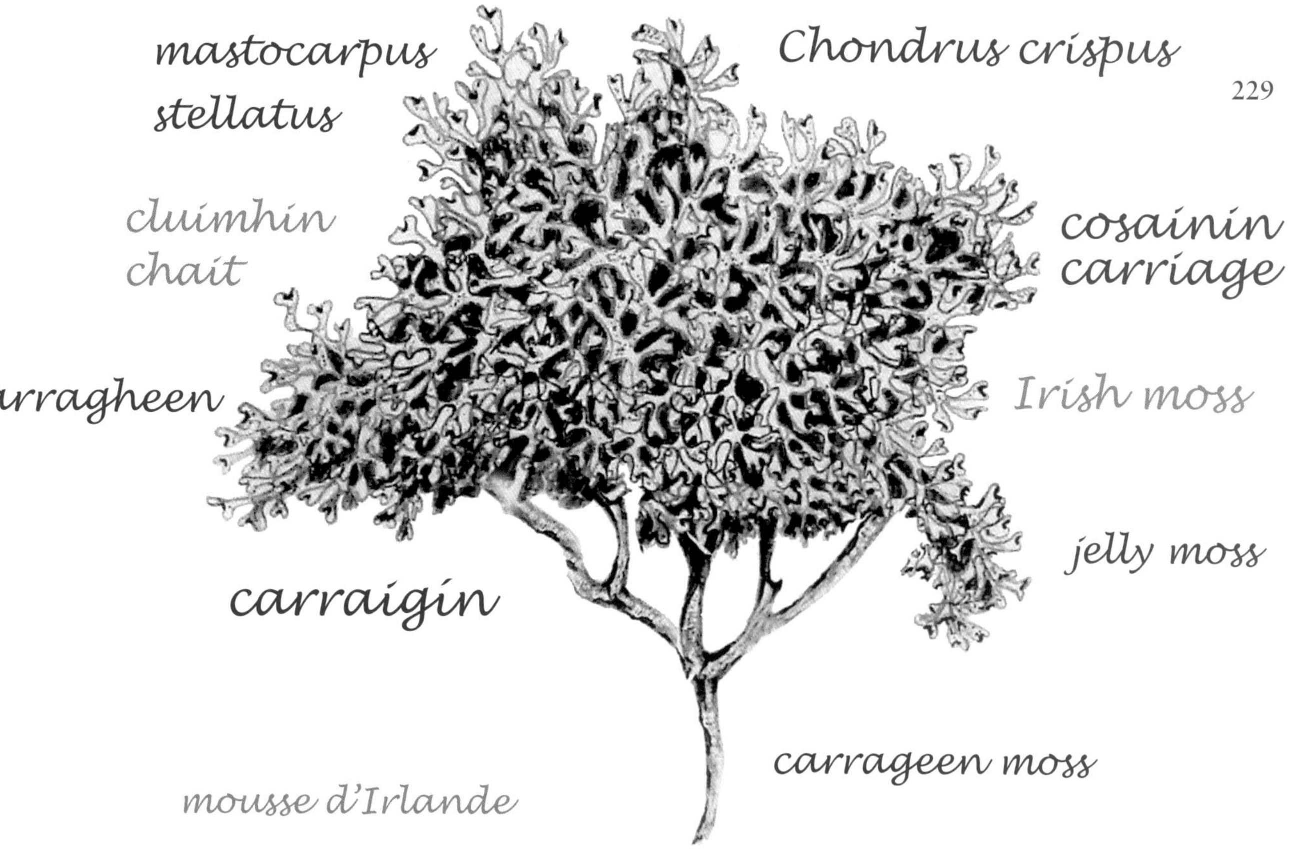

Caoilte Breatnach, writing about folklore from Kinvara, Co. Galway, reports that carraigín was 'plucked', (never picked) and sold in Galway for six pennies a stone. Dangerous work, the harvesters sometimes risked getting cut off by incoming tides as they plucked the plant off the rocks and into sacks as quickly as possible, often damaging their hands in the process. The main buyers were French cosmetic and pharmaceutical firms who used the carraigín for gels and cough mixtures, and London breweries that used it to purify beer.

In certain parts of Donegal, washed boiled carraigín, known for its nutritious qualities was fed to calves during lean times to supplement their diets, and during the years of the great potato famine, 1846–49, carraigín is said to be one of the three plants that kept many from total starvation, the other two being charlock and nettle. Traditionally it was also used for the treatment of burns where it was boiled, stored in a cold place and applied to the affected area when needed, according to **Peggy Hughes** from Carrickfergus.

Máirín Uí Chomáin who has an oyster recipe on page 154 and is a fluent Irish speaker, has demonstrated the traditional way of making carraigín pudding on TV. She makes a collar of greaseproof paper around the top of the bowl which when removed allows the pudding to sit a few inches above the top of the bowl. She always decorates with a little candied angelica on top.

These days, carraigín is as popular as ever, and current research tells us that the old folk were correct in their assessment of its healing properties; it is both antiviral and an expectorant (helps expel phlegm) and was the seaweed of choice to hasten recovery from chest infections. Boiling carraigín in the presence of acid alters its structure and there is debate among scientists as to the health effects of consuming carraigín that has been altered in this way.

After much scientific scrutiny, regulatory agencies worldwide suggest the extract of carraigín is safe. To remain updated on the subject there are several ongoing publications available for review such as: the reports of the Joint Food and Agriculture Organization / World Health Organisation Expert Committee on Food Additives, reviews by Cohen and Ito, Weiner and Burges – Watson and the documented research carried out by Tobacman. They all offer interesting opinions on the debate. Until the studies can prove conclusively either way, it is advisable to add any acidic ingredients like lemon after boiling and when the carraigín has cooled somewhat.

Instinctively, our ancestors got this right too, as the old recipes all cite adding lemon only when the boiled carraigín had cooled ... I recommend carraigín for medicinal purposes and as an occasional sweet treat.

Food writer **Lucy Madden** from Hilton Park, Co Monaghan author of *The Potato Year: 365 Ways of Cooking Potatoes*, has a favourite cough remedy recipe given to her by **Kevin** and **Mary Rickard** of Clew Bay, Co. Mayo:

1 loosely filled pint glass of ***dried carrageen moss,*** *soaked in water for about 6 hours.*
900ml (1 1/2 pint) milk
300ml (1/2 pint) water
2 tablespoons of sugar
juice of a lemon
1/2 – 1 teaspoon vanilla extract, optional

1 Place the carrageen in a saucepan. Cover with 600ml (1 pint) milk and all the soak water. Bring to the boil and simmer for 10 minutes.

2 Put the mixture through a strainer, making sure that you get all the thickened liquid by scraping the bottom of the strainer with a spoon. Discard the contents of the strainer. Allow to cool slightly.

3 Add the sugar, the remainder of the milk, the lemon juice and the vanilla if using. Decant into little serving bowls and chill in the fridge – this will make enough for a week by eating one a day until the chest is clear.

There was always a paper bag of carraigín moss in our kitchen press. When the west of Ireland winter brought its coughs and colds, my mother made us caraigin puddings with skimmed milk, a little honey, rum, raisins and chocolate powder or vanilla in a visionary effort at producing a palatable healthy treat. I

never liked the consistency, but her flavours were great. I remember it being very wobbly and there were little pools of liquid in the dish as you got near the end.

Mary Sexton from Mullaghmore, Co Clare swears by her cough mixture recipe which she got from the local priest **Fr. Clancy.** Her version has ginger; another tribute to the wisdom of folk medicine, ginger having anti inflammatory properties. The recipe also includes local honey, glycerine and a drop of rum or brandy.

Like the Irish themselves, caraigin has travelled, and become integrated into the folk medicines of other countries. Several recipes abound, especially on coastal areas, like Prince Edward Island, Canada, where the carraigín is called 'Irish Moss' It was even exported as far as New Zealand for making the famous Bonnington's Irish Moss cough mixture.

While visiting Prince Edward Island I was treated to a Jamaican cocktail of what they call 'Irish Moss'. This is actually a different seaweed which they believe to have aphrodisiac properties. I also met the women who run the 'Seaweed Pie Café' and Irish Moss Interpretive Centre and who use freshly harvested carraigín moss to make their sweet pies.

At the Scituate Maritime and Irish Mossing Museum just outside Boston, the story is told of how Daniel Ward, an immigrant from Derry in the 1820s, recognised the carrageen moss growing off the coast as a potential source of income for the then terribly poor Irish community. So the tale goes, with a lucky find of gold from one of the many shipwrecks off the coast, Daniel purchased the moss dories, creels, rakes and other equipment that started up the profitable Irish moss industry in north America.

There is less 'mossing' in Scituate these days, but interest in the whole plant was revived by a company in Halifax, Nova Scotia, who grow naturally coloured Irish moss and export it to Japan where it is eaten as a salad.

As carraigín transcends centuries and is so steeped in folklore and memories it is fitting that some of the most respected chefs in Ireland keep it firmly in their repertoire as a special treat on their desserts trolley.

carrageen moss pudding

from Myrtle Allen

'Carrageen did not grow on the shores of Cork Harbour where I grew up, but when I married, I moved close to the East Cork coastline. All along here, people used it and treasured it for its properties. They picked it on the rocks at low tide, dried and bleached it on the short grass on the cliff tops and stored it in jute sacks to be used daily until the next summer came. It was good for sick calves, sore throats and keeping cancer away, they said. I weaned my babies onto it and made it into delicious puddings.

'Ballyandreen Bay was the place to get carrageen. There, Dinny Hasset always had some to sell to me. When he grew too old to go down on the rocks, I found Annie Dawe. Hers was always the best. She had her secret places to pick and to bleach. She calls the best variety 'the gentleman' which I think is *Chondrus Crispus* and the coarser one 'the lady' which I believe to be *Mastocarpus stellatus*. Annie doesn't pick now but I still have her carrageen.'

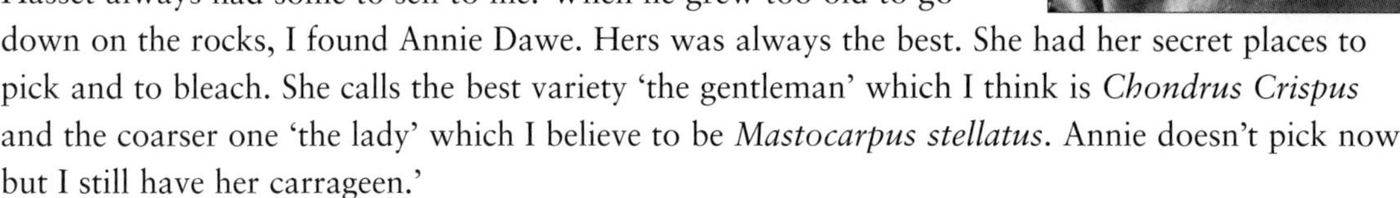

Part of every Irish recipe repertoire from the time of our Grandmothers and beyond; this version comes from the hallowed kitchens of Ballymaloe House, Co. Cork, Ireland.

'The gentleman.'

Seaweed used: Carrageen moss
Serves 6

3.5 – 4.5g carrageen moss, depending on variety (Myrtle suggests using 3.5g of the finer variety of carrageen moss, or 4.5g of the thicker one)
850ml (1½ pint) milk
½ teaspoon vanilla essence or vanilla pod
50g (1½ oz) sugar
1 egg, separated

1. Soak the carrageen in cold water for 10 minutes, then remove and put in a saucepan with milk and a vanilla pod, if using.
2. Bring to the boil and simmer very gently for 15 minutes, semi–covered, taking care that it does not boil over.
3. The carrageen will now be swollen and exuding jelly.
4. Pour through a strainer into a mixing bowl.
5. Rub the jelly through a strainer and beat it into the milk with the sugar, egg yolk and vanilla essence, if using.
6. Whisk egg white stiffly and fold it gently into the mixture; it will rise to make a fluffy top. Transfer to serving bowl.
7. Serve chilled with a fruit compote, or a sweet sauce.

lemony carrageen moss pots

from Clodagh McKenna

'You can buy carageen dried, in health food stores. This recipe is so light and delicious that it's perfect after a heavy dinner.'

Seaweed used: Carrageen
Serves 6

8g (1/4 oz) ***carrageen moss***
700ml (1 1/4 pints) milk
4 tablespoons castor sugar
6 lemon balm leaves, or
the grated zest of 3 lemons
1 vanilla pod
2 eggs, separated
extra ***carrageen*** *to decorate*

1 Soak the carrageen in lukewarm water for 15 minutes.

2 Drain and place in a saucepan with the milk, 1 tablespoon of sugar, lemon balm and vanilla pod.

3 Bring to the boil, then reduce the heat and simmer for 30 minutes.

4 Strain the liquid through a sieve into a bowl, pushing the natural gelling material from the carrageen moss through the sieve.

5 Put the egg yolks in a bowl and beat in the remaining 3 tablespoons of sugar. Whisk in the strained milk mixture.

6 Whisk the egg whites until they form stiff peaks. Fold them into the mixture with a metal spoon. Use a figure of eight movement to get rid of any blobs of egg white.

7 Fill 6 little pots with the mixture and chill in the fridge for about 1 hour or until set.

8 Serve decorated with tiny sprigs of carrageen moss.

Clodagh McKenna, chef and media presenter, is the author of *The Irish Farmers' Market Cookbook* and *Fresh from the Sea*.

www.clodaghmckenna.com

nut and apple carraigín mousse

Vegan chef, Mike Harris cooked this surprise dish for a Community Food Project Harvest celebration. He used agar to set the original recipe and was curious to know how I would use carraigín as the setting gel. Here are both recipes, one using agar and one with carraigín. This will allow you to convert any agar recipe to carraigín using these recipes as guidelines.

It is a great autumn recipe when the windfalls are plentiful.

Mike previously ran the award winning Heather's restaurant in London.

THE RECIPE WITH AGAR
Serves 6 – 8

450g (1lb) Bramley apples
285ml (10fl oz) water
115g (4oz) raw cane sugar
2 heaped teaspoons ***agar agar flakes***
juice of 1 lemon
85g (3oz) cashews, or nuts of choice, ground roughly

A note on proportions

1 tablespoon of agar flakes = 1 teaspoon of agar powder. This amount will set 250ml (8.5fl oz) of liquid. Acidic fruits need more and some fruits such as pineapple and mangoes need to be cooked or they won't set.

1. Peel, core and slice the apples, place in a saucepan and cook in just enough water to cover them.
2. When tender, add the sugar and the remainder of the water and bring to the boil.
3. Sprinkle the agar on top and cook for 1 minute. Pour into the liquidiser, add lemon and cashews and blend thoroughly.
4. Pour into ramekin dishes, allow to cool, then refrigerate for 30 minutes.

THE RECIPE WITH CARRAIGÍN
Serves 6 – 8

25g (1oz) ***carraigín***
500ml (17½fl oz) water
100 – 115g (3½ – 4oz) raw cane sugar
100ml (3½fl oz) water
450g (1lb) cooking apples
Juice of 1 lemon
85g (3oz) cashews or nuts of choice, ground roughly

1. Wash the carraigín under a running tap and soak for 10 minutes in cold water. Remove and check for shells. Place the carraigín into a saucepan with 500ml of water, bring to the boil, then simmer gently for 30 to 40 minutes until well softened. Stir occasionally to avoid sticking. It will practically melt down. Strain off the liquid, pushing the last bit through the sieve. It will measure about 200ml (7fl oz).
2. Place the sugar, 100ml (3½ fl oz) water and apples in a saucepan and stew to soften.
3. Mix the remaining ingredients plus stewed apples in the liquidiser.
4. Pour into ramekin dishes, cool, and refrigerate for 30 minutes. Serve with ice cream or cream.

Cook's Tip
Toasted almonds worked really well in the test kitchen too as an alternative.

carrageen, honey and yoghurt panna cotta
with fresh figs in port
from Denis Cotter

Café Paradiso is a unique and critically acclaimed vegetarian restaurant in Cork city. Opened in 1993, their cooking has evolved into a unique and personal style over the years, resulting in the publication of three celebrated and award winning cookbooks.

This style has been strongly influenced by the producers of local vegetables and cheeses. Café Paradiso was listed in the Bridgestone Guide's 100 Best Restaurants from its first year and holds the guidebook's highest 'icon' status.

Seaweed used: Carrageen
Serves 6

500ml (17½fl oz) cream
1 vanilla pod, split
150g (5oz) runny honey
200g (7oz) sheep's' milk yoghurt
500ml (17½fl oz) milk
1g (few sprigs) of carrageen, rinsed
extra honey, to serve

1 Place the cream, vanilla, honey and yoghurt in a pan and bring slowly to a boil, then remove from the heat.

2 In another pan, bring the milk and carrageen to a boil and simmer very gently until the milk becomes slightly viscous, about 7 – 9 minutes. It is important that the milk is not allowed to become too thick at this stage, so as to avoid setting the panna cotta too firmly.

3 Combine the liquids and pass through a fine sieve three times to remove all the carrageen.

4 Lightly butter six dario moulds and place a piece of parchment in the bottom of each. Fill the moulds and chill for 8 hours.

FIGS IN PORT

1 orange
200ml (7fl oz) port
175g (6oz) sugar
1 cinnamon stick
6 – 12 figs, fresh

1 Peel the rind from the orange in large strips. Put these in a pan with the port, sugar and cinnamon. Bring to a boil and simmer for 15 minutes. Leave to cool to room temperature.

2 Quarter the figs, put them in the syrup and leave for 15 minutes.

3 To serve: Carefully unmould the panna cotta and place each one on a plate. Drizzle a little honey over. Arrange some figs around the panna cotta and pour some of the syrup over them.

baked pears with green tea and sugar kelp

A somewhat sophisticated dessert made with very little effort and simple ingredients that give a perfect result every time.

Allow the oven to do the work, then sit back and enjoy the compliments.

Serve with a dollop of mascarpone cheese.

Seaweed used: Sugar kelp
Serves 4

25ml (1fl oz) pear concentrate plus extra for drizzling
175ml (6 1/4 fl oz) green tea
1x10 – 15cm (1 x 4 – 5 inch) piece dried sugar kelp, snipped into 2.5cm (1 inch) pieces
4 firm pears
1 tub mascarpone cheese

Preheat oven to 180°C/350°F/Gas 4

1 Mix measured pear concentrate into tea and pour mixture into an ovenproof dish. Add sugar kelp and stir. Core the pears and place upright in the dish. The pears should be fitted snugly together.

2 Drizzle some concentrate over the pears and bake in the oven for 50 – 60 minutes. The pears are ready when the point of a sharp knife slides into the fruit without pressure.

3 Remove the pears to a serving dish, add a dollop of mascarpone and spoon over cooking juices.

Sugar kelp, known as 'sweeties', was used by the children in the Scottish Hebrides Islands in former times, who sucked it for its sugary/salty taste.

baked lemon cheese cake with nori

Cheese cake is one of the great favourites when it comes to desserts, and this version is no exception. With its traditional crunchy base and creamy topping this dessert is colourful, delicious and can be very quickly prepared. The seaweed gives a firm texture and the seaweed and lemon combination is both perfectly complementary and offers a great depth of flavour.

Seaweed used: Nori, flaked or ground
Serves 6

Base

85g (3oz) butter, melted
225g (8oz) digestive biscuits, crushed by hand or food processor into crumbs
*1 teaspoon **nori**, flakes or finely ground (see bookmark)*

Filling

85g (3oz) castor sugar
2 eggs, beaten
zest of 1 organic lemon
juice of 1/2 – 1 lemon
1/2 teaspoon nori, ground
500 (1lb 2oz) full fat cream cheese

COOK'S TIP

Filo pastry also works well as a base. Follow packet instructions and sprinkle nori between buttered layers of filo.

Preheat oven to 175°C/350°F/Gas 4

To prepare the base

1. Melt the butter in a saucepan. Add the biscuit crumb and nori and combine.
2. Using the back of a tablespoon, press the mixture into the base of a 22.5cm (9") buttered loose bottomed tin.

To prepare the filling:

1. Beat the sugar and eggs together until pale and thick.
2. Whisk in the lemon zest, lemon juice, ground nori and cream cheese. Use a hand whisk or beat with wooden spoon until smooth.
3. Pour the mixture over biscuit base and bake in the centre of oven for 30 minutes.
4. Remove from the oven – the cheesecake centre will shake slightly. Run a round bladed knife around the edge of tin to loosen cheesecake – this will prevent it cracking when cooling.
5. Allow to cool in the tin on a wire rack. When cooled, remove the sides of tin and refrigerate. Decorate with lemon slices or dark chocolate curls.

chocolate molasses meringues

I have always had a horror of making meringues because of the amount of sugar required and wondered what a 'healthier' version of chocolate meringues using seaweed and molasses sugar would be like.

The result is delicious and won't harm your immune system too much. Of course you can undo the good work, add a dollop of cream, and treat yourself to the perfect meringue... And don't forget to serve with a dark chocolate sauce!

Seaweed used: Nori
Serves 4 – 6

4 large egg whites
40g (1½ oz) molasses sugar
40g (1½ oz) brown sugar
135g (4¾ oz) castor sugar
*10g (4½ tablespoons) **nori**, ground (see bookmark)*
10g cocao powder
1 teaspoon dark chocolate, grated finely

Preheat oven to 150°C/300°F/Gas 2.
Line two baking sheets with tinfoil.

1. Whisk the egg whites to soft peaks. Mix the sugars together and ensure all lumps are broken down. Add 2 tablespoons at a time to the egg whites, beating well after each addition, until the sugar dissolves and the whites stand stiff.
2. Fold in the seaweed, cocao and then chocolate using a metal spatula. Drop one heaped tablespoon of the mixture onto prepared baking sheets to form 2cm (¾ inch) mounds. Space the mounds roughly 5–10cm (1 – 2 inches) apart. Shape into nests with a spoon.
3. Place in the oven and bake for 1¾ hours. Turn off the oven and allow to go cold.
4. Remove, cool completely and store in an airtight tin.
5. Serve with summer berries and your favourite chocolate sauce.

sweet flaked millet and duileasc pudding

This is a nourishing, old fashioned pudding that can be eaten for breakfast instead of porridge. It's equally good as a filling dessert after a light supper.

Millet is a very nourishing food which is easy on the digestive system. Apples can be substituted for pears as a variation.

For this recipe, either millet flakes or whole grain millet can be used equally successfully.

If you are making the sushi dessert however, use whole grain millet for best results.

Seaweed used: Duileasc
Serves 6

750ml (1¼ pint) rice milk or milk
1 teaspoon arrowroot or double this amount if using whole millet
150g (5oz) millet flakes or 200g (7oz) whole millet, well rinsed and drained
1 tablespoon molasses
8g (¼ oz) ***duileasc,*** *snipped very finely*
25g (1oz) raisins
1 teaspoon coriander seed, ground
2 firm pears peeled, cored and chopped roughly 280g weight when cored
zest of 2 organic lemons

1 Blend the milk and arrowroot together in a saucepan. Add the millet and heat gently to bring to a boil.

2 Stir in the molasses, duileasc, raisins and coriander. Add the pears now if using millet flakes as they cook faster than whole millet. If using whole millet add the pears 10 minutes before the end of the cooking time, and bring back to a simmer. Stir in the lemon zest close to the end of the cooking time in both cases.

3 Cover the pan and simmer gently for 15 minutes if using millet flakes or 50 minutes if using whole millet, until cooked. Fluff gently with a fork and allow to stand, covered for 10 minutes to absorb all the flavours.

4 Serve with a blob of blueberry jam or natural yogurt.

sushi dessert

using sweet wholegrain millet with duileasc, raspberry jam, chocolate drops and cream

My daughter Kate put this together as a hungry six year old and it has become a firm favourite with family and friends alike.

Seaweed used: Nori
Serves 8

wholegrain millet
4 – 8 sheets nori
chocolate drops
raspberry jam
dollop of cream
allow half a nori roll per person or if rolling into a cone shape use less filling and allow 1 cone per person

1. Prepare Sweet Millet Pudding with duileasc using whole grain millet as described opposite. This takes about 50 minutes.
2. Place 2 nori sheets into the oven or under a grill for 30 seconds or so, turning often if using grill. Be careful not to burn it. Nori should still be green in colour when toasted.
3. Quickly spread the hot millet dessert on the sheet and sprinkle with chocolate drops. Add a little jam and a dollop of cream if you are feeling decadent.
4. Roll up as for sushi but leave it quite loose or roll into a cone shape. The chocolate drops will melt into the millet.
5. Eat hot.

winter solstice fruit salad
with kirsched sea spaghetti

My mother and I concocted this salad to bring a breath of summer to the table when the December days are at their shortest and the trees and bushes are bare.

The summer garden fruit stores well in the freezer, and responds well to overnight soaking in the luxurious mix of cherry brandy and syrup. Kirsch or maraschino cherry brandy works best.

The addition of brandied sea spaghetti, marinated overnight, adds an exotic touch to this ultimate slow food fruit salad.

Seaweed used: Sea spaghetti
Serves 6 – 8

Kirsched sea spaghetti

20g (3/4 oz) ***dried sea spaghetti****, rinsed in cold water and snipped into 2.5cm (1 inch) pieces*
100ml (3 1/2 fl oz) of water
1 teaspoon honey
dash of kirsch or cherry brandy
dash of raspberry syrup

Fruit salad

200g (7 oz) dried figs or prunes or a mix of both
200g (7oz) unsulphured apricots
55g (2oz) good quality sultanas
300ml (1/2 pint) green tea
a squeeze of lemon juice,
a generous dash of pineapple juice,
1 teaspoon dark molasses sugar or honey
A good dash of Kirsch or cherry brandy
raspberry syrup, optional
2 handfuls frozen summer fruits: a mix of gooseberries, blackcurrants and raspberries
1/4 stick cinnamon
1 medium sized tin of sliced peaches,

To prepare and leave overnight

1 Soak the sea spaghetti in the water, honey, kirsch or cherry brandy and syrup and leave overnight on top of a cool range, or in a cool oven, 40°C/150°F.

2 Soak the prunes, apricots and sultanas in green tea, lemon juice, pineapple juice, honey, kirsch and raspberry syrup if using.

3 Defrost the frozen summer fruits at room temperature, overnight if possible.

Next day

4 Simmer the dried fruits and defrosted summer fruit, except the raspberries, gently together in the soak liquid with 1/4 stick cinnamon for 20 – 30 minutes or until the gooseberries or other hard fruits are cooked.

5 Add the prepared brandied sea spaghetti, remove from the heat and allow to cool a little.

6 Transfer to a large serving dish and add the raspberries, the sliced tinned peaches, and the peach juice. Mix all together gently. Taste and add honey if necessary. Add kirsch to taste and serve at room temperature.

Serve with a dollop of mascarpone cheese, custard, crème fraîche or millet and dulse pudding.

sticky figgy pudding with brandied Alaria

This wonderful pudding retains the richness of an old fashioned winter treat – the brandied Alaria and praline topping making it a dessert fit to grace the most discerning of Christmas tables. Do go to the bother of making the topping as it makes it extra special.

Seaweed used: Alaria
Serves 4 – 6

Brandied Alaria:
25g (1oz) ***dried Alaria,***
25ml (1fl oz) brandy
25ml (1fl oz) water

To prepare the brandied Alaria: (left overnight)
Using scissors, snip the dried Alaria into 5mm ($^1/_4$ inch) pieces and place in a bowl. Add the brandy and water and soak overnight.

Pudding

225g (8oz) dried figs, sliced finely
115g (4oz) walnuts, chopped
1 carrot, grated
1 eating apple, grated
115g (4oz) butter
1 tablespoon molasses
1 tablespoon runny honey
85g (3oz) molasses sugar or dark sugar
175g (6oz) plain flour
2 teaspoon baking powder
$^1/_2$ teaspoon bread soda
2 eggs

To prepare the pudding

1. Grease a 1.5 litre (2$^1/_2$ pint) pudding basin. If steaming in an oven, preheat to 180°C/350°F/Gas 4
2. Combine the brandied Alaria, figs, walnuts, carrot and apple in a large mixing bowl and set aside.
3. Melt the butter with the molasses, honey and sugar in a small saucepan and set aside to cool. Meanwhile mix the flour with the baking powder and bread soda.
4. Tip the slightly cooled butter and sugar mixture into the mixing bowl with the fruit and walnuts. Mix to combine, and beat the eggs in one at a time.
5. Add the flour, a little at a time until very well combined, then tip into the prepared pudding basin. Secure the lid snugly using a layer of greaseproof paper if necessary.
6. To steam: Place the pudding basin on an upturned ovenproof saucer in the bottom of a large saucepan. Add enough boiling water to come two–thirds of the way up the basin. Simmer for 2 hours, either in the oven or on the stove. Top up with water as necessary.
7. Serve the pudding by turning out onto a flat plate.

Praline Sauce
115g (4oz) molasses sugar
55g (2oz) walnuts
115g (4oz) butter
a generous dash of cream

To prepare the praline sauce

1. Melt the sugar in a saucepan over medium heat.
2. Add the walnuts and swirl around in the sugar until coated, taking care not to burn the mixture.
3. Lift out the coated walnuts with a slotted spoon and place onto greaseproof paper. Allow to harden into praline.
4. When the mixture has cooled, fold the greaseproof paper over the praline and break it up with a wooden rolling pin.
5. Melt the butter with the sugar still remaining in the saucepan, add the cream and simmer until it forms a toffee sauce.
6. Spoon the sauce over the pudding and add the crushed walnut praline. Best served piping hot.

christmas puddings with brandied sea spaghetti

My sister Margaret is queen of the puddings. She has it down to such a fine art that we now just wait with anticipation for the moment when she hands them out.

To be honest I was never a Christmas pudding fan but hers are light, totally exotic, and definitely worth the effort. This Christmas pudding, in addition to an array of succulent fruit, also contains brandied sea spaghetti, which must be prepared a day in advance and left overnight in a warm place, such as the hot press.

Seaweed used: Sea spaghetti Serves 6 – 8

Brandied sea spaghetti: (left overnight)

20g (¾ oz) ***sea spaghetti****, rinsed in cold water and chopped into 5mm (¼ inch) pieces*
100ml (3½ fl oz) boiling water
1 generous teaspoon of honey
a good dash of brandy

Pudding

1.8kg (4lb) pudding bowls x 2
Enough greaseproof paper and tinfoil to cover the mouth of each bowl, leaving a 2.5cm (1 inch) overlap

450g (1lb) butter
225g (8oz) soft brown sugar
450g (1lb) raisins
450g (1lb) sultanas
225g (8oz) glace cherries
450g (1lb) dried fruit, any combination, see dried fruit suggestion below
juice of 1 lemon
225g (8oz) mixed nuts, almonds, pecans, walnuts
115g (4oz) crystallized ginger
1 teaspoon allspice
1 teaspoon ground cloves
225g (8oz) breadcrumbs
About 225ml (1 cup) of alcohol, brandy or whiskey, grappa or any good spirit. Not wine or beer
225g (8oz) plain flour
6 eggs
1 large carrot, grated

Dried fruit suggestion

85g (3oz) sour morello cherries
55g (2oz) baby figs, chopped
85g (3oz) dried pears
85g (3oz) dried cranberries
85g (3oz) dried blueberries
55g (2oz) dried peaches

To prepare the brandied sea spaghetti

Soak chopped seaweed in the water, honey and brandy, cover, and leave overnight in a cool oven 40°C/105°F or warm place, like the hotpress.

To prepare the pudding

1 In a large mixing bowl cream the butter and sugar together. Stir in the fruit and nuts followed by the spices and breadcrumbs. Add the alcohol and the flour. Stir well, cover with a clean towel and leave overnight in a cool place.

2 Next day add the eggs 1 at a time. Crack each egg into a cup, check for freshness, and beat each in, mixing well. Grease the pudding bowls with butter.

3 Add the brandied sea spaghetti and grated carrot, stir very well again and fill the mixture into the pudding bowls.

4 Cut circles 2.5cm (1 inch) wider than the lid out of tinfoil and greaseproof paper. Fit this layer of greaseproof paper followed by the layer of tinfoil, leaving an overlap of 2.5cm (1 inch) over the top of the bowl. Secure lid snugly over the 2 layers.

5 To steam: Place each covered pudding bowl in the bottom of a large saucepan. Add enough boiling water to come ⅔rds of the way up the bowl. Cover with a lid and simmer for 4 – 5 hours. Top up with hot water every hour. Water should be simmering up the sides of the bowl but not over it.

COOK'S TIP

Steam the pudding on the stove or in the oven for 1 hour on day of serving to warm it thoroughly.

condiments, marinades and sauces, snacks and titbits

condiments

Irish and international harvesters produce combinations and individual packets of flaked and ground seaweeds, or you can purchase larger pieces to toast and grind yourself.

Whatever you decide to do, put it on the kitchen table and use it on everything instead of salt and pepper. If you make your own you can vary it from batch to batch and experiment until you have your perfect condiment.

Put this dry condiment on the table in a little dish or shaker. Seal any extra in an airtight container and refill as required.

Sprinkle on whatever you have for breakfast, lunch and dinner; over eggs, fish, pizza, soup, vegetables or rice.

Preparation

Prepare the seaweed until it is brittle by following the instructions supplied on the bookmark and grind a combination of the following in a pestle and mortar or coffee grinder:

*2 parts **Alaria***
*1 part **bladderwrack***
*1 part **channelled wrack** – optional*
*2 parts **duileasc***
*2 parts **nori***
*1/4 part **sugar kelp***
*1/4 part **kelp***

Depending on preference and requirement, add more or less of each seaweed. If a low salt diet is required choose washed nori as your main seaweed and also rinse the other seaweeds before drying and grinding. If the requirement is for calcium, then Alaria has the highest content. For a full spectrum of trace elements, minerals and vitamins, choose as wide a range of seaweeds as possible.

VARIATIONS

Use sesame seeds mixed with the condiment as an interesting form of gomasio or try ground pumpkin seeds mixed half and half with the seaweeds. Don't leave any crushed seeds out to the air on the table as they may go rancid. It's better to use them up at a single sitting or store in the fridge in an airtight container and use over a few days.

A note about salt

- The current recommended daily intake of salt in Ireland and the UK should not exceed 6gms per day. However, North America has recently advised a lower daily intake, between 1.5gms – 2.3gms per day, depending on age and health history. Most excess salt intake comes from the salt added to processed foods.
- The North American recommendation is to encourage people to read labels to be more aware of what is added to food, avoid unnecessary excess salt and to use fresh ingredients in their daily food preparation. If your diet includes a lot of processed foods, consider regularly replacing some of your processed meals with a healthier seaweed option from the recipe section of this book.
- If you opt for unprocessed foods in general, but love salt, try adding lots of flaked seaweed to your salt mill. Nori, in particular, gives a salty flavour to food or use a duileasc and salt mix from the suppliers listed.
- Most seaweed is dried with natural sea salt attached. If you are on a salt restricted diet, then rinse seaweed pieces under the tap to remove salt before preparing and using.

Include bladderwrack if possible, as in addition to being nutritious it also binds helicobactor pyori, a fairly common bacteria, and helps to eliminate it from the body.

real mayonnaise

from frank and betty melvin

Frank and Betty Melvin from Co. Sligo have been harvesting for a lifetime and were the first harvesters in Ireland to put a range of Irish seaweeds on the market. Prior to that, imported Japanese seaweed was the only option. Among the first in Ireland to be granted a harvesting licence they have supported this book from the start in many ways, not least by supplying almost all the seaweed necessary for the formal testing.

Seaweed used: Carraig Fhada duileasc or a mix of seaweeds
Makes 300ml (1/2 pint)

2 fresh eggs
Salt and pepper
1/2 teaspoon mustard powder
1 teaspoon cider vinegar or lemon juice
230ml (8fl oz) olive oil
3 tablespoon of ***dried duileasc,*** *chopped finely or 3 tablespoons of a selection of* ***mixed seaweeds,*** *chopped finely*

1. Place the eggs in a food processor. Add the salt, pepper, mustard and cider vinegar or lemon juice. Process briefly to combine.
2. Set the food processor on a low setting and add the oil in a slow steady stream until it thickens to mayonaise. Add the seaweeds.
3. Enjoy with anything.

Keep refrigerated and use within 1 week.

VARIATION: WASABI & GARLIC MAYONNAISE

125g (4oz) seaweed mayonnaise as above
1 small garlic clove, crushed
1 teaspoon wasabi paste, add a little more if necessary but be careful as it is very hot

Mix ingredients well together.
Great to jazz up a salad.
Keep refrigerated and use within 1 week.

dulse* crisps

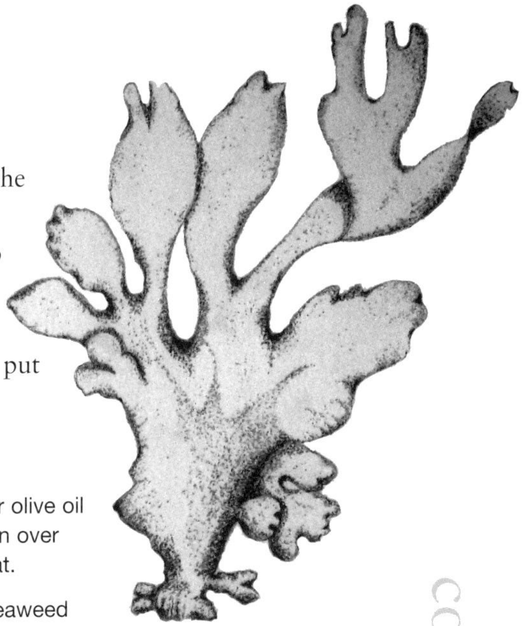

No doubt about it, the potato crisp in all its variations, is one of the greatest tasting snacks of our times.

If it's salt you're after, but could do without the fat, why not go for the naturally occurring tang of duileasc which also crisps up a dream with very little effort on your part.

To help yourself make the psychological break, you can always put your duileasc crisps into a little foil lined bag that rustles...

Seaweed used: Duileasc*
Serves 2 – 4

butter or olive oil for cooking
*packet or two of **duileasc**, snipped into 2.5cm (1 inch) pieces*

1 Heat butter or olive oil in a heavy pan over moderate heat.

2 Toss in the seaweed pieces and fry for a minute or 2 until they change colour.

3 Remove from the pan and allow them another minute to cool and crisp up further.

COOK'S NOTE

Crisps can also be made from seaweeds such as Alaria and sea spaghetti. Kelp and sugar kelp can be used too, but need to be soaked in plenty of fresh water for 30 minutes, drained and well dried on kitchen paper.

Note on duileasc crisps

In true Northern Ireland fashion, **duileasc*** is pronounced and spelled dulse in the province.
Eat these right away on their own, added to food, or between two slices of buttered bread as a crisp sandwich.

kombu condiment

This indispensable condiment comes from Justin Keating, retired politician, who makes it in fairly large quantities and uses it in the French sense as 'anything that goes on the table, wet or dry, which is a pleasing supplement, and not part of the main meal.' It will keep for two weeks in the fridge and can be used with meats, cheeses, vegetables and fish. In fact, your only limitations here are your taste buds.

Seaweed used: Kombu/kelp

'None of this is set in stone. Seaweeds vary. Tastes vary. I experiment with this recipe all the time and it always turns out well.'

Makes 1 jar

40g (1½ oz) kelp, dry weight, snipped as finely as possible
10g ginger, chopped finely or grated
100ml (3¼ fl oz) water
50ml (2fl oz) shoyu (soy sauce)
30ml (2 tablespoons) lemon juice,
a dash of mirin or white wine vinegar
30ml (2 tablespoons) local honey

1. Rinse the kelp, and soak in plenty of water for about one hour. Rinse again and place in a saucepan with the ginger and measured water.
2. Cover and boil for 15 minutes. Check if it has become tender enough to eat. Boil for longer if needed as kombu varies in toughness.
3. Using a wooden or plastic spoon mix the shoyu, lemon juice, vinegar and honey together and taste for sweetness.
4. Transfer kelp with cooking liquid to a jar with a lid.
5. Pour the shoyu mixture over the kelp in the jar and stir with wooden or plastic spoon to mix well.
6. Refrigerate. The condiment will be ready to use after 12 hours and will keep for 2 weeks in the fridge.
7. Use the seaweed and the marinade together until used up.

COOK'S TIP

Don't use ordinary commercial soya if you can get shoyu, tamari or, for a fishy change, some nam pla. To save on preparation time the kelp can be cooked in large pieces and blended with a hand blender when tender enough to eat. Transfer to a jar as above.

kelp party snacks

I attended the Constance McFarlane symposium on seaweed on Prince Edward Island where I collected this useful and delicious recipe.

Seaweed used: Kelp
Makes 16 pieces

2 tablespoons soy sauce
2 tablespoons honey
16 slices of roast beef the same size as the kelp
16 pieces of ***kelp*** *cut into 6 – 8.5cm (2½ – 3½ inch) pieces, soaked in cold water for 30 – 60 minutes and simmered for 15 – 30 minutes to soften*
16 cocktail sticks

Preheat the oven to 190°C/375°F/Gas 5

1. Combine the soy sauce and honey to make a marinade.
2. Place a piece of roast beef on a piece of kelp, smear with marinade, roll up and secure with a cocktail stick. Place in an ovenproof dish.
3. Roll up the remaining beef and kelp and place in the dish, then pour the marinade over them.
4. Place in the oven and cook uncovered for 20 minutes until almost all the liquid has evaporated.
5. Serve warm or cold.

FACT
Research on the nutritional role of alginates from brown seaweeds has shown them to be potentially beneficial to gut health by contributing to water binding and decreasing transit time. Decreased transit time is a positive factor in preventing colon cancer.

Irene Novaczek, marine scientist and environmentalist.

COOK'S TIP
Recipe can be easily doubled or trebled.

toasted nori snack

'Particularly nice with a pre-dinner drink and works really well with left over nori sheets.'

Seaweed used: Nori
Serves 2

1 teaspoon sesame oil
***2 nori sheets**, torn or cut into small pieces about 1 – 2cm (1/2 – 1 inch) square is ideal*
1 tablespoon sesame seeds
1 – 2 teaspoons soy or tamari
2 spring onions, sliced thinly
pinch of sugar
pinch of chilli pepper, optional

1. Heat a heavy frying pan over high heat and add the sesame oil, nori pieces and sesame seeds. When the sesame seeds start to pop take the pan off the heat.
2. Cool for 20 seconds before adding the remaining ingredients. Mix well.
3. Note that if the pan is very hot, it may sizzle when the tamari is added, but this is fine. You will need to soak the pan afterwards.

Serve cold.

Duika Burges Watson

nori marinade for beef

As with all marinades, this tenderises the meat and brings out a fuller flavour. Wasabi can be uncomfortably hot for first time users, or where too much has been added to the recipe, so be strict with your measurements on this one.

Seaweed used: Nori
Makes enough for 4 servings

1/2 teaspoon wasabi paste, (Japanese horseradish)
50ml (2 1/2 fl oz) soy sauce
Worcester sauce, a dash
3 tablespoons balsamic vinegar
1 clove garlic, chopped
1/2 teaspoon wholegrain mustard
***1 sheet of nori,** soaked for 1 – 2 minutes in boiling water, drained and chopped finely*
4 portions of beef, can be whole steaks, strips or cubes to stir-fry

1. Mix the wasabi paste, soy sauce and Worcester sauce together in a small bowl.
2. Add balsamic vinegar, garlic and wholegrain mustard. Add the nori and mix well.
3. Toss the beef in marinade and leave to soak 1 to 8 hours in the fridge.
4. Cook the meat as per selected recipe.

The recipe comes from Odhran who was taught how to cook by his father, Gene O'Donnell.

a visit to two harvesters

We visited Maine Coast Sea Vegetables and tasted their wonderful candied seaweed snacks fresh from the oven, the recipe for which can be found in their book Sea Vegetable Celebration by owner Shep Erhart and chef Leslie Cerier.

sea salsa verde

This salsa recipe was contributed to Shep's book by Susan Asanovic and is a great way to use up a glut of tomatillos. Substitute jalapeño peppers with red pepper or mild chilli peppers if you need to. The salsa also works well with ordinary tomatoes if the tomatillos are unavailable.

Seaweed used: Nori / laver
Serves 4

25g (1oz laver)
3/4 lb (about 15) tomatillos
1 – 2 tablespoons fresh red jalapeño peppers, chopped
1/2 a red onion, chopped
1/4 – 1/2 teaspoon ground cumin or to taste
3 tablespoons fresh lime juice
4 cloves garlic, chopped

Preheat the oven to 150°C/300°F/Gas 2

1. Toast the laver in the oven for 5 to 8 minutes until crisp, or dry roast it in a medium skillet (pan), turning occasionally until crisp.
2. Remove the papery husk from the tomatillos, and steam them with the laver until soft.
3. Blend until smooth in a food processor or blender. Mix in the remaining ingredients.

pepper dulse sauce for fish

A trip to Roscoff, Brittany, France brought me in contact with Ronan from the Seaweed Discovery Centre who invited me to join him for a cookery session.

While enjoying all the well known seaweeds in a variety of dishes Ronan particularly likes the less well known pepper dulse.

Seaweed used: Pepper dulse
white sauce (see page 140 for how to make it)
*1 tablespoon **pepper dulse,** chopped finely or to taste*
salt to taste

Add the pepper dulse and salt to the white sauce. Taste and adjust seasoning if necessary. Serve with white fish.

gooseberry, apple and alaria chutney

Mary Luthers, from Bluebell Organic Farm in Co. Leitrim, looks very French in her blue and white check apron and creates a continental atmosphere at the Sligo Market each Saturday with her delicious array of home baked produce. Influenced by her French grandmother who wrote a culinary encyclopaedia, this fruity chutney is one of her favourites.

Seaweed used: Alaria
Makes 18 x 350g jars

1.5kg (3½lb) organic gooseberries topped and tailed
1kg (2lb 4oz) organic apples, peeled and chopped
250g (9oz) organic cranberries
250g (9oz) organic sultanas
400ml (14fl oz) organic cider vinegar
4 teaspoons of salt
1kg (2lb 4oz) organic onions, peeled and chopped
1 teaspoon fresh organic turmeric root, grated
1 teaspoon organic ginger, ground
1kg (2lb 3½oz) organic unrefined sugar
40g (1½oz) Alaria, snipped into 5mm (½inch) pieces

1 Put the prepared fruit into a heavy based preserving pan with the vinegar, salt, onions and spices and cook gently until the fruit is tender.

2 Add the Alaria and the sugar. Bring to the boil and then simmer very gently for about two hours or until the chutney thickens.

3 Pour into hot sterilised jars, seal and store in a cool dark place.

COOK'S TIP

Adding the Alaria at this stage keeps a slight bite in it. Use recipe to deal with a glut of fruit or scale recipe down as required.

two rice recipes

Use 370g (13oz) organic wholegrain basmati rice, rinsed and cooked in double the volume of water for 40 – 45 minutes. Divide the cooked rice in half and use one half to make each of the recipes below. While the rice is cooking assemble the ingredients for the additions.

This is a nice way to have variations on a dish without spending too much time.

RICE WITH MUSTARD OIL AND SEAWEEDS

Seaweed used: Alaria, mixed
Serves 4

400g (14oz) cooked rice of choice, organic wholegrain basmati works well
1 – 2 tablespoon olive oil
1 teaspoon mustard
*2 teaspoons **Alaria** or **mixed seaweeds,** crushed roughly or flaked*

1 Mix the olive oil and mustard to a paste. Set aside.

2 While the cooked rice is still warm stir in the olive oil, mustard and the Alaria or mixed seaweeds. Stir gently to mix and serve with any dish.

Aisling O'Connor Organic Gardener

COOK'S TIP

Don't crush the Alaria to a powder, it works better if more flaked rather than ground.

RICE WITH MUSTARD OIL, TOMATOES AND SEAWEEDS

This is a variation on Aisling's recipe opposite and is delicious both warm and cold.

Seaweed used: Alaria, mixed
Serves 4

400g (14oz) cooked rice
1 tablespoon olive oil
1/2 teaspoon mustard powder
*2 teaspoons **Alaria,** crushed*
5 mm (1/2 inch) of red hot chilli pepper, chopped very finely
10 sun–dried tomato halves in olive oil, chopped, or use dried and rehydrate them by soaking them in warm water for 20 minutes
a good handful of fresh basil leaves, torn roughly

1 Mix the olive oil and mustard powder to a paste and stir into the rice.

2 Add the Alaria, chilli peppers and tomatoes, then the basil. Stir gently.

COOK'S TIP

If using rehydrated sun–dried tomatoes add 1 teaspoon of toasted sesame oil or 1 tablespoon of toasted sesame seeds.

sleabhac* pesto for pasta

This mix of sleabhac, goats' cheese, walnuts and coriander combines to a rich and unusual pesto for which you will find many uses.

Seaweed used: Sleabhac/nori*
Serves 4

*2 – 4 tablespoons of cooked **sleabhac** or 1 – 2 sheets of **nori** prepared as a paste*
4 – 6 tablespoons olive oil
1 – 2 cloves garlic
25 – 55g (1 – 2oz) walnuts
handful of coriander
shavings of smoked goats' cheese or Parmesan
parsley

1. Put all the ingredients into the container of a hand held blender and process until blended to a pesto.
2. Warm over low heat and stir into freshly cooked and drained pasta.

pesto with ground Alaria

Great with salads, pâté, savory scones, meats and pasta

Seaweed used: Alaria
Serves 4 – 6

115g (4oz) pine nuts, lightly toasted if desired until aromatic and slightly coloured
4 – 6 cloves garlic
*1 – 2 teaspoons **Alaria,** ground very finely*
about 175g (6oz) fresh sweet basil, tough stalks removed
1 sprig of mint
about 150ml (1/4 pint) olive oil
a dash of pumpkin or walnut oil (optional)
85g (3oz) Parmesan cheese (optional)
a dash of lemon juice (optional)

1. Place the cooled pine nuts in a food processor with the garlic. Process until combined. Add the Alaria, basil and sprig of mint. Process to combine.
2. Run the processor on low speed and gradually add the olive oil until well incorporated. Add the flavoured oil, Parmesan and lemon juice if using. Process again.
3. Place in jars and cover with a layer of olive oil to keep fresh. Refrigerate. Pour off the oil before using and replace oil after use. This keeps the pesto fresh for longer.

roasted tomato and almond pasta sauce with Alaria

This recipe came about as a solution to a recent glut of tomatoes. We tend to use either all sweet small cherry tomatoes or a mix of these and plum. Use whatever you have. It is plate–licking good.

Seaweed used: Alaria
Serves 4 – 6

1 head garlic, with skins left on
450g (1lb) tomatoes, use a mixture of plum and small ripe sun gold if you can
25g (1oz) hazelnuts, roasted briefly and skins rubbed off in a tea towel
25g (1oz) almonds, blanched in hot water and skins rubbed off
1 tablespoon tomato puree
2 teaspoons ground Alaria (see bookmark)
1/2 – 1 teaspoon chilli flakes
2–3 tablespoons olive oil
basil leaves, a handful
1 – 2 garlic cloves, optional

1. Roast the garlic and tomatoes separately until they soften. Place the nuts into a food processor and process to break them up but not too finely.
2. Squeeze the garlic out of the skin by snipping the top and place in a food processor. Add the tomatoes and process again. Add the tomato puree, Alaria and chilli flakes and pulse briefly.
3. Add the olive oil and basil and pulse briefly to mix. Fresh garlic can be added after the nuts are processed (optional).
4. Serve with pasta.

When we were growing up on the west coast of Ireland in the seventies, our parents very enterprisingly installed a glasshouse in the garden, so we always had a wonderful supply of glowing red tomatoes in late summer. As youngsters, however, we were not keen on the constant round of watering and weeding that goes with the territory, and were silently delighted when a neighbouring herd of cows broke in one morning, and more or less demolished the structure. We didn't know it at the time, but that was the end of the tomato summers.

edible seaweeds

visiting the shore

While the bracing Atlantic breeze and the beauty of the rolling waves can be enjoyed free of charge, it must be remembered that it is illegal to remove any naturally occurring material from any part of the foreshore without a licence from the Department of the Marine. Regulations differ the world over so check with the appropriate department in your country.

A list of the licensed harvesters who collect and supply seaweed for commercial use in this country and beyond is on page 282.

This 'edible seaweeds' section gives an idea of where the seaweeds grow; and when and how they are harvested sustainably by the suppliers.

Go to the beach, bring a picnic lunch and enjoy a wonderful day identifying treasures on the shoreline.

Care at the shore

- It is advisable to listen to the sea area forecast before starting out as there can be rough seas and heavy swells at times on any coastline.
- Local knowledge of the area is useful.
- Don't go alone.
- Wear suitable non–slip boots and warm rainproof clothing.
- Never turn your back on the tide.
- Follow the tide out and turn back before it turns.
- If you turn a rock over be sure to turn it back carefully.
- Take your litter home but not any animals (marine life) – they just won't survive.

Tides and the moon

Every 2 weeks there is a spring tide which is the best time to harvest seaweeds. The biggest tides of the year are usually February/March, followed by September/October, but any spring tide is usually suitable for harvesting all edible seaweeds. A spring tide does not refer to spring time but a 'springing' of the water.

Usually two days either side of the full moon or new moon are the best tides for harvesting but sometimes this varies slightly. Become familiar with a local tide book.

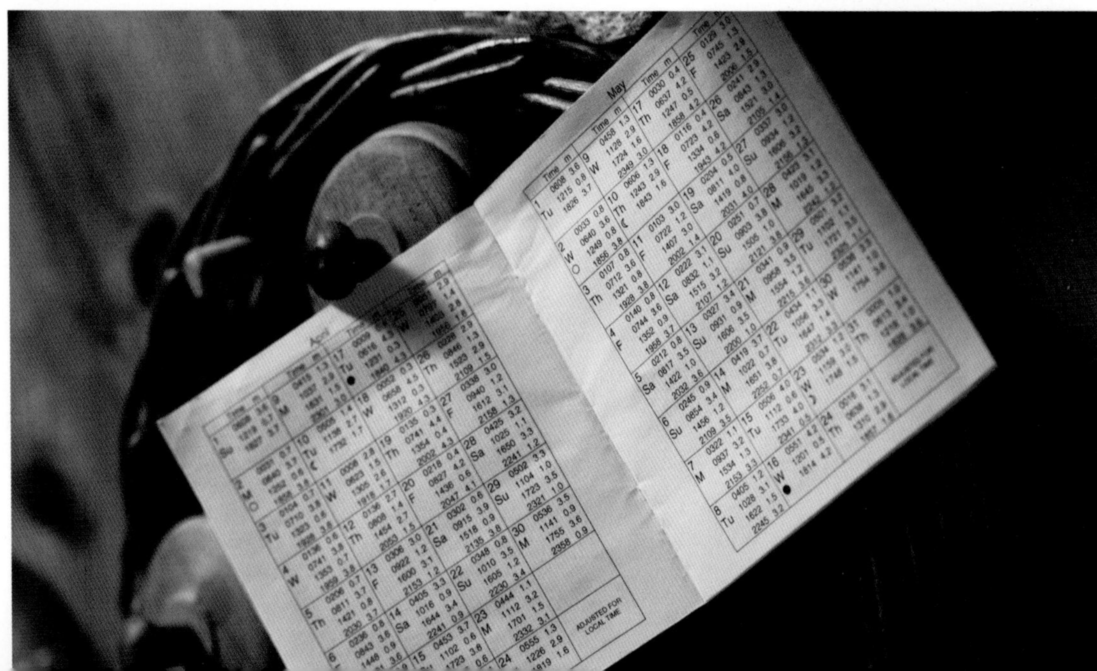

seaweeds for culinary use

The large marine algae, of which there are over 600 identified off Irish shores, are divided into three, conveniently identified by colour:

- **Brown algae (about 147 species)**
- **Red algae (274 species)**
- **Green algae (80 species)**
  Of these those suitable for culinary use are...

BROWN ALGAE
divided into
kelps (laminarians)
Laminaria digitata
Laminaria hyperborea
Saccharina latissima
Alaria esculenta
Wracks (fucoids)
Fucus vesiculosus
Ascophyllum nodosum
Pelvetia canaliculata
And **other**
Himanthalia elongata
Sargassum muticum

RED ALGAE
Palmaria palmata
Porphyra species
Carraigín: chondrus crispus
and Mastocarpus stellatus
Pepper dulse:
Osmundia pinnatifida

GREEN ALGAE
Ulva lactuca and Ulva rigida
Ulva compressa
Ulva intestinalis
Codium

duileasc

Description

- Small red seaweed 6 – 12 inches long.
- Dark purple – red, soft, flat leathery fronds with a small disc–like holdfast. Dark pinky–red fronds when dried.

Location

- Mid intertidal. Grows on rocks and on other seaweeds, especially the kelps.
- Can survive in low light levels, but will not survive drying out for long periods.

Sustainably harvested

- Usually from late spring to autumn.
- Using a very sharp knife half of the plant is harvested longitudinally. Half of the reproductive leaflets are left intact so the plant can regenerate quickly.
- Care is taken as the holdfast is poorly attached to rocks and so easily dislodged when harvesting.

Creathnach is the smaller plant found growing on small mussels known as diúilicíns. In the west and north west of Ireland there was a preference for eating this smaller sweeter plant which was torn off frequently with a small mussel shell attached. Having a dentist for a father we were actively discouraged from eating creathnach and subjecting our teeth to such abuse.
It is a seaweed steeped in history.

See memories of duileasc on page 186

Also known as...
***Palmaria palmata*, dulse, dillisk.**
The smaller plant: creathnach, shell dulse

Carrageen moss is a generic term for *Chondrus crispus* and *Mastocarpus stellatus*. They are harvested as carrageen moss and used for the same purpose which is mainly to set liquids.

Description

- Small bushy fan shaped seaweed with flat fronds. Height 7 – 15 cm. Colours range from pink to dark purple to cream. When submerged under water the tips of *Chondrus crispus* often have a beautiful violet iridescence (see photo page 228).

Location

- Lower shore – sometimes under the large brown seaweeds or in rock pools.
- Can be found to a lesser extent on the midshore.

Sustainably harvested

- Traditionally in spring at the high tides of Shrove Tuesday and St Patrick's Day, but usually harvested in Ireland now during the summer months and into early autumn.
- Cut with a sharp knife, the 'holdfast' is left intact with base of plant to regenerate. If the plant is pulled that is the end of the life of that plant.

The gelling properties of carrageen moss have made it a well known seaweed and many of us consume it without even knowing it is in foodstuffs such as ice creams and salad dressings.

See memories of carraigín on page 228

Also known as...
Chondrus crispus (and *Mastocarpus stellatus*), also known as clúimhín chait, irish moss, carrageen moss, carragheen, mousse d'irlande, jelly mousse, cosáinín carraige

carraigín moss

Sugar kelp

Forest kelp

the kelps

There are three large kelps:

1 Laminaria digita (oarweed)
2 Laminaria hyperborea (forest kelp)
3 Saccharina latissima (sugar kelp)

Also known as...
tangle kelp, feamnach dhubh, sea tangle, sea ribbon, leathrach coirrleach, kombu (in Japan)

Oarweed

1 *Laminaria digitata*
oarweed

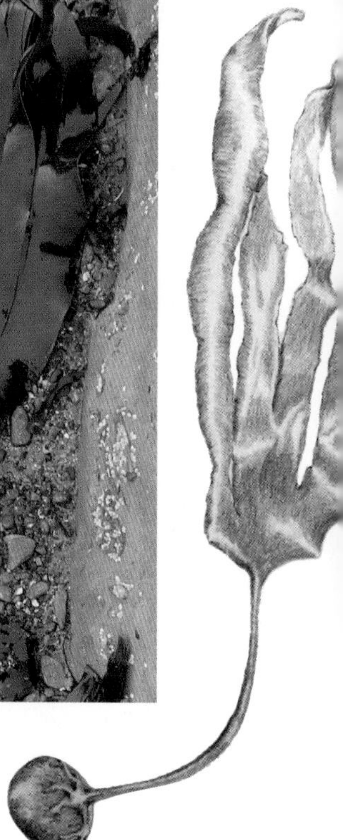

Description

- Golden–brown up to 2.5 m long and 60 cm wide across the frond. Stipe is smooth, flexible and oval in cross section. The frond is similar to a giant palm with giant flat shiny slippery leathery strap–like fingers (digits).
- Dark green–black when dried.

Location

- Extreme lower part of the shore.
- Because the plant is so large the holdfast is very large and is securely attached to rocks.

Sustainably harvested

- During low spring tides all year round.
- The upper three quarters of the frond is cut by knife well above the meristem leaving the lower part of the frond, the stipe and the holdfast intact to regenerate quickly.

2 *Laminaria hyperborea*
forest kelp

Description

- A large, erect gold–brown kelp that can reach a length of up to 3 m. Fronds are similar to *Laminaria Digitata.* The stipe is very different in that it is a long stiff rough textured stalk that is usually covered with epiphytic seaweeds such as duileasc. The stipe is round in cross section and can be snapped by hand when fresh.
- Children chase each other with these rods on the beach and dogs chew on them like sticks.

Location

- Form dense forests below the low water line.

Sustainably harvested

- During spring the old growth is still attached to the new growth and often figure–of–eight fronds are thrown up on the shore during the May storms. These, and the old fronds are known as the May weed.
- Harvested in a similar manner to Laminaria digitata (oarweed).

Also known as ...
may weed (detachable blades), sea rods (stipes), ceanna slat, múrach bealtaine, múrach fómhair, feamainn bhúi, leathach dearg, barraí raic, slat(a) mara, sraith bhuí, also similar to kombu

3 *Saccharina latissima*
sugar kelp

Description

- It has a thin short stipe. The single fond has a distinctive wavy crinkly appearance like a huge long frilly tongue, 2 – 4 m in length.
- Sometimes it has a white dry powder on the surface (a mix of natural sugar and salt).

Location

- Extreme lower shore and in gullies and rock pools.
- It has a small holdfast and very short thin stipe which is less than 60cm long.
- It is easily torn off rocks in stormy weather.

Sustainably harvested

- From spring to autumn.
- Older plants can look battered from storms and yellowed at the edges as the year progresses.
- Similar to the Laminaria digitata and hyperborea the upper half of the plant is harvested leaving the lower third, the stipe and the holdfast, intact to regenerate

Also known as ... sweet kombu, sugar wrack, poor man's weatherglass, cupog na gCloch, lásaí, rufaá, madraí rua, coirrleach, sea belt and kombu royale

Description

- Dark brown or dark green in colour.
- Characterised by a firm defined midrib running through a narrow single frond usually less than 2 m in length. 'Alaria' is latin for 'wings' since the reproductive 'leaves' at the base look like wings.
- It has a small holdfast and short thin stipe.

Location

- Extreme lower shore.

Harvested

- Grows quickly during the winter months and is harvested in mid spring to early summer when it is at its nutritional prime.

Sustainably harvested

- Only the upper third to two thirds of the frond is harvested by cutting carefully with a sharp knife. It is absolutely essential that the remainder of the frond, the reproductive wings, the stipe and the holdfast are left undisturbed to ensure that the plant can reproduce and regenerate.

NB The name Wakame is only used for Undaria pinnatifida not for the Alaria species, although it is always sold under the name Atlantic wakame.

Also known as...
***Alaria esculenta*, atlantic wakame, wing kelp, murlins, honeyware, láir, láracha, tangle, dabberlocks**

Alaria

nori

(so called in Japan and worldwide) is a member of the *Porphyra* species.
Nori is also known as... sleabhac, laver and sleabhcán black butter, purple laver, purple sea vegetable, sladaí, sleadaí. In Wales it is known as laver

There are about 115 species of nori worldwide. In Ireland 6 – 8 species have been identified to date. Nori contains lignan compounds, a type of antioxidant which can prevent and fight cancer.

Description

- Delicate, almost transparent small seaweed about 20 – 30 cm long.
- Colour ranges from very dark green to brownish purple to chocolate black when ready to harvest.
- Dried as thin, papery black or dark green nori sheets for making sushi

Location

- Lower and mid shore. Several species are only found at the high shore.
- Grows on rough surfaced rocks and boulders, mussels and concrete breakwaters almost covering them completely.
- From a distance it can look like a black plastic bag has melted onto the rocks.

Sustainably harvested

- After the first frost which is usually around Christmas.
- Usually harvested until April.
- Plucked from the rocks ensuring that a little is taken from each rock.

See memories of sleabhac on page 50

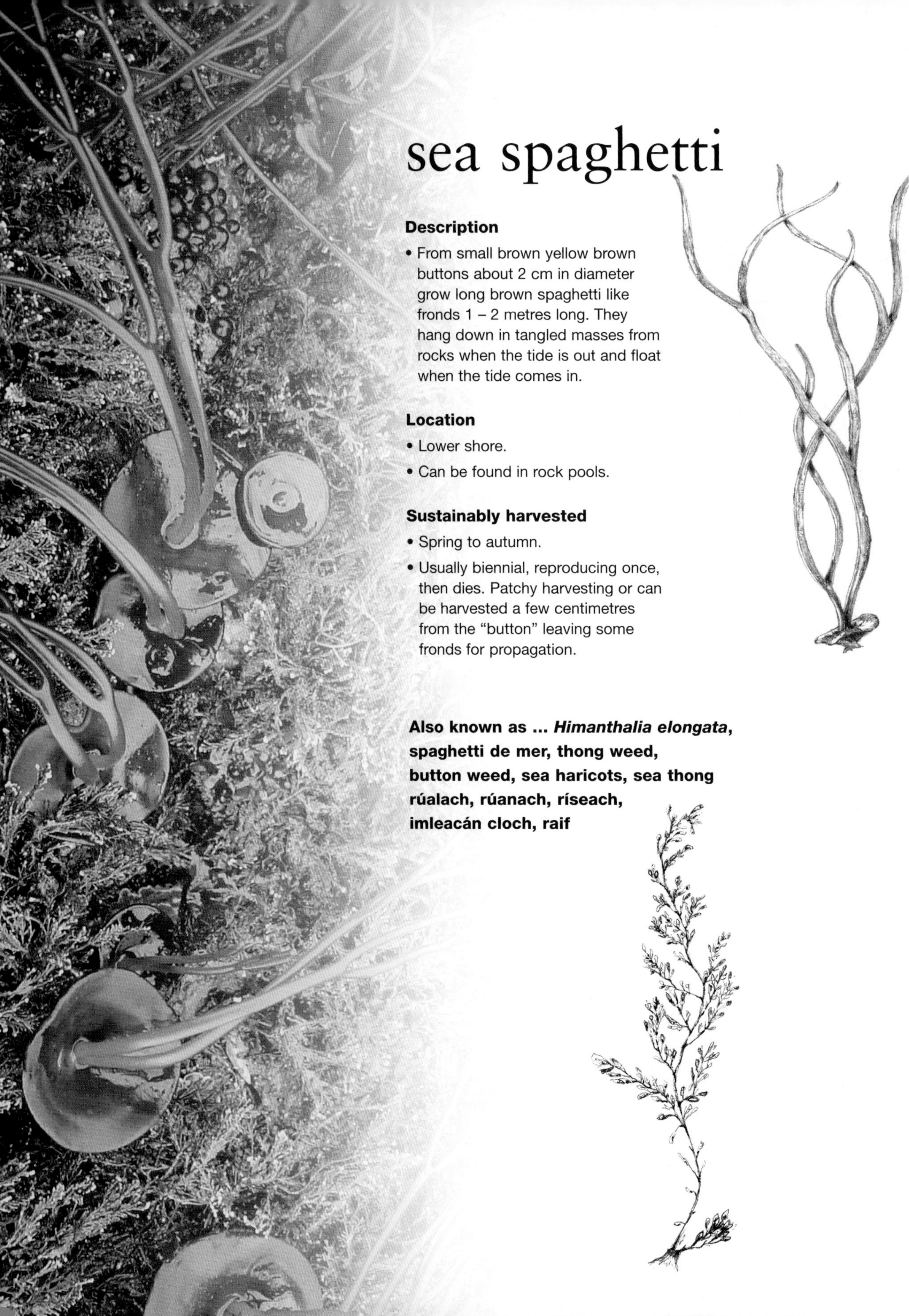

sea spaghetti

Description

- From small brown yellow brown buttons about 2 cm in diameter grow long brown spaghetti like fronds 1 – 2 metres long. They hang down in tangled masses from rocks when the tide is out and float when the tide comes in.

Location

- Lower shore.
- Can be found in rock pools.

Sustainably harvested

- Spring to autumn.
- Usually biennial, reproducing once, then dies. Patchy harvesting or can be harvested a few centimetres from the "button" leaving some fronds for propagation.

Also known as ... *Himanthalia elongata*, spaghetti de mer, thong weed, button weed, sea haricots, sea thong rúalach, rúanach, ríseach, imleacán cloch, raif

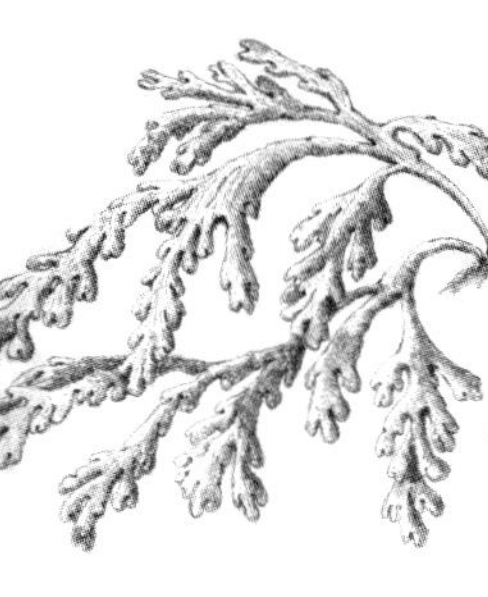

pepper dulse

Description

- A flat dull red, purplish brown to almost black frond branching in one plane. The colour and shape vary considerably depending on the environment.

Location: mid intertidal

- Occurs in rocky shores, mid to lower shore and in crevices.
- In the middle shore where it is exposed to longer periods of sunlight it may be a more yellowish–green in colour and have stunted growth, only a few centimetres high.
- In shaded places and in the lower water it can reach 20 – 30cm and be almost black.

Sustainably harvested

- Spring to autumn.
- There is little information available on how to harvest it sustainably.
- We cut two thirds of the plant with a sharp knife leaving the remainder of the plant intact.
- Patchy harvesting is also recommended.

Also known as ...
Osmundia pinnatifida

sargassum

Description

- Greenish brown to dark green. Low temperatures limit its spread otherwise it can grow around 7 cm per day.

Location

- Grows on rocks and on other seaweeds.
- Found in mid to lower shore and often found lying unattached in rock pools.

Sustainably harvested

- In summer and autumn.
- It is spread when pieces simply break off.
- The pieces are self–fertilising and release spores while floating along. As it can reproduce within the first year of life, it is currently overtaking the native species – see the "extra note" below.
- Attempts to eradicate it from British waters have been unsuccessful and removing it by hand is both time–consuming and needs to be repeated, probably indefinitely.

Extra note

It is a recently invasive species from the pacific and regarded as a pest as it outgrows and chokes native species of plants and animals.

Also known as... ***Sargassum muticum*** **(fucoid)**
Japanese weed

channelled wrack

Traditionally fed to pigs during times of hardship it was given the name Muirin na Muc. Like most seaweeds it should be used to supplement food, like a natural multi–mineral and multi–vitamin, and not replace food.

The trace element selenium is currently attracting a lot of attention regarding its potential anti cancer properties.

Description

- Small brown wrack ranges from olive brown or yellow to a dark green brown.
- It is the smallest of the wracks and is also the farthest up the shore. It doesn't grow more than 15 cm in length. The fronds are partially inrolled like a channel or a gutter hence its name.

Location

- Found on the upper shore and splash zones.
- The channels hold water and help the plant survive long periods of time without tidal cover.
- The surface area of the plant also helps to hold water.
- Animals bordering the shoreline have been observed freely grazing on this seaweed in addition to other seaweeds and their usual grass. There is photographic evidence of sheep not just eating channelled wrack, but out at low tide sampling the large kelps.

Also known as...
***Pelvetia canaliculata*, dubhlamán, caisíneach, cow tang**

Sustainably harvested

- Spring to autumn.
- Use a sharp knife used to cut a little from a few plants, ensuring some swollen, glandular fruiting bodies are left on the tips of each plant.

bladderwrack

Description

- Olive–brown drying to greenish black. Can be bright yellow drying to a deep russet colour. Up to 60 – 80 cm in length.
- Has a short thick stipe and a wavy edged frond which is branched and has a prominent midrib. On either side of the midrib are the air bladders, generally in pairs.

Location

- Mainly midshore.

Sustainably harvested

- Just less than half the frond or the tips from half the fronds are taken, leaving the remainder of the plant intact to ensure its survival.
- Reproductive bodies grow from the plants also in pairs.
- On wave–exposed coasts plants can be sparse and have no bladders.
- Plants can be either male or female.

Fucus Vesiculosus inhibits the adhesion of Helicobacter pylori on the gastric mucosa and is currently under research as a treatment to safely eliminate h pylori from the body as an alternative to triple therapy.

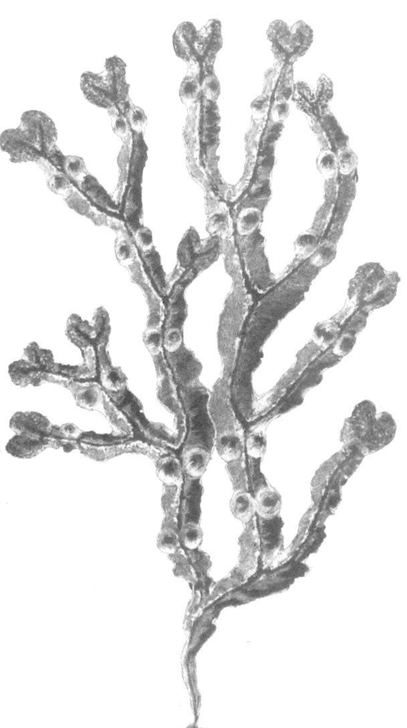

Also known as... *Fucus vesiculosus*, sea wrack, feamainn bhuilgíneach, feamainn dhubh, feamanach na gclog, cosa cruadha, cosa dubha, clogach, dúlamán, feamla, feamra, múrach dubh, bladder fucus, dyers' fucus, red fucus, swine tang

sea lettuce

Description

- Easily recognised green seaweed up to 45 cm long. Pale green when young, bright green when mature and dark green when old. Looks like land lettuce with wavy edges. Composed of only two layers of cells with a perennial holdfast, the fronds can be as broad as they are long.

Location

- Anywhere on the shore but mainly in the mid to lower zones of sheltered or moderately exposed shores.
- Attaches to rocks and other seaweeds.

Sustainably harvested

- The upper two thirds of the plant is cut with a sharp knife.

The young plants are tasty in springtime but have more Vitamin C if left until the early summer months. Can also be harvested into the autumn if the plants look green and healthy.

Also known as ...
***Ulva*, *Ulva lactuca* or *Ulva rigida* are the two most common in Irish waters.**
Sea lettuce, glasán (for any ulva).

sea grass

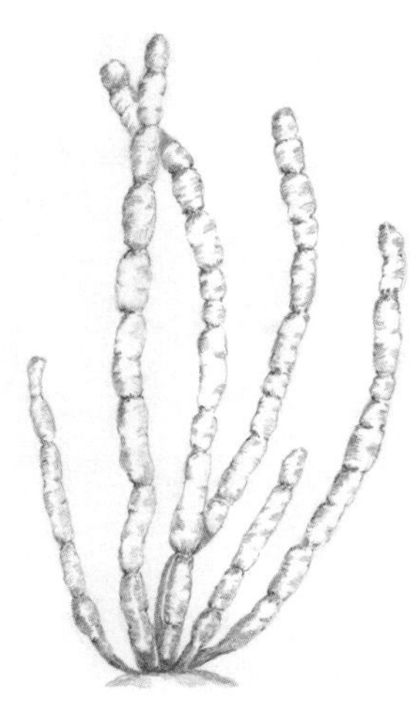

Description

- A bright green mat. It is slippery as anyone who has slipped on a green mat of seaweed already knows. Maximum length 15 – 30 cm.

Location

- Grows on rocks and sheltered pools in almost all zones.

Sustainably harvested

- In spring and autumn as it can bleach white over the summer months.
- Plucked like nori.

Also known as ...
***Ulva*, *Ulva compressa* and *intestinalis*, glasán, líneáil ghorm**

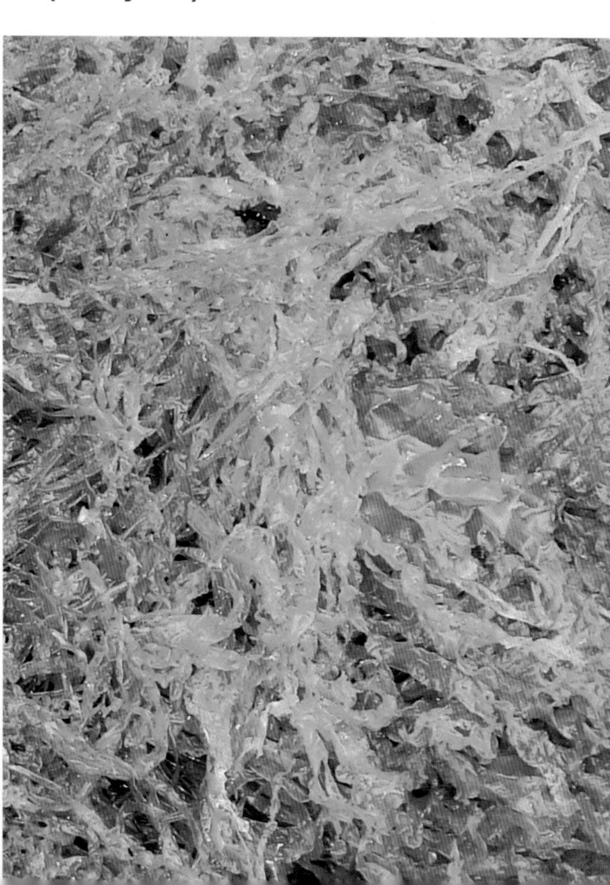

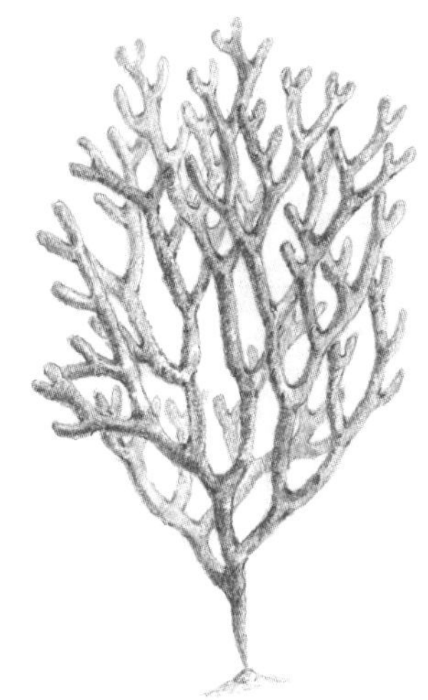

velvet horn

Also known as ...
***Codium fragile*, two sub-species: *atlanticum* and *tomentosum*.**
Green sea velvet, sponge seaweed, spúinse, fleece,

Description

- Deep green in colour it is up to 45 cm in length. It has a distinctive waterlogged spongy texture and felt–like appearance.

Location

- Grows on rocks and on other seaweeds, especially the kelps. Can survive in low light levels, but will not survive drying out for long periods.

Sustainably harvested

- Spring until autumn.
- Using a sharp knife, less than half the plant is removed.
- Patchy harvesting is also recommended.

Ascophyllum nodosum

Also known as ...
***Asco*, egg wrack, knotted wrack, rockweed, feamainn bhuí, sea whistle, yellow tang, feamainn bhuí bhoilgíneach**

Description

- Olive green to yellow it takes 3 – 5 years to grow up to 2 metres in length.
- Long, tough elastic–like, slender fronds. The fronds contain long, egg–shaped bladders which contain gas and are characteristic of the plant.

Location

- Found in the middle shore.

Sustainably harvested

- From spring to autumn.
- A sharp knife ensures that at least 15 – 25cm of the plant is left intact and some plants are left untouched.
- Asco grows apically and so the oldest part of the plant is near the base. New growth is at the tips.
- One bladder is generally formed each year which gives an indication of the age of the plant.
- The reproductive bodies grow out laterally from the fronds, from November to May, and are the size of sultanas.

We have traditionally used Asco as a fertiliser for the garden and so vicariously eat it through eating our vegetables.

Nutritional Charts /range of values

	DUILEASC	SEA SPAGHETTI	NORI	LAMINARIA DIGATATA	ALARIA	CARRAIGÍN	SEA LET
Protein (% dry matter)	12–21	6–11	15–37	8–14	9–20	11–18	15–25
Fat (%)	0.7–3	0.5	0.12–2.48	1	1–2	1–3	0.6–1
Carbohydrate (%)	50	61	50–76	48	46	55–66	42–46
Vitamin C (ppm)	150–280	75	130–1110	12–18	100–500	10–30	100–200
Beta–Carotene (ppm)	456	240	4500	336	41	–	310
Vitamin B1 (ppm)	7	–	3–6	5	5.5	–	2.5
Vitamin B2 (ppm)	2.5	–	10–29	22	0.3–1	–	12.4
Vitamin B3 (ppm)	2–19	–	50–98	34	5	–	98
Vitamin B6 (ppm)	9	–	112	86.3	62	–	0.1
Vitamin B12 (ppb)	89000	–	10000–20000	120–600	50	600–4000	6000
Vitamin E (ppm)	–	33.3	3300	8.9	–	–	9.1
Calcium (ppm)	2000–8000	8910–9282	2000–8000	12,400–13,200	11,670	9000–1300	7300
Iodine (ppm)	150–550	185	150–550	800–5000	165	200–300	240
Iron (ppm)	56–350	22–40	56–350	50–70	126	170–210	870–137
Magnesium (ppm)	2000–5000	5670–6944	2000–5000	6400–7860	8960	6700–8351	2800
Phosphorus (%)	–	–	–	–	–	–	1
Manganese (ppm)	10–155	1–16	7–83	1–16	1–14	2–28	347
Sodium (%)	0.8–3	3–3.4	0.5–3.2	2–5.2	4.6	2–2.6	1.1
Zinc (ppm)	28.6	55	41	28.6	34	71.4	20
Copper (ppm)	10.8	4.3	7.9	5	6.8	5.6	7.3
Potassium (%)	7.8	3.5	3.5	11	7.4	3	0.7
Energy (kJ/100g dry matter)	1187	1299	1657	1260	1447	1445	1047
Alginic acid (%)	–	–	–	Mannitol 7.5	–	–	–
Laminarin	–	–	–	0–18%	Retinol 0.75 ppm	–	–

A GRASS	BLADDERWRACK	SUGAR KELP	SARGASSUM	ASCOPHYLLUM
18	5–10	6–11	–	5–12
1.7	0.5–2	0.5	2.6–3.8	2–4
	62	61	–	42–64
122	100–700	13–18	–	500–1650
	present	–	36–60	35–80
	–	–	9 ppb	1–5
	–	–	–	5–10
	–	–	–	10–30
	–	–	–	0.1–0.5
7000	–	–	6	0.8
	–	–	–	260–450
	2500	8910–9282	1300–1500	1000–3000
	500	5000	30	700–1200
	150	100	92–139	101–176
	1	5670–6944	10,000–160,000	5000–9000
	0.35	–	0.14	0.15
	130	1–16	6–15	10–15
	4	3–3.4	1.5–1.7	3–4
	14–80	30	7–16	70–240
	4	3	9–11	18–35
	4.3	5	7.9–9.5	2.3
	–	861	–	–
	18–22	18 (Mannitol 14)	–	26
	Fucoidan 16–20%	16%	–	10%

The Vitamin and mineral content of all seaweeds varies considerably throughout the year. This chart gives an indication of this seasonal and environmental range.

Source of classification and nutritional analysis is from *A Guide to commercially Important seaweeds on the Irish Coast,* by Jim Morrissey, Stefan Kraan and Michael D. Guiry. Other values are from personal communication with Stefan Kraan.

Research is ongoing worldwide to determine exactly how bio-available these nutrients from seaweeds are in humans.

sheep getting nutrients from grazing seaweed

Suppliers

Suppliers of sustainably harvested seaweeds from Ireland. Even if you don't live in Ireland, it's worth contacting the companies to see if they supply somewhere in your country or if you can purchase from them directly. Many have an online ordering service and dried seaweed is so light it is is easy to post to anywhere in the world.

IRELAND AND NORTHERN IRELAND

Algaran Teoranta

(Rosaria Piseri)
Cashlings, Kilcar, Co. Donegal
t:: +353 74 9738961
e: rosaria@algaran.com
w: www.algaran.com

Bláth na Mara

(Máirtín Concannon)
Onacht, Inis Mór
Aran Islands, Co. Galway
t: +353 (0)99 61411
m: +353 (0)87 6163481
e: blathnamara@eircom.net

Bláth Na Mara company is a small company that hand harvests and processes seaweeds found along the Inis Mor coastline. A range of seaweeds are harvested and dried for use as sea vegetables.

Carabay Seaweed Health Products

(Graham Casburn)
Unit 5, Liosban Ind. Estate, Galway
t: 091 773370
e: sales@carabay.ie

Carrageen moss and dillisk harvested from the west coast of Ireland for culinary use. Also do a range of garden fertilisers.

Carraig Fhada

(Frank and Betty Melvin)
Carrig Fhada, Cabra, Rathlee Easkey, Co. Sligo
t: +353 (0)96 49042
e: carraigseaweed@eircom.net

Hand harvested by Frank and Betty from shores on the West Coast of Ireland. A range of dried seaweeds in small packs perfect for home cooking. Available in health food shops around the country.

Cleggan Seaweed Company

(John King)
Dock Road, Cleggan Fishing Village, Connemara, Co. Galway
t: +353 (0)95 44649
e: info@clegganseaweed.com
w: www.clegganseaweed.com

Offering five varieties, hand harvested from the Connemara shore at low tide, air dried naturally. Also producing 'sea pickle' in jars. Available through shops.

Cybercolloids Ltd

(Ross Campbell)
Site 13, Unit 4A,
Carragaline Industrial Estate,
Carragaline, Co. Cork
t: +353 21 4375773
e: info@cybercolloids.net

Dolphin Sea Vegetables

(Gus Heath)
Unit 54, Glenwood Centre
Spingbank Industrial Estate, Dunmurray,
Belfast BT17 0QL
t: + 44 (0)2890 617512
w: www.dolphinseaveg.com
e: info@dolphinseaveg.com

A small family run business based in Belfast, Dolphin Sea Vegetables offer a wide range of hand harvested seaweeds for culinary use. Also range of seaweed skin care and cosmetics. Supplying into retail and available direct from website.

Erris Seaweed & Shellfish

(Gerard Heneghan)
12 Barr na Trá, Ballina, Co. Mayo
t: +353 (0)97 84976

Feamainn Cairn

(Maureen Connolly)
Ballinavode, Belmullet, Co. Mayo
t: +353 9781258
e: seaweedmaureen@eircom.net

Glasraí Mara Port Láirge

(Nicholas Paul)
Ballinagaal, Ring, Co. Waterford
t: 058 46168
w: www.glasraimara.com

Based in an Irish speaking 'Gaeltacht', their name means simply 'Waterford Sea Vegetables'.
Wide range for culinary use. Nicholas enjoys seaweed sprinkled over soups just before serving.

Irish Seaweed Processors Ltd

(Tony Barrett)
Rossmore Quay, Woodford,
Co. Galway
t:: +353 909 749071
e: tbarrett@irishalgae.com
w: www.irishalgae.com

LoTide Fine Foods

(Seamus Moran)
Moyna, Kilmeena, Westport, Co. Mayo
t: +353 (0)98 42616
w: www.lo–tide.com
e: info@lo–tide.com

LoTide harvest Atlantic seavegetables for supply into speciality food shops around the country and the UK. Browse Seamus's website for the full range available and try the duileasc and winkle recipe in particular.

Marigot Ltd

(Michael Ryan)
Strand Farm, Currabinny,
Carragaline, Co. Cork
t: +353 21 4378377
e: celticsm@indigo.ie

On the Wild Side

(Olivier Beaujouan)
Kilcummin, Castlegregory, Co Kerry
t: +353 (0)66 7139028
e: seatoland@hotmail.com

Olivier collects the wild produce of the sea and land to make a range of speciality food with seaweed including pates and tapenades. Available in farmers' markets.

Quality Sea Vegetables

(Manus McGonagle)
Cloughglass, Burtonport, Co. Donegal
t: +353 (0)74 9542159
w: www.seaveg.co.uk
e: maire@seaveg.co.uk

Manus harvests on the Donegal coastline. In addition to supplying packets of dried seaweed, he also grinds and blends a variety of seaweed condiments.
Available in health food shops and through his website.

Roaringwater Bay Seaweed Co – op

(Diana Pitcher)
P.O. Box 7, Skibbereen, Co. Cork

Situated on the shores of Roaring Water Bay on the South West coast of Ireland, the co–operative supplies varieties of seaweed to the food, pharmaceutical, beauty and livestock industries.

Spanish Point Sea Vegetables

(Gerard Talty)
t: +353 (0)65 7087395
m: +353 (0)85 1648648
e: gerard.talty@gmail.com

ON THE NET

Many Irish seaweed products can be found around the world.

Ask in your local health or speciality food shops what they can order in for you if you can't see seaweed on display. You might also find the following websites helpful:

www.alcasoft.com/seaweed
www.aquaveggies.com
www.bckelp.com
www.clearspring.co.uk
www.dulse.com
www.edenfoods.com
www.loveseaweed.com
www.mitoku.com
www.naturespiritherbs.com
www.ohsv.net
www.rolandsdulse.com
www.ryandrum.com
www.seagreensonline.com
www.seaveg.com
www.seaweed.net
www.seaweedireland.com
www.organicseaweeds.com.ar

Index

* denotes Gaelic words and spelling

acknowledgements

A project as large as this one that evolved over many years finally came to fruition as a result of the input of many many people....a true wider community effort.

Sincere thanks to.... all guest contributors of recipes

Dr Stefan Kraan Irish Seaweed Centre for being such a constant great resource and for keeping a watchful eye on my findings and documentation from the ever-changing seaweed shoreline

The very wise seaweed experts spread across the globe who who shared so much and could also be called upon at any hour of the day or night to discuss a seaweed question:

Dr Jane Teas
Dr Duika Burges-Watson
Dr Alan Critchley
Mr Ross Campbell
Dr Sarah Hotchkiss
Dr Peter Smyth

Martin Walsh, BIM the first phonecall was made to him with the idea of a book and without any hesitation he said 'yes'

All of the rest of the BIM staff, especially Geraldine Lane and Helen Brophy, and Ian Mannix for recipe testing.

Una Fitzgibbon and Eimear O'Donnell from Bord Bia for great ideas, and all the Bord Bia staff involved in this project.

Dermot Hurst, Marine Institute for encouragement.

Noelle Cawley and Paul Mc Loone from Fáilte Ireland for getting the message to the world about Sligo Seaweeds

Rebecca and John – former managers of the Organic Centre who nurtured the project when it was evolving, and Hans and Andy who maintained the support of the book.

All participants on courses everywhere for their genuine appreciation of the evolving seaweed recipes.

Rita Byrne and Joan Mc Carrick for sharing personal research.

Frances Morris for wholeheartedly sharing her own work and ideas.

Nick Cann for his enthusiasm and love of the project and for his sterling work in getting it under way... always with a sense of humour.

Gaby Wieland for introducing me to her version of a green smoothie just at the moment when I needed it.

The Erne Garavogue Slow Food Convivium who wove recipe testing into a sensational seaweed slow food lunch.

Grange National School staff most especially Patsy Currid and Kate's infant teacher Karen Keeney who baked seaweed cookies with the children.

St Angela's College for their facilities and expertise, especially Clodagh Fitzgerald and Patricia Prendergast.

Dr Anthony Breslin and Dr Peter Wright for their support and encouragement in getting the project completed.

The Public Health recipe testing team, Mary, Celia, Sheila, Carmel, Fionnuala, Aidan, Tracy, Roisin, Joan and Martina.... and Beatrice for putting a notebook in my hand and telling me to go home and write down what I cook for dinner.

Very special thanks to

Donal Conaty who lent his professional journalistic experience to the project from the initial to final draft.

Siobhan Morris for her timely and tireless hard work on the proofs of this book which had a gestation period five times longer than baby Otto!

THIS PROJECT IS SUPPORTED BY

Romas and Yumiko for their dedication and hard work in capturing the beauty and essence of delicious seaweed food.

Mary Roche for being such a force of creative energy-testing recipes and scrutinising drafts.

Eithna O Sullivan – for recipe preparation, locating props for photo shoots and for her stunning catering for the book preview lunch.

Mike Harris for assisting Eithna with seaweed recipe preparation.

Grit Glass for recipe testing, creative photo shoot preparation..... and dog walking when needed

Anna Galligan – for testing recipes, assisting at photo shoots and setting up the plan for recording and editing recipes.

Thanks are due to the following who helped with testing recipes, research and just about anything else that needed doing: Dan Nelson, Michael Roberts, Dr Mari-Lynn Thomson, Rose Gallagher and Joan Epping.

Berni Chambers, Síle Haran and Mary Mahon for helping to make the preview such a success.

.... my neighbours for being there when needed, especially to Anne and Philip for supplying all sorts of ingredients – even milk and baking powder in emergencies!

Sincere and heartfelt thanks

to the Waters and Rhatigan families and extended families in law who gave of their time and artistic talents to the project when most needed.

To my husband Johnny, – the unshakable anchorman of the project who had to undertake the most unexpected of tasks: for sharing his respect, understanding and vast practical knowledge of the sea and everything to do with it. His is a quiet wisdom, reflected in many, many pages of this book, and appreciated more than words can say. Great chef too.

To our daughter Kate, who was so full of inspiring ideas for the book.

To Margaret provider of a warm kitchen, great meals, and lots of ideas and enthusiasm, always.

To Catherine – a true wordsmith whose insight into the very soul of the project could only have come from a sibling. Her attention to detail, understanding of the subject and vision of the finished work made my work so much more enjoyable.

Daithi and Frances for sharing so generously from their own personal work collection.

To Geraldine for creating her seaweed illustrations especially for the book – truly magical pieces.

To Martin for his wizardry in animating the vaguest of concepts, and for breathing life and colour onto the pages.

And to Andrea for supplying a one man help desk: research, drawing up charts, contrary computers and requests for photos were all efficiently processed.

The contact details of the production team involved in this book are available on my website. Check the website for updates in the world of seaweeds and please contact me with seaweed news or old recipes or ways of doing things with seaweeds that may get forgotten in the future.

Website design **www.prannie.com** by Deirdre Waters

Final thanks to Wendy Dunbar for adding the all important finishing touches and to Claude Costecalde, Booklink, for providing extreme dedication to book publishing.

Carraig Fhada Seaweed, Betty and Frank Melvin
Quality Sea Veg, Manus Mc Gonigle
Dolphin Sea Vegetable company, Gus Heath
St Angela's Food Technology Centre
Marketing Sligo Forum, Co Sligo Tourism
Aer Arann
SJM Food Services and Strandhill Golf Club
The Organic Centre
Sligo Market
Tobergal Lane Café
Mullaghmore Sea Farm
Voya

PHOTOGRAPHY

Romas Foord: 3, 4, 5 left, 11, 17 top right and left and bottom right, 18–19, 21, 23, 31–32, 37, 39 left, 40–41, 43, 54, 61, 65, 67, 81, 83, 88 bottom, 91, 99, 105, 120-126, 128-129, 131-132, 135–136, 141, 149, 151, 155, 157, 164, 167, 170–179, 185, 191–192, 196–197, 204, 207, 212-213, 217, 226, 233, 237, 240, 245–246, 249–250, 262–264, 288, cover portrait
Yumiko Matsui: 5 right, 6, 17 bottom left, 28, 38, 44–48, 55, 57, 59, 71–74, 85, 91–92, 96, 112-118, 145, 147-148, 153, 156, 158, 161, 182, 194–195, 199–203, 209-210, 215, 218, 225, 238–243, 253–255, 257–258, 260

CONTRIBUTING PHOTOGRAPHERS

Prannie Rhatigan and Johnny Waters, 1, 2, 24, 27, 49, 51 top right and bottom, 52, 56, 68 top left, 87, 90, 93, 138–139 bottom right, 162–163, 180–181, 187 bottom, 211, 228, 231 top, 266–277; Dr Andrea Oestreich, 39 right, 68 right, 69 left, 108–109, 190, 198; Michael Morrissy, 51 top left; Dr Mari-Lynn Thomson, 76–77, 88 top, 130 bottom; Doug Hamilton, 86; Rory O Donnell, 70, 79, 100, 101 2nd on top and 3rd on bottom, 127, 150, 160; Mike Waters, 101 1st and 3rd on top and 4th on bottom, 154 bottom, 189, 223, 252, 261; James Connolly, 22, 69 right, 101, 1st and 2nd on bottom, 142, 154 top; Martin Byrne, 103, Ciaran Davis, 25; Dr Duika Burges Watson, 187 middle; Marty Flaherty, 139 bottom left; Dr Alan Critchley, 231 bottom; Brian Morrison, 220 bottom, Malachy Harty, 232 top; Cullen Allen, 232 middle; Dr Stefan Kraan, 279; Frances Morris, back flap of dustjacket.

Bord Iascaigh Mhara, Bord Bia and Fáilte Ireland as the lead supporters of the book in addition to the others who support this book are not responsible for the contents of the book and cannot accept responsibility for omissions or inaccuracies contained therein.

Photography: Romas Foord
Yumiko Matsui
Editor: Catherine Rhatigan
Sub editors: Donal Conaty
Siobhan Morris
Initial design and art direction: Nick Cann
Design and layout: Martin Byrne
All Seaweed illustrations and watercolours: Geraldine Greaney
Apart from watercolours on pages 62–63, 94, Frances Waters O Dowd; watercolour page 42, Kate Waters; poster on page 265, Margaret Rhatigan; watercolour on cover, Daithi O Dowd
Phycology Advisor: Dr Stefan Kraan
The dedicated team of advisors and proofreaders:
Mary Roche, Dr Celia Keenaghan, Pam Nelson, Dr Ann Shannon, Fr Christy Mc Hugh
Index: Martin Byrne, Dr Andrea Oestreich, Catherine Rhatigan

Published by Booklink
Publisher: Dr Claude Costecalde
120 High Street, Holywood, BT18 9HW, Co Down, Ireland

Printed in Slovenia on paper from sustainably managed forests
ISBN 978-1-906886-22-6

This book is dedicated to my father Johnny Rhatigan, a man ahead of his time in so many respects regarding the safeguarding of the environment, and with whom we spent many many happy hours on the shore.

And to my mother Shelagh Tuohy Rhatigan, a stalwart in all weathers, who worked magic on simple fare and whose nourishment of us extended way beyond the kitchen table.